Praise for *The Boy Kings of Texas*

"With *The Boy Kings of Texas,* a new and important truth about those Rio Grande Valley border towns like Brownsville and McAllen has finally emerged, one that takes into account the brainy boys of the barrio who read Cyrano de Bergerac between waiting tables at the Olive Garden, and play hooky at the Holiday Inn in order to discuss foreign films. Sure, there have always been stories about smart kids who want to leave town or risk going nowhere in life. In the Valley, where there is also a high chance of succumbing to border violence, Martinez unveils the lives of smart kids who feel they need to leave town or else simply die of boredom."
—*Dallas News*

"*The Boy Kings of Texas* is a spirited confession in the tradition of smart, self-deprecating comedies about young manhood like Robert Graves' *Good-Bye to All That* and early Philip Roth. Martinez weaves artful comic asides with anecdotes about poverty so crushing that it leads to the death of his friends."
—*Texas Observer*

"This compelling, often heart-warming book explores how Martinez and his family tried to find their place in Brownsville. . . . *The Boy Kings of Texas* alternates between serious, often violent stories, such as the uncle who beats up Martinez in a cocaine-fueled rage, and humorous stories showing his family's softer, loving side. Often, the most moving chapters combine humor with a dark undertone. For example, Martinez writes about how his sisters dealt with their own feelings of inferiority by creating two blonde, Anglo alter-egos."
—*San Antonio Express-News*

"There is no easy resolution to this personal journey told through a series of anecdotes that range from hilarious to heartbreaking. Martinez simply splays out the different chapters of his life with a raw honesty that dispels the myth of the big happy Hispanic family and critiques the codes of machismo that lead to reckless choices. An incredibly engaging read and full of colorful characters that keep the writing vibrant. . . ."
—*El Paso Times*

"Martinez's story is heartrending and uncomfortable, but he maintains a surprising sense of humor that keeps his reader cringing and rooting for him. A starkly honest memoir of growing up on the Texas-Mexican border in the 1970s and '80s, with a wry twist."
—*Shelf Awareness*

". . . offers experiences that readers will find informative and emotionally engaging."
—*ALA Booklist*

THE BOY KINGS
OF TEXAS
A MEMOIR

DOMINGO MARTINEZ

LYONS PRESS
Guilford, Connecticut
An imprint of Globe Pequot Press

To buy books in quantity for corporate use
or incentives, call **(800) 962-0973**
or e-mail **premiums@GlobePequot.com.**

Lyons Press is an imprint of Globe Pequot Press.

Text design: Sheryl Kober
Project editor: Kristen Mellitt
Layout artist: Justin Marciano

Library of Congress Cataloging-in-Publication Data is available on file.

ISBN 978-0-7627-7919-2

Printed in the United States of America

10 9 8 7 6 5 4 3

For Velva Jean

and because of Sarah

Gramma in Matamaras, late 1950s

CONTENTS

Prologue ix

Chapter 1: Border Justice 1

Chapter 2: His Favorite Place 10

Chapter 3: Grampa 13

Chapter 4: Curses 21

Chapter 5: Vulgaria 25

Chapter 6: ¡Oklahoma! 40

Chapter 7: Gramma and the Snakes 58

Chapter 8: Poo and Piglets 64

Chapter 9: Christmas with Grandma 70

Chapter 10: The Mimis 85

Chapter 11: Dan's First Fight 99

Chapter 12: The Oklahoma Joneses 105

Chapter 13: In Which Mom Is Introduced
to the Barrio 112

Chapter 14: Faith 122

Chapter 15: Football 145

Chapter 16: The Artless Dodger 155

Chapter 17: Dan's Second Fight 163

Chapter 18: Delta City Repeat 180

CONTENTS

Chapter 19: Room 124 191

Chapter 20: Neighborhood Heroes 218

Chapter 21: Cheering up Philippe 224

Chapter 22: Crying Uncle 252

Chapter 23: Afterward 282

Chapter 24: Sleeping with Monsters 288

Chapter 25: Dad's Warning 302

Chapter 26: Dan's Second to Last Fight 317

Chapter 27: The House that Rock 'n' Roll Built 336

Chapter 28: Bioluminescence 340

Chapter 29: Home 358

Chapter 30: Mom's Story 367

Chapter 31: Origins 378

Chapter 32: Cheating 385

Chapter 33: Cheating II 390

Chapter 34: Keep on Truckin' 392

Chapter 35: Ten Years Later 394

Chapter 36: Dan's Last Fight 397

Chapter 37: Settling Accounts 408

Epilogue 429

Closedown 437

Acknowledgments 442

About the Author 444

PROLOGUE

It began as a joke, when I was in my late twenties.

I thought I'd make my older brother Dan laugh by learning a song in the long-forgotten Spanish from our youth, then belt it out unexpectedly some afternoon when we were having beers.

The song was by Vicente Fernandez and was an unofficial anthem for the Mexican farming class, back when Dan and I were growing up on the border of Texas and Mexico in the 1970s and 1980s. When it came on the radio, it would make anyone listening stop what they were doing and sing along at top volume with Mr. Fernandez in pure, animal joy, like an overemotional call to arms.

The song was, or is, rather, *"El Rey,"* ("The King"), and was originally written by José Alfredo Jiménez, a near-illiterate troubadour who wrote over one thousand songs, it is reported, even though he never learned to play an instrument.

The song was so popular on the border that even my grandmother, who was not known for her *joie de vivre*, would bounce along happily in a mock waltz and sing out as the spirit overtook her, in uncharacteristic glee:

Con dínero, o sín dínero . . .(If I'm rich, or if I'm poor . . .)

✤

One afternoon, after blaring the song repeatedly on my stereo in order to retrace those disused paths of language—much to the confusion of my neighbors in Seattle, I'm sure—I made one of the most startling discoveries of my early adulthood.

Vicente Fernandez, I was told by my friend, David Saldana, who grew up in the Chicano movement of 1960s California, was sort of a farmer's Frank Sinatra, and sang the *rancheros* and *corridos* traditional to that class. (David, who grew up in urban areas, was more partial to Juan Gabriel, who was considered "posh.")

What I could not have known growing up and hearing Vicente Fernandez all around me in South Texas was that he was singing the paean of machismo, the topographical map of the rural Mexican male's emotional processing.

Right in front me, after a quick online search, was the lyrical genome for machismo. José Alfredo Jiménez had mapped the emotional DNA of the border male, had illustrated clearly what had so viciously plagued my father, and, well, his mother, who was as butch as they come.

Here was the source code for everything I was trying to escape: the generational compulsions and impulses of alienation, narcissism, self-destruction, emotional blackmail, and a profound conviction that everyone else in the world is wrong—*wrong!*—wrapped in a deep, all-consuming appeal to be accepted, protected by an ever-ready defensive, fighting posture, perfectly captured in a song. I was stunned at the accuracy; Jiménez, in his illiteracy, was nothing short of brilliant.

This is the song, and my bad rendering to the right[1]:

---

1 Music and lyrics by José Alfredo Jiménez; translation by Domingo Martinez.

El Rey	The King
Yo sé bien que estoy afuera	I know very well that I'm on the outside
pero el dia en que yo me muera	but on the day I die
sé que tendras que llorar	I know that you'll have to cry
Llorar y llorar	to cry and to cry
llorar y llorar	to cry and to cry
Diras que no me quisiste	You say you never loved me
pero vas a estar muy triste	but you're going to be really sad
y asi te vas a quedar	and that's how I demand you stay
Con dinero y sin dinero	If I'm rich or if I'm poor
hago siempre lo que quiero	I will always get my way
y mi palabra es la ley	and my word is law
no tengo trono ni reina	I have neither a throne nor a queen
ni nadie que me comprenda	nor anyone that understands me
pero sigo siendo el rey	but I will keep on being the king
Una piedra del camino	A stone in the journey
me enseñó que mi destino	taught me that my destiny
era rodar y rodar	was to roll and roll
Rodar y rodar	to roll and to roll
rodar y rodar	to roll and to roll
Después me dijo un arriero	Then a mule-driver once told me
que no hay que llegar primero	that you don't have to be the first to arrive,
pero hay que saber llegar	but you have to know how to arrive
Con dinero y sin dinero	If I'm rich or if I'm poor
hago siempre lo que quiero	I will always get my way
y mi palabra es la ley	and my word is law
no tengo trono ni reina	I'm without throne or a queen
ni nadie que me comprenda	nor anyone that understands me
pero sigo siendo el rey	but I will keep on being the king

It loses quite a bit in the translation, but dear God, this is really what they felt. This was truth, and it was the water Dan and I swam in, growing up.

We were the sons of kings.

Chapter 1

BORDER JUSTICE

They were children themselves, my mother and father, when they started having children in 1967 on the border of South Texas. Dad had just graduated from high school and in a panic asked my mother to marry him because he wanted to avoid the Vietnam War draft. Mom had eagerly agreed, in order to escape something even worse.

They had three girls in three successive summers, and were then happily surprised by a boy the following year. Having done her duty in producing a son for her husband, Mom was allowed some ten months off from incubating yet another child. Or maybe Dad had finally discovered condoms. Perhaps they'd bought a television. Whatever the reason, there was a full eighteen months before I was born, the fifth child and a second son, at least for a while.

Most of the kids had been born in August or September, roughly nine months after Thanksgiving, when the Dallas Cowboys traditionally played. Dad had been a Cowboys fan since their inception, and their winning streak in the late 1960s coincided with the conception of most of his children. The year I was next to be born, the Cowboys didn't win, so I was conceived sometime during grain season, when he was maybe flush with cash and had come home drunk, which is possibly the reason I hate sports and am very fond of bread.

✥

Collectively, we have vague and dreamlike memories from those early days of the burgeoning family, but one stands out for all of us. In it, Dad surprises us one afternoon by bringing home the smallest puppy we had ever seen. We stand around him and watch him feeding it with a bottle, and after a while he cups it in the palms of his hands and offers it to one of my sisters while the rest of us watched this and cooed enviously: There was no way she was going to keep this dog to herself, we had all subconsciously decided.

The puppy was black, with tiny brown feet, and as we had only recently been introduced to English when the oldest kids entered kindergarten, we were limited on possibilities when it came time to name it. The name "Blackie" caught on quickly, and we were immensely satisfied with our creativity at giving the dog a name in English.

We were big on names back then. We each went by a *nom de guerre* as kids. The eldest, Sylvia, was called *la flaca*, or "the skinny girl." Margarita, the second oldest, was *Tata*, or *Tita* when we were feeling kinder to her, because as toddlers, Sylvia would look at her and yell, "*Ta! Ta! Ta! Ta! Ta!*"—in Spanish, of course.

The third girl, Maria de los Angeles, was called *la guera*, or "blondie," in a way, because she was fair skinned and born with light hair. My older brother Daniel was called *¡Denny!,* always with that exclamation point. Dan grew up startled. And I was, as Domingo Martinez, Jr., called *Yuñior,* eventually to be called "June," when we made the switch to English.

I was a boy named "June."

This must have been about 1976, maybe 1977. When we got him, Blackie, a Chihuahua blend mixed with something equally rodentian, was still just a few weeks old. I remember we tried our best as a family to be as good to the dog as possible, even though I was just four or five years old. The dog was a new project; the pack of children had never quite come together like that before, and we tried to outdo one another showing kindness to the new family pet.

The dog, on the other hand, very likely would have disagreed, because in a family with five children under nine years of age, and parents who were no more than children themselves, Blackie must have thought he was a victim of relentless torment. But such was the love we knew.

Margarita, or Marge, as she was eventually renamed, had previously insisted on a dog, as she developed an early fixation with lap dogs that would last her whole life. I think Mom gave in to her as a way of an apology after Dan threw a large D-sized battery at Marge while they were playing under the laundry shack. It split her forehead open. Dan threw the battery out of jealousy, as he felt Mom was giving Marge far too much attention. Dan has always been a bit too protective of the things he loved.

So we were all surprised when Dad brought the tiny puppy home in a blanket, coddled it as it fed adorably on a disproportionately gigantic bottle of warmed milk, and then ceremoniously handed him over to Marge, who murmured lovingly at the dog and quickly forgot the huge cut on her forehead, though I don't believe Mom really ever did. Mom was also quite overprotective of her favorite things.

Meanwhile, Blackie began his adjustment to the loud, large family. He was molecular in size—perfect for children—and we loved him to death. We doted on him constantly: We fed him and pet him until he was so annoyed at our attention that he snapped at us, yapped at us.

We didn't care.

Marge made sure Blackie slept with her at night on her thin, yellow cotton blanket. He would curl up in the ribbed crook between her knees and growled every time she moved, so she'd wake up with a stiff back but she would never tell anyone about it. I would force a bowl of leftovers at Blackie when everyone else was gone, lying on the floor on my stomach so I could see eye-to-eye with this black and chocolate rat with the cold nose. He'd get annoyed with me and snap at my hand and face with his vicious, tiny teeth, but I didn't care, because we all loved him, this yappy puppy with the heart of a wolf.

Mare, the third oldest and youngest of the girls, had always been a bit sickly and asthmatic. She had been delivered at home by a midwife, and it had been a difficult birth. She had come through with a caul, and because her umbilical cord was wrapped around her neck, she was blue and had to be resuscitated. Now at age six, she had developed allergies to almost anything with dander, and as such, she wasn't very close to the dog, but Mare and Marge were best friends, so Mare loved the dog by proxy. Sylvia, as the oldest, joined in on the care and feeding and tormenting of the dog, but from a distance. Syl had the burden of being the oldest child, and that took up most of her focus, pushing the uncertain and undetermined boundaries.

Dan took care of the dog, too. He put Blackie in a big basket and carried him around the front yard and through the pervasive junk field from Grampa's trucking business that perpetually surrounded our house. There were bits and parts of derelict dump trucks, machinery, backhoes and axles, open barrels of spent oil and split tires that wound in a trail through the back of our property. Somehow, every morning, Dad and Grampa would manage to put eight ailing dump trucks and a front-end loader/backhoe to work, out of the dismal lot. Dan would carry the dog in the basket on a tour of this, the only path we knew as kids with absolute certainty.

As he walked by with the dog in the basket, the oily Mexican mechanics and drivers who worked for Grampa would look up from their greasy business and snicker at Dan, because they saw him as a developing pansy. A young man showing affection— any sort of affection, even to a puppy—was not macho, even at six. His tight shorts didn't help, either. But hey: It was hot, and the kid grew fast.

✦

Some months later we couldn't find Blackie one morning. We happily orchestrated a search party like we'd seen in cartoons and then spent the better part of the morning searching loudly around our house and in the native, still-wild property across Oklahoma Avenue. It was Gramma who finally found him, ripped to shreds behind her pigsty, bleeding from his eyes and ears, his tail chewed off completely. Dad was the first to respond to Gramma's screams, the first to cry out, which immediately gave those of us who weren't already doing it the cue to wail uncontrollably. None of us knew the dog had meant so much even to him, and though it came as an unsettling surprise to us in our collective horror to see our father crying, we each continued to anguish independently at the foul murder of our beloved Blackie.

But then Dad became quiet, uncharacteristically composed, as he dug a hole behind the pigsty where we would bury Blackie with the minimum pathetic honor a family of children could summon.

None of us questioned who'd been responsible. We all knew who had done it, who had been the villains behind such terrible violence. It was the dog pack that lived with *Elogio,* Dad's stepuncle, a few houses to our west. We all knew this without evidence or even discussion, and needed neither for our conclusion. Elogio's dogs, about five or six of them, terrified the dusty length of Oklahoma Avenue.

Elogio and his four sons clearly felt that Dad and his family did not belong in the Rubio barrio, since Gramma had married into the barrio when Dad was already four years old, a child from another man. Elogio was our Grampa's usurping younger brother, and he wanted control of the family trucking business that Grampa had built. As Grampa's stepson, Dad challenged Elogio's succession. It was a Mexican parody of Shakespeare, in the barrio, with sweat-soaked sombreros and antiquated dump trucks.

Elogio's near-feral dogs made it unsafe for anyone to walk on that dirt road. They would charge full speed at cars driving by. They were fearless and dangerous. Somehow, Blackie had managed to escape our house, and the dogs found him and tore him to shreds.

"Lo reventáron," Dad had said to my mother when she showed up, describing in Spanish what had happened to Blackie. *"Reventáron"* is a difficult word to translate into English, and the very thought of that word gave me anxiety attacks in my adolescence, when the word would bubble to the surface of my thinking, after this experience. It's a combination of sensations, actually: It's part ripping, part tearing, but with an elastic

resistance, like pulling apart a rubbery, living membrane—an image like bleeding rubber. When I would remember the word later, I thought the same thing was going to happen to my mind.

And that was what these dogs had done to Blackie, from what Dad had seen. That was his postmortem assessment. Bit down on each end and split the tiny mutt apart.

Dad wrapped Blackie in a white blanket as we all stood around weeping, unsure of what to do. He lowered the tiny bundle into the hole while we surrounded him, crying all the while, and then he filled the grave with the coal-colored loam upon which Gramma's land was built, having been carved out of a larger cornfield. He affixed the small cross Gramma had fashioned from dirty, soiled planks over the small grave, and then he clutched his crying wife and children to him as Gramma said some sort of fiery prayer calling for vengeance, in Jesus's holy name.

Dad must have been about twenty-six then, watching his family cry like that. And it's only now, really, that I understood why he cried as much as we did, even though he was not exactly what you would describe as an animal lover.

There was another message in this horrible pet murder, something more disquieting that attacked the very position of Dad's family in this barrio, something I understand now, from this distance. I know now why he wept like that, for that dog, for us.

The Rubios had kept these dogs unfed, unloved, and hostile. Presumably it was to keep burglars away from their prototypical barrio home: a main house, built by farmhands many years before, with subsequent single-room constructions slapped together according to the needs of the coming-of-age males and their knocked-up wetback girlfriends. As such, the houses were consistently in varying stages of construction and deconstruction, because the boys never left home; they just brought their illegitimate children and unhappy wives along for the only ride they knew, the one that headed nowhere.

The dog pack resulted from the same sort of impulsive decisions and behavior: They'd bring a feral puppy home when some overwhelming sense of crypto-macho sentimentality overtook them, and then they would leave the dog disregarded and abandoned, much like the families they were creating.

And now, whether consciously or subconsciously, the dog pack had grown to a level of domination on that street, establishing their position in the pack order of this barrio.

And those dogs had attacked our dog. And it would have to be answered.

The next morning is one of the few memories I have of seeing my father as an adult, as a man, as he climbed somberly into his dump truck. It's the best truck of the lot, oversize and red, fancy for the barrio business. His CB handle is "Too Tall," but the other drivers have difficulty with English, so instead they call him *tútol*.

As he pulls out of the driveway, Mom stands in the door of our house and tells me to walk out to the road, to watch as my father drives off just after the school bus had picked up the rest of the kids earlier that morning. Dad pulls out onto Oklahoma Avenue, the dirt billowing behind him as he makes his way to the state road about a mile west, a route that would take him past the Rubios' house. I stand in the road and watch as Dad's dump truck rumbles off while the low morning sun beats down on the tailgate, making the red paint glow orange through the dust cloud.

As if on cue, the wild dogs run at the dump truck when he drives past the Rubios' house, barking and snapping at the tires. Except this time my father slows his truck with menacing purpose and leans out of the driver's side window with a .22-caliber revolver. I hear him shoot repeatedly, shoot every single dog as close to the head as he can. And as they all lay there dying, gray and brown lumps in the dusty early morning road, he continues his drive to work, and I don't ever remember feeling so proud of my father again.

Chapter 2

HIS FAVORITE PLACE

In those rare moments when my father was gripped by paternal obligation, he would attempt to bridge the widening gap that was developing between us with an awkward father/son exchange, more often than not by asking whether I'd had my cock sucked yet or had bedded a cousin. I was fourteen, and that gap was widening daily.

My father wasn't a complicated man, you can be sure. I think at this time he actually took pride in his coarser urges. Or, more accurately, in his ability to get them satisfied. And he would teach his boys this quality, so help him Jesus.

But one day, he catches me off guard when he asks, "Where's your favorite place?"

I don't have to think about it too long on that stifling South Texas afternoon. I knew it could be anywhere other than these talcum-powder farm roads he had us constantly traveling, tending to his deteriorating trucking business. We were Sisyphean wetbacks with a back load of dirt or sand or grain or corn, grimly traveling the same fields, the same roads, the same faces.

Yet his question has an uncharacteristic lure of soul-searching, something that might even be approaching the thoughtful. So I try to answer with some due sense of hope, introspection. But I have to be careful.

The last time he asked something similar I got a knuckle to the temple for answering his spirit-lifting questions truthfully. "In ten years from now, who are you gonna be?" That's a translation from his Spanish. I think he was drunk.

I was ten, sitting in the passenger side of his red dump truck, and we were driving. I thought about his question for a moment, looked around at the dismal, shortsighted South Texas surroundings, at the complete absence of hope. I muttered, "Dead, hopefully," mostly to myself. I didn't think he'd heard me, but then he suddenly exploded into one of his tantrums, which resulted in a lump on the side of my forehead. So today, I'm more cautious, but cryptic.

"I think my favorite place is the water bed at night," I say.

Back then, it really was. Those summer nights down there could get suffocating. My sisters had all gone off to college and I'd moved into their bedroom, where they left a disco-era waterbed, undulating and slowly leaking away. At night, I could lie there and look at the stars through the badly screened windows, and think about escaping. About what life was going to be like when I was able to get away from this place. But Dad has never been one for romanticism. He doesn't take the bait.

"Mine's inside a nice, warm pussy," he tells me with a big smile, like he's just said the smartest thing he's ever thought, and I should be equally impressed.

Instead, I am horrified at this declaration. Even today I cringe when this memory forces its way to the surface. It is visceral, twists my stomach into knots. His face is beaming with boyish satisfaction as he slowly, deliberately, in a singsong exclamation, enunciates the words "Nice. Warm. Pussy."

THE BOY KINGS OF TEXAS

We are sitting in the cab of his dump truck. I am opposite
him. He is haloed by the nuclear sunlight behind him. It is close
to 100 degrees outside and no one in my family lives any farther
away than twenty miles from where we now sit. I simply cannot
run far enough away from this man. His mustachioed upper
lip curls when he forms the word *warm,* and for a moment his
mouth becomes vulvular, creating the image of female pudenda,
and I think I might try to turn gay to get as far away from my
Dad as possible. It's the only plausible solution.

Oh dear God, please, I pray silently, *turn me gay. Please turn
me gay.*

Chapter 3

GRAMPA

The last time all four of Grampa's brothers had met like this, they had come home drunk and beaten him bloody. Tonight is different, though; instead, they are in his bedroom, watching him die.

He has come home after a three-day bender with his mistress that very nearly killed him, and he is slipping into diabetic shock, but no one has realized it yet.

His brothers are large men, the color of coffee and cream, and every one of them a type-1 diabetic. Some of their wives sit in silent concern around Gramma's table, attempting to comfort her as Gramma wails in desperation, drawing attention from the dying man to her own fears of being left alone. I am maybe seven or eight years old, and I remember thinking that the light in the bedroom was unnaturally bright for Grampa and Gramma's house, which was usually dark and sepulcherlike, crawling with old religion.

✣

"Lo golpíaron," Gramma had said with something like inevitability in her voice the night they had beaten him up and he had come home bloody and bruised. The brothers had all been drinking, and at some point, they'd set upon Grampa, as head of their

clan. She took Polaroids of his bruises and cuts and took a wet towel to his head while he breathed heavily and tried to sleep, all while I watched. Ten years later she would do the same for me.

They had beaten Grampa because he was their boss as the oldest brother and he controlled the trucking business he'd built with a GI loan. Obviously the brothers had a problem with Grampa's terms.

That night their bedroom stank of metabolizing alcohol, sickness, isopropyl, and sage. The smell of sage meant that Gramma was casting spells again. She burned the sage with other plants and assorted bits of witchcraft in a cast-iron skillet and ran around to every corner of both their house and ours chanting Our Fathers and Hail Marys in Spanish. *Buena suerte*, she said, for good luck.

When we got sick, she'd take an egg from the refrigerator and rub it on us, on our arms and legs and in our palms and feet, while praying, always praying. She'd rub some green aromatic alcohol on our temples and on our necks while chanting Catholic prayers in Spanish. It would lull us into a beta-heavy trance, and then she would call us back, back into the land of the living: "*¡Vente, Junior, no te quedes!*" ("Come back, Junior: Don't stay behind.") "*Aye voy.*" ("I'm here.") She'd say that three times, and you would return to consciousness, feeling oddly calm. Then she would crack the egg into a glass of water and study the tendrils and yolk, for omens, or signifiers. But Gramma wasn't wishing anyone good luck the night Grampa came home beaten purple.

She took those Polaroids and hung them in her homemade altar as if she needed further encouragement for her hatred of his brothers and their families, needed proof in praying for repri-sal. Her altar was a triangular, four-shelf unit that went floor to ceiling, a disorganized cluster of South American and Catholic saints, blood images, and hateful mementos like these photos aligned with postcards of Jesus, statues of the Virgin Mary, and rancid egg yolks suspended in water for interpretation.

✤

The night he's dying, though, there's no time for witchcraft, but there are lots of cries to Jesus and far too many people in Gramma's kitchen. They're all around the kitchen table, which is covered in a clear plastic that protected a flowery tablecloth underneath, some cigarette burns in the plastic. A porcelain coffee cup sat at the table, the lip stained with that morning's instant coffee. Grampa did that, left a trail of coffee from the lip.

The last time I had seen this many people at their house was a few months earlier, when Grampa was first caught cheating with *la viéja,* or "the crone," as near as could be translated to English. That's how his mistress came to be known in the neighborhood; we all knew who was meant when someone said, *la viéja.* The old bitch.

"Witchcraft!" Gramma had cried that afternoon. "*La viéja* uses witchcraft to control him!" Gramma had been crying and all those same people were there, and I had wandered in because of all the commotion in the driveway and Gramma was a mess, her hair wet from histrionics, looking like she was wearing a black wig that had fallen forward. She was wailing a long, high sound that was far more animal than human, a sound like a race car grinding its way up through its gear cycle—*huuuuuuuuu huuuuuu huuuu*—and she came at me suddenly, like the witch in the dream I kept having, all black hair and tears, and cried, "*Poongui!*"

That was what Grampa called me. Never found out why. Might have been a word he picked up in Korea. Spelled as closely as it can get, phonetically. She came at me and kissed my cheeks and clutched me to her, her face hot and uncomfortably damp, sticky with drying saliva and tears, and then a new wave of sobs hit her and I became scared. I didn't know what was happening. I scanned the room for someone familiar, hoping for my mother. I saw her there, out of place with a look of mild disgust on her face. I felt I did something wrong by coming here. Most of the people in the room were strangers to me because we kept away from Grampa's family, knew them only by reputation. That night they had the beatified look of churchgoers. There was more drama in the barrio, with Grampa coming home from a fling, a bender, and nearly dead. All was as it should be. It had a pacifying effect on them, to see someone else going through what they were all going through, though not publicly, not like Gramma.

The next few weeks after the night he was caught are weird. Gramma is going to the *cúrandera* daily, the family witch doctor, and I have to accompany her when I can because that's my role as the youngest boy.

The *cúrandera* is known as *La Señora*. See, there's the difference. The "good witch" and the "wicked witch" in *The Wizard of Oz* sort of thing. *La Señora*, or "The Lady," is the good witch. *La viéja*, or "The Old Crone," is the bad witch. It's a classic tale of good versus evil, except with garlic. Gramma goes to *La Señora* for consultation, for help, for direction. But Gramma has darker thoughts than *La Señora* can get behind.

She's casting midnight spells with nail clippings and ear-wax, cheap powdery perfumes and dead toads in jars, carrying her 9 millimeter pistol in her car. She prays for strength. She prays for death. Not for herself or him. Maybe him. She prays to Pancho Villa, she prays to bad saints. One afternoon she and I are out driving along the port of Brownsville by that bar where *la viéja* supposedly met Grampa, near Portway Acres where she is rumored to live when Gramma sees that other woman driving by and Gramma guns the engine in her huge blue LTD and gives chase, screaming and blaring her horn, trying to run *la viéja* off the road.

The woman turns onto a dirt road and rockets off, leaving an atomically billowing cloud of dust behind her while Gramma drives her LTD into a ditch and punches the ceiling repeatedly and depresses the horn until you think she'd kill the battery, so long did it howl.

This sort of stuff is happening a lot more often now. We never catch a good look at that other driver, just the car, and we never know what she really looked like; we just see just images of a squat woman in a battered maroon car who turns tail whenever she sees Gramma's blue LTD. It might not even really be the right person, just someone scared of the prowling lunatic in the LTD. My older brother Dan has many similar stories.

Gramma's house becomes a coven. The altar in the corner starts to bloom like a death flower, all rosaries and death spells with the Polaroids of Grampa all beaten up and drunk taped up all around. Basil, rosemary, lilac, rue, and peppermint are tied in bundles and placed under pillows; sage smoke saturates everything in both houses. Raw eggs hang suspended in half-empty glasses of water for interpretation, their milky tendrils growing rancid in the South Texas heat and giving the dark house a rank odor of putrescence, like something's already dead here, already decaying wetly, we just don't know what it is.

No one talks about Grampa's disappearances. He goes off for two, maybe three days at a time. Dad is quiet, Mom is nowhere. Am I going to school at this time? I had to be. Busy with my own second grade dramas, likely, as were the other four grandkids.

When he does come home, Grampa is drunk and penniless, and once he returns without his shoes. I remember seeing him sitting on the concrete well that night, just outside their porch, with Gramma throwing his things out the front door while he nodded off, snoring quietly as he waited for her to finish.

He notices me looking at him and smiles.

"*Poongui,*" he says in Spanish. "*Bien paca.*" (Come here.) I do, and he hugs me quietly while Gramma howls from within the house. He smells of beer and cigarettes.

This was about a week before Grampa died. The night his brothers were all called over, he'd been gone two or three days. I hadn't noticed. We lived across the driveway, but Gramma and Grampa came and went on their own. Grampa had given my dad half the property as a wedding present so he and his new wife could build a new house. Our front doors faced each other, but they said very little anymore; they looked away from each other's lives in what passed for politeness.

There are lots of cars in the driveway parked over by Gramma and Grampa's house that night, and that's what catches my attention. Something going on over there. I walk over to see what's happening even though it's late, like eight o'clock. Richard's first of many wives is there, and she holds me back, tells me not to look. Richard is Dad's younger stepbrother, the one who beats me up years later. His wife is seventeen and knocked up. Her name is Patty. She smells soft, very pretty for the area. Fair. All the men like her, pretend not to flirt. The family is talking about taking Grampa to the hospital across the border because it would be cheaper. He's sick, really sick. Where is Dad? I don't see him. He's not there. Gramma is mad, throwing things around and crying that loud, wailing cry again. Grampa's whole family is there—his brothers and their wives, maybe one of their kids. I see Grampa through the doorway of his bedroom for a moment, when they finally decide to drive him. They should have called an ambulance hours ago, they shouldn't move him, but they do. I see him make a painful effort to get up off the bed, swing his legs over the side, and he can hardly do it. His face is aortic, totally purple, like he's been beaten up again; his neck is a deep crimson, and the rest of his body is deathly pale, freckles on his sagging, overweight torso. He sees me and tries to smile. "*Pookie*," he tries to whisper. It hurts him. This makes me cry, even today.

They get him to a clinic in Matamoros, and they immediately send him to that bleak, dirty green hospital. He dies within an hour, of diabetic shock, on a tile table. Someone is holding his hand and his last words are, "*¡Sueltáme, Poongui!*"—telling me to let go of his hand, imagining I'm there, even though I'm across the border watching television now. He needed to go. It was time for him to say goodbye, and he said it to me. It was March 26, 1980. They tell me this, when they come back, one man short, that his last words were of me, like I should be proud. And I am proud, strangely, even today, but I don't know why. Maybe because he was the last person I loved without complication, before I learned that love was a negotiation. He was someone I never failed, never hurt, and I still can't let him go, let go of his hand when I dream of him. And I can't remember much of him when I'm awake, only feelings. I wouldn't recognize him if I saw him.

At the funeral, only Gramma cries louder than I do, probably because she kept his insulin from him as punishment for his last bender and didn't mean to kill him, not really.

Chapter 4

CURSES

When we received the chain letter, it took my parents one or two days to discuss it with the rest of the family and organize a response. This freshest of hells was met with the same resignation that every other ill omen to strike the family had been received, as we were hit often with the relentless misfortunes of Catholic beliefs.

That the chain letter was simple and idiotic superstition would never occur to Dad or Gramma or even Mom: They played by the rules of faith, and faith, like everything else, has a positive and a negative side, a good and a bad, a yin and a yang, Budweiser and Miller Lite.

So it naturally followed that their prayers for good fortune would sometimes bring them bad. In this, they were unquestioning.

The whole family was therefore collected one dark and eerie evening (What made it eerie? The television had been turned off) around the typically cluttered and unused dining room table, and we were each asked to produce what we could. The chain letter called for twenty-five duplicates, each to be mailed off randomly and within the week of the letter's arrival. We were slow in writing out the unfamiliar words of the badly written chain letter because none of us, save the preteen girls, were too confident in our writing, in either English or Spanish. So we sat there, that night, as a large Catholic family in the yellow dining room light, with the somber reverence of pilgrims genuflecting before a particularly testy saint.

I was about eight, so I was required to produce only one copy, if that. My sisters proudly cranked out about five each, in that large, pouty-lipped flowery script of the junior high nymphet.

Personally, I was in dire trouble. My left margin drifted dangerously toward the center of the page and then drunkenly over-corrected back to the left, the letter stumbling like a tourist pouring himself out of a Mexican bar, ending in a tired, horrible scrawl of, well, an eight-year-old.

See, I wanted to do my part to set this right, to participate in the salvation of the family, because continuing the chain would bring better fortune and ignoring it would bring the bad, the chain letter explained. This became very important to me that night.

When I finished, Mom looked at my work and remained characteristically quiet, but I could immediately see she wasn't exactly satisfied, though she accepted it, also very characteristic of her at this time.

We had to reproduce the twenty-five copies of the chain letter like fifteenth century monks, writing them out in long hand because the technology of copier machines had not yet infiltrated the barrio. Mom folded my work and reluctantly stuffed it into an envelope to be mailed to some unfortunate soul with a last name like *Salazar* in McAllen, Texas. I kept wondering the whole time, if it was illegible, if that recipient didn't take it seriously, would the curse still take hold? Would my childish scrawl disqualify the magic number twenty-five and would it be my fault the family was still spiraling toward indigence? It frightened me to consider that we had left this to chance.

✦

Seven years later, my older brother Dan pulls me aside and says, "Do you remember the chain letter we got right after Grampa died?"

Of course I remembered the fucking thing. I had to smile inwardly at the idea of a chain letter written by an eight-year-old landing in the mailbox of what was probably an equally superstitious Catholic family (chances were) and the fear that it would trigger, the *Exorcist*-type horror that would settle upon the person opening the envelope. He would struggle at first to make out the childish script, very likely wrestling with a language barrier. Then the weight of the potential curse would settle coldly into his heart, its evil beyond measure because it was written with the hand of a dreadful, pestilence-bringing child, like in that other movie, *The Omen*. . . .

"I think that's what started this whole thing, was that letter," Dan starts telling me in quick secret. It's morning, before school, and we're helping a very panicked Dad change tires on one of his trucks.

"Grampa died right before that, the business started to fall apart, and things just got really bad, right? It was right after we got that letter," he says.

"But we sent out all the letters."

"I don't know what happened, but something went wrong."

Immediately I thought of my work, somehow unacceptable to the cosmic decorum of chain letters because of the bad margins, the cross-outs, the candy stains, the little drawings of an X-wing fighter I made at the end—had it all been my fault?

"But it's been seven years now," he says. "I think it's almost over." He is very satisfied with this, convinced, and I can see he's serious.

I almost join in his little moment, am almost convinced of the same thing, if I weren't still turning over the possibility of being single-handedly responsible for all that we are going through, all the panic and fear and shame.

That's when Dad appears around the corner dressed in a torn, veil-thin V-necked cotton undershirt that is covered in oil, stinking that high, gamey smell of still-metabolizing Budweiser and threatens to throw a grease-covered half-inch wrench at Dan for wasting time. We were supposed to be rotating the bad tire that couldn't hold a charge with the good one that could hold half of one before we got off to school. We both immediately get back to work, me crawling under the truck to assemble the hydraulic jack under an axle while Dan, because he was stronger, loosens the huge bolts. Dad stops, leans against the door of the cab, takes a long drink from a glass of cold gritty water. He is eventually satisfied we're back on task and returns to reinstalling the water pump, muttering curses continuously with every breath.

Dan and I don't talk again, lest we should become the focus of the real curse that befell us when Grampa died seven years ago, and the family's care was left to our father, the unattended boy-tyrant now in charge of our lives.

Chapter 5

VULGARIA

El Jardin was the happiest I'd ever been, as a child. Every memory surrounding that school was like an afternoon spent in an idyllic garden of innocence, like the name suggests, if you know Spanish.

I even remember coming down with a terrible fever once and being picked up at school by my father and mother, who brought me home and showed me the sort of attention no single child in our family ever dared ask for, with soup and compresses and blankets arranged on a couch. My older brother Dan came and quietly attempted to play tic-tac-toe with me and showed me his new Dallas Cowboys picture book. My sisters brought Blackie to me and sat him in my lap. But the dog would always fuck off in less than a minute, and I would lapse, awake later on my back, looking up at my mother's face. She'd have a look of sadness, a smile pressed into her face like she was looking at . . . I'm not sure. I wasn't sure, then. *It couldn't be me*, was one of the first things I thought when I woke up and saw the look on her face. It was almost a look of loss, of letting go. The sadness of a mother worried for her sick child, a display of tenderness. I was unfamiliar with it.

I quickly became accustomed to school and the long days, though I have a clear memory of one morning, in kindergarten, of looking out the window and watching the cars slip by with muted sound on the road parallel to El Jardin. It's the very heart of the morning, the dew is about to be singed off the ground by the South Texas sun, and I remember feeling like something was dying, something was changing, and the day, how it carried on with us indoors as we learned numbers and the alphabet and recited the dates (I still remember the first day of 1980, in the immersion English program, trying to get my mouth around that number). I remember the sadness that I felt that day, some type of dread tugging at my heart, looking out in that morning, like I wasn't sure I was where I was supposed to be. I still have that feeling every few years and it has lost nothing of its dread intensity after all these years, like it's dug a trench back to that very first time I noticed it.

�֓

What I could never adjust to at that time was CCD, the "church" school. These classes were on Saturdays, and I didn't see why I had to go to church school after having been to elementary school all week long. Catechism was spent in a dirty room in the Christ the King Church complex, and I was mingled with city kids that I wasn't comfortable around, and I answered every question asked like Hermione Granger until the church leader wouldn't pick on me anymore. I was annoyed for having to be there, because it annoyed my mother to have to drive me there, too. Christ the King Church was a clear fifteen miles or so from our house on Oklahoma Avenue, way in the bad part of Brownsville, but Dad had a reverence for the reverend, Father Juan Nicolau, because Father Nicolau would let the congregation go early on the Sundays the Dallas Cowboys were playing. The shepherd knew how to play to his sheep; you had to hand it to him.

CCD for me ended one Saturday evening, when it began to grow dark and I had spent over twelve hours waiting for my mother to pick me up.

After dropping me off at 8:30 that morning, the family had gone about their business and Mom had completely forgotten the youngest of her brood, as I was not numbered among the muster for dinner, haphazard as dinner might be. I didn't show up, no one had seen me all day, and I'm sure Mom must have had one hell of a shock when she realized she had forgotten to pick me up at ten that morning.

The first part of that day, immediately after class, I spent reassuring the people there that my mother would show. She was usually late, I said, but I was used to it. Not to worry.

When they left, though, they were worried.

I sat and went where I usually did, into my head, and imagined all sorts of ways to get myself ingratiated into the story lines of popular movies I'd seen. *"How to fix it so that an eight-year-old can wield a gun and fly an X-wing in Star Wars"* was my usual pastime, and I liked to be alone to do it. This lasted a few hours. But by two that afternoon, I was starving, bored with the goddamned Wookies, and throwing rocks at cans. *The next car will be mom*, I thought. *Next car. OK, next car. Next one.* Stupid fuckin' church school. Actually, now that I think about it, I don't think it ever occurred to me that they'd forgotten about me; I thought that they were just late, so it didn't occur to me to call. I just had faith they would show. They were just busy with other things at the moment.

The afternoon grew very hot, and soon I was sweating, delirious with hunger, and cursing my family in a way I don't think many children are capable of cursing. I lay on my side on the concrete steps and watched the entrance to the deserted church compound and cried, my resentment growing with each passing car that was not the family Bonneville.

By nightfall, I was done crying and was in a sort of stoic trance, sitting up against the door of the classroom, watching the sulfur lights of the parking lot come on one at a time. Mosquitoes were swarming and I put my arms inside my thin T-shirt, using my shoulders to squish them from my face. My heart started to grow firm here, my resentment metastasizing into a cold jelly around it, and I went into a sort of fugue. I don't even remember being picked up by my mother, or what she said. I have a dim image of the car finally turning into the parking lot, with its lights on and two people in the car, I think Mom and Dan. There was no tug at my heart to see them.

✣

The summer before the third grade, a new school starts to go up in a field about two miles away, near my friend/enemy Charlie's house. In a matter of a few months, the new school starts to take shape. It's flat, laid out in straight geometrics and smells of fumes. I see it out the window of the dump trucks when we drive by, new landscaping and wire fences and concrete pillars holding up a concrete veranda.

I dread the idea of leaving El Jardin, think it couldn't possibly happen. El Jardin is old, tactile, made of red brick, and built in the 1940s with a large auditorium and wooden hallways. It's one of the very rare things in Brownsville that is old, has history. My father went to elementary school there, it's so old. It's our area's own little Oxford. There are trees all around it, paths and hidden trails, with a snack bar run by an old woman from her house next door.

At El Jardin, I was one of the top students. Kids from all aspects of suburban Texas life mingled there—the farmers' kids and the field hands' kids and the kids from families who didn't live off the land, whatever it was they did. It was like Sesame Street there. We coexisted happily, and every three days there was something called "bilingual education" and the kids who had trouble with English would be taken into a different class and helped along while the rest of us—all the white kids and me—would work on different projects, usually a book we'd all read together or a fun word problem. It was blissful learning like that. Every few months, the Mexican kids would take a reading test from a counselor to determine their ability in English comprehension and whether they could be relieved from the "bilingual" status, as it had an air of dishonor to it. I was never "bilingual." I did my best to forget Spanish from the start.

That was because my brother and sisters had already made the conversion to speaking English and I was bringing up the rear, humiliated constantly because I couldn't distinguish the "*ch*" sound from the "*sh*," and it became very competitive in our house, learning as much of Our Master's language as we could. English in that area was the language of money, domination. Six-foot Mexicans would wither when its sounds were spoken by a five-foot-tall white man, make them hunch their shoulders, lower their heads, and move in the direction opposite of the English. Even my father, who understood its themes and suggestions, spoke it reasonably well for the area—even he would send me to collect payment from white people because he was frightened to get into conversations. English was power. And I was doing very well with it at El Jardin.

I was really confused growing up in Brownsville; I didn't identify with the Mexican culture. We were Americans, we were light skinned, and we spoke English: I thought we were white. I was sure of this. So much so that, when I am around ten years old and Dan and I are watching Eddie Murphy doing stand up, and Murphy lapses into the tried-but-true "black people dance like this / white people dance like this" schtick, I laugh loudly and say to Dan, "He's right! He's so funny! We really do dance like that!" Meaning us white people.

Dan doesn't miss a beat, says, "You stupid motherfucker; we're not white."

Here, my world collapses. "We're … not?"

❖

The new school is finished at the end of summer. It's called "Vermillion," named after an unpaved side street that runs parallel to it. No one knows what *vermillion* is. I look it up in the dictionary and find it's a color, coppery red like mildly coagulated blood. I don't want to go there. Just have a bad feeling about it.

But then comes the notice to our home about bus-scheduling changes and redistricting. My parents cower from anything written in form letters and in English so it's decided: I go to Vermillion for the third grade and on. I can't believe it. I know no one else who's going there except a cousin or two. I might as well be moving to a new city at ten years old.

The first day of school at Vermillion is confusing, like an internment camp for foreigners. I had been redistricted into the city's new school for poor, immigrant families. These kids have been told by their parents to be appreciative of the chance they're getting, to listen to their teachers and administrators, so the kids are solemn, like they're in church, frightened of the opportunity just given them.

Hardly anyone here speaks English but the principal. The teachers can hardly carry on the day's curriculum without lapsing into the pidgin Spanish spoken in border towns so that the kids can understand.

All the kids wear their one new shirt or pair of pants bought for their third-grade year. They look like tiny replicas of their parents, tiny old men in guayabera shirts and women in loose cotton dresses. I'm at my desk in the front, lightheaded from the fumes of the new paint and the adhesives on the linoleum floor. The morning sun is a violent, yellow thing that floods the room undeterred because the fucking school is in the middle of a field and there are no natural obstructions to keep the sun in check, so the windows, when shut, glow like they're about to blow. The whole thing just made for a migraine.

I'm there for an hour, and I can't help but start crying from exasperation. It's like starting all over again. I don't know anyone and my Spanish is really, really bad now because I was told that it was wrong to speak it in America, and we are in Texas. I just put my head down and sniffle. After all that work I put into it, I would regress back into speaking Spanish and be humiliated, left behind by my family, I felt.

After a few days, though, things turn routine and I take a look around. These are tough kids, the sort of ten-year-olds even adults are afraid to correct, and classes are quickly divvied into the kids near the front who are willing to learn and listen, and the kids who don't see a reason to be here and are waiting to get home to get back to work, in the back. Or they're here for the two free meals. There's one white girl from the trailer park and I immediately align myself next to her. "Shannon." I like Shannon—she's kind of trashy though she's just a kid, but we get along fine. We share pencils and paper and write notes to one another and the other kids immediately start calling us "*the gringos.*" Not an optimistic launch.

Eventually things settled down and I made friends with some of the boys, but mostly my immediate peers were the upwardly mobile girls who lived near me, out in the sticks. It was still a tough school; don't get me wrong—but I learned how to swim in it quickly. Kids got stabbed there, with that little nail-cleaning tool in the rear part of the nail clipper or a stubby pencil. But for the most part, we were kids, doing kid things. We developed a very high-stakes and competitive game of marbles before classes. We played basketball and volleyball in a very organized fashion (I did the organizing). We became ingenious at manufacturing flexible but indestructible pens and pencils, as the game of the day was a sort of "pen smashing" competition, where you'd flick your opponent's pen with your own, over and over again, until one of them splintered. So we engineered things like pens filled with glue, pens filled with buckshot, pens from Mexico, pens filled with dirt, pens wrapped in rubber bands or tape, and even pens that could write. I was never really good at that game.

The other thing we did was competitive cursing. This I was good at. Cursing in English, I've come to find, is fairly unimaginative and usually indicates a loss for a retort, a failure of description or command of language, so instead the curser resorts to the general and unspecific, to the emptiness of phrases like, "Fuck you, you cock-sucking motherfucker." Et cetera.

In Spanish, however, the art form, when it is done well, comes from painting the rudest word picture using anything but vulgar words. Say, for instance, someone is being unreasonably proud of him- or herself. In English, one might say this person's "full of shit," or, "up himself." In Spanish, the phrase would be something like, "... *no le cabilla un arroz de punta*," ("... you couldn't fit a grain of rice up his ass point first, puckered as it was.")

Conversely, if a person is out of luck, in English he's "shit out of luck," or "screwed," or maybe "up shit creek." But in Spanish, the popular colloquialism is that the person " ... *tiene la madre en rasta*," (" ... has to drag his mother around"), the suggestion being that the person is so poor, he's got his family in tow, no vehicle. (I learned about the second part to this phrase when I called my father when I was out of work in Seattle, had to admit to being very nearly broken down, very much out of luck and out of work, and said, "*Tengo la madre en rasta*." He surprised me by chuckling, and finishing the sentence, " ... *y la tía en la manó*." (...and my aunt in hand.)

These are timid examples, though. We could get very dirty, very biological, very *Aristocrats* in our verbal assaults. For me, somehow, because it was in Spanish it didn't seem wrong, and I got very good at it—especially in Spanish, but also in English. This is what these kids understood at this new school, this is what I was good at among them, and I had developed a reputation as the "put-down" champion, so much so that I could make kids cry or attack in just a few seconds. Normally I'd have an audience, so the attacks were usually thwarted by my friend Arthur, or Agripino and his bunch, led by a kid nicknamed *El Chicloso* ("gummy asshole"), because he always smelled like poo.

(I remember once feeling really, really terrible when this one kid, Teodóro, challenged the position of champion and I annihilated him in one or two rounds during P.E. He was inconsolable when we got back into the classroom, putting his head down and sobbing loudly. The teacher finally attempted consolation, asking, "What happened? What's wrong? What's wrong, Teodóro?" He wouldn't speak, so she finally asked the class what had happened, and my cousin Dora raised her hand and said, "Domingo said his mother's anus looks like cauliflower," which was something I'd heard my Gramma say to a police officer a few weeks before. A few years later, I was driving around with Dad and he had some sort of business with a man who turned out to be Teodóro's father, and as I was sitting in the passenger seat the whole time my father was calling Teodóro's dad *Panocha*, which was apparently his accepted nickname, which means "twat." His dad's name was "Twat," and he cried when I said his mother's anus looked like a cauliflower? I just don't understand people sometimes.)

This continued for many months, and I had established myself among these kids in a way that I had not considered myself capable when I first got to Vermillion. I had changed, certainly, but I was able to turn off the vulgarian side of me with an easy, very smart switch, and the minute I stepped off the school bus and entered the house, another switch was flipped and I was clean-mouthed, pissed off and quiet. The minute I got on the bus in the morning, it was showtime: I would be there all week. I still managed my academia to the extent I could—I was the top student, a good athlete, and well-liked by teachers, students, and administrators—but I was also well-respected by the farm kids, who didn't buy into this American "upward mobility" thing, this "education," who might have otherwise picked on me, thought me soft. I spoke their language, after all.

This created a duality in me that left me feeling soiled and conflicted. I remember one lunch I was sitting with Agripino and Arthur, two of my closest friends at the time, and we were trading marbles while eating our lunch when this scraggly curly haired problem white kid named Billy sat directly across from me. Knowing now what we do about learning disabilities, I think it's likely that Billy was dyslexic and was acting out from his frustration, because there was nothing else really wrong with him except he couldn't write and couldn't read. But he had nothing else so he had decided to be tough.

He sat there and stared at me. The table got quiet. Billy squinted his eyes in the theatrical way that children do when they're pretending to be tough, like they've seen on TV, and he dramatically stabbed his plastic spork into his Salisbury steak, splashing the gravy on the table.

It was on. But I had this one won before it started. Instead of a verbal assault, I diversified by kicking him square on the knee under the table and then tucking back my legs and opening them astride the chair, pulling them back without moving my upper torso so Billy didn't see what I'd done, and he tried to kick me back, and hard, but instead his kick went high and he kicked the underside of the table, scraped his shin hard on an under-support. Dyslexic he may have been, but gullible he certainly was.

The blow was clearly quite painful, and he began yelling loudly. The new female principal came up and grabbed him by the arm, said, "Now what are you yelling about, Billy?"

Billy pointed at me and said, "He kicked me under the table!" That was partially true. Mostly true.

The female principal, whose name is lost to history, pointed to me and said, "This is the nicest and smartest boy at this school. This boy would not have kicked you." She pulled him out of his chair and he began screaming. As he was being led away, he managed to pull back his jeans and reveal a huge scarlet scrape, bleeding from where the skin on his shin had been peeled back from kicking the underside of the table.

I felt the weight of the world there, the cross-over consequence of my dual personality, and I wanted to chase the kid down, apologize, and tell the principal the truth, but instead, Arthur said, "Damn, Dom; you got rid of him quick." But I didn't have much time to feel sorry for Billy, as my own rue was already in the cosmic mail.

✤

Dan and Mare were also at Vermillion for their sixth-grade year, but it was as if they were already in junior high, at another school. We never overlapped, never saw one another. My reputation as a gutter-mouthed vulgarian would inevitably show up on their radar, I understood. It was too small a school, and kids, they liked to talk. For the record, I wasn't comfortable being a hoodlum-in-training. I preferred to be the Nancy-boy academic, but the suction of appealing to the neglected element, of having their respect and keeping them quieted, keeping them from looking at me like a target, like someone they'd like to have a go at, that sense of . . . well, survival . . . that was more powerful, and I felt I could walk that line like Johnny Cash. This was a question of survival: I was a soft kid, thin for my age, and fairer and smarter than the rest of them. They felt I was not one of them, not one of the Mexican kids, nor was I one of the others, the white kids, and so I adapted. This was adaptation for the border town.

But I didn't think anyone was capable of understanding, so instead I parceled it out, compartmentalized, and I dreaded the day my family would find me out.

It was Mare who got the word first. One of the girls in my grade found out Mare was my sister, and I must have pissed off that girl at some point because she told Mare everything, in great delicious detail.

I remember that afternoon. I am sent on an errand with this kid named Juan. Juan is scary. He must have been fourteen or so, but was passing off as a ten-year-old. He wore thin cotton shirts that were hardly ever buttoned, a black comb in his back pocket, didn't speak a word of English. You could very easily see Juan having lived in some ramshackle hut out in the Mexican frontiers, a horseman, cattleman, something, and already having been fully realized. There was something elegant about him, something sinister and beautiful, like he was already a man very clearly defined. He scared me and most of the teachers, too. So this afternoon, we're asked to get the projector from the library, and as we're walking down the exposed hallway, we're alone and we're having an easy exchange—this guy that speaks to no one—and he says through a smile, *"Esté vato,"* which really can't be translated, more of a *Get a load of this guy, man* sort of mock shoulder punch, very blokish, and well, I felt that I had done my work. Like I'd arrived, like I was safe.

When I get home, Mom yells to me from her bedroom. The door is shut, because it's the only air-conditioned room in the house. I put my books down and am changing into my afternoon clothes. I'm not expecting anything when I walk into her bedroom and almost recognize the look on my sister's face, one of delight at reporting gossip, tattletaling, and I certainly do not recognize the look on my mother's face before her blow catches me on the jaw. It was the look of divorce. It was the look of hatred only a mother could give her child.

She hits me again, when I recover. She slaps me on the ear, leaving it ringing. She slaps me again, high on the cheek. She backhands me on the lower jaw, nearly chipping my tooth. She slaps me on the eye. She slaps me so many times I lose count, lose a sort of consciousness as I slip back into that cold around my heart, confused, now that I got the beating at home—in this room, it wouldn't be the last time—that I thought I had avoided at school. And the tug from my heart, this time it did snap, snapped like a winter that has never really gone away. This is finally where I went cold.

My father gave my brother and me spankings about three, maybe four times a week. They were painful at first, but eventually you got used to the routines, the motions, you cried loudly so he'd stop and sometimes they'd bruise but mostly they just made your legs rosy—he'd use a belt, sometimes a stripped branch from a tree, if it was available.

A few of those stories really got into my brain, got into my psychology. As I grew older, it became a power play: How long could you take it before you cried? He'd hit you repeatedly, then you'd cry, then you'd get one or two more: That was where the lesson was. That was how I learned justice. And I eventually understood it to be a regular Catholic exercise: You did bad, you got your licks, you did your *mea culpa* for a while, then things settled down. This pattern was repeated until you understood the thing about Jesus: You do it, He pays for it. That's why you should feel guilty. He took your licks for you. Awfully good of him.

But Mom's beating, that I don't think I ever recovered from. I felt that if she only could hear about it, if she knew what that school was like, I was certain she would have understood—Mom was the only bastion of reason and safety and to an extent, love, in that household. Mom was supposed to be the opposite of Dad, but then: this. It was betrayal from a place I had never expected.

The look on Mare's face as I left, I don't think even she was prepared for what Mom's reaction would be. Mare went to the kitchen, got a wet towel and came back, and put it to my face as I cried quietly into it. A little later, Mom came out of the room. She sat next to me on the couch, lifted the cold wet towel from my face like she did when I was younger and had the fever, and looked at me, looked at what she had done to my face. The look on her face, it was a cluster of things, like she was forgiving herself and forcing herself to forgive me, and it was the complete opposite of the look she had given me when I was badly fevered. I couldn't look at her again for ten years.

Chapter 6

¡OKLAHOMA!

There's a custom in this part of the world that never fails to raise eyebrows when I describe it to those who didn't grow up here, and usually fails to impress anyone who has.

Down on the border, it is quite common for a family to swap or trade children in a sort of biological "regifting" program, usually when an unwanted issue has visited unexpectedly, and it is also used as a system of barter. If an indigent family cannot afford to feed yet another mouth, or finds itself in need of something and has a newborn for exchange, then they might exchange it with a childless couple who is willing to swap. And they will do so totally without oversight or consequence. Well, without immediate consequence.

Children here are a commodity slightly more precious than livestock, I think because eventually a life-insurance policy could be placed upon them, and then they further mean a guaranteed revenue stream once past elementary school, when they are capable of manual labor, or exhibit some skill at driving.

This is an admittedly cynical posture to take, sure, but growing up among this displaced strata of people, this is what I felt, or felt eventually, when I was able to describe it. It was not that they were incapable of feeling love—I'm fairly positive most did *love* their children, but I think they were simply incapable of translating it into everyday communication when there was work to do, or the possibility of sex in the offing.

Gramma, as bad luck would have it, experienced this familial redistribution firsthand in the late 1930s during the Depression, and then more than once. Gramma was swapped around until she could be placed with a family that could find her useful, and feed her in return. By the time she was ten years old, she was sent to live with her uncle at a farm adjoined to her father's, equally poor, but burdened with wild children whom Gramma would presumably nanny.

She would do this, it was decided, for half a tortilla a day. For the other half, her brother, Felípe, an Irish twin ten months older than she, would work the ramshackle dust-boned animals.

In later years Gramma would tell us of this time, how, for punishment, she and Felípe would sometimes be tied to a pole buried in the ground and whipped without mercy, their hands bound together while made to walk around and around. Marge teared up when Gramma told us this story, sobbing, holding her hands to her face, saying, ". . . *they were like slaves!*" But I couldn't really feel anything for Gramma at that time, although I'm sure Marge did, because she didn't have the sort of history I had with Gramma. For Marge, the image of Gramma getting whipped like a Mexican Kunta Kinte was poignant, but to me it was *mot juste,* because I couldn't feel pity for her after having experienced a similar childhood at her hand.

Gramma had grown up tough and mean as a result of her circumstances. She had to become tougher than her environment, or she would have starved. Her metric for wealth, as a result, became food, at a very early age, like you see in survivors of POW camps, who horde secret caches of food in an otherwise suburban existence.

Gramma went on to describe how she spent the early part of her adolescence as the unwanted cousin come to live with a mean, wild-boy tribe of haranguers, these five cousins of hers, who would torture and assault her every chance they had, would keep her subjugated, inferior, reduced, and reminded of why she was there. She had to watch her cousins during the day, while everyone who was capable (boys over age twelve, girls over age fifteen) would work the land, the fields, the farm.

She was responsible for their welfare, and it was a tough job because there were so goddamned many of them, and some of them were actually older, like her cousin Elvíra. Elvíra was fourteen, and blossoming. One day, she decided to cross the woods through a short cut that separated her from the rest of the kids, returning home from some errand or chore, and Gramma had decided to follow her. When they arrived at the wooden fence, which served as a boundary between their farm and their neighbor's, Elvíra was suddenly grabbed from behind in ambush by the eldest son of that neighboring family, a lean boy in his twenties, who set about to tumble her in the field, right there. But this was Gramma's family, and she was having none of it. She grabbed a log and brought it down hard on the back of his head while he was trying to pin down her cousin.

He flopped over, rolled onto his back, and she grabbed Elvíra and they both ran home, Elvíra clutching what was left of her dress closed over her new breasts. When they got home, they told her father, who grabbed his 30/30 and set off in his truck, but the boy had already run off, and he was never heard from again.

Gramma was regaled, heralded at home as the guardian of her cousins, but it was short of the mark. Gramma was not going to let some wiry fieldhand's unchecked libido get between her and the one-a-day tortilla that was keeping her and her little brother alive, no sir.

Some years later, when Gramma was nearing the fertile age of sixteen, it was with some fairy-tale alarm that the unruly tribe of cousins would get surprise and periodic visits from a wandering and charismatic cowboy smuggler during the hours when the kids were out doing what they usually did each day, which was make someone miserable near the Rio Grande.

They first noticed him because he kept coming around and asking if the kids had seen the American Border Patrol, or maybe the "*reínches*," which is what the border Mexicans called the Texas Rangers, and then if they had, where, how often, how many, et cetera. But he had no need for their sidekick intelligence. He was circling around because Gramma had somehow caught his eye, a fact that eventually surfaced and quickly bewildered everyone.

The kids would gladly and loudly report anything they'd seen, make up information just to keep him hanging around; he was the area's Billy the Kid. Everyone knew him by sight there: Daniel Martinez, *El Caballero*. The Gentleman Cowboy.

At nineteen years old, Daniel, my grandfather by blood, was already a *caballero*, a sort of localized knighthood acquired by his obstinate refusal to acknowledge the law on either side of the border, and excellence in his field. He wore Stetson hats and exotic animal hide as boots, a very big deal at the time, like spinning rims on an Escalade. Daniel was a *coyote*, bringing people and liquor and cinnamon and animals across the Rio Grande

River, called *el río bravo* in Mexico. It was, at this time, a huge, swollen, and undammed thing, a proud and dangerous partner in Daniel's enterprise, utterly unconcerned with human welfare, a warm and brown liquid dragon.

My grandfather was a lean, light-skinned man with wavy black hair, and he towered over the regular men of the area at an easy six feet, clearly of Spanish lineage. He was the area's Robin Hood, the bandit-hero, and he was well received everywhere he went, it seemed. Daniel was a born river person, totally unafraid of the whims of the water that now divided Mexico from white people, and he understood its moods and temperament intimately, and he took advantage of this gift.

The Border Patrol had its issues with Daniel Martinez. For years he had helped hundreds of Mexicans across the river to travel north and work more jobs up in the States, floated over booze by the gallons during Prohibition and carried bundles of cinnamon, parrots, and reptiles—anything that could turn a profit in the United States. The "border town" was a brand-new thing to the area, some mythic division created during the Civil War, and he and his own fathers were simply making the best of it, very much a Rhett Butler of the area, and he was very good at it. Just look at his boots. Then, for reasons lost to history, he set eyes on Virginia Campos, and he fell in love. . . . Or the sort of love he was capable of, as a full-grown boy king of early Texas.

The only stories I have of my grandfather are those of guile, of exquisite slipperiness, and of a near mythological ability to evade the law. He was Brer Rabbit, with a fondness for the river, which I actually have to admit I possess as well. I like the water. I am good under the water, and it doesn't scare me in the least, whatever the form or velocity. Its depths and hydraulic violence do not frighten me. Water kills you when you fight it, saves you when you go with it. My father doesn't have this appreciation of water, I've seen. Things like this skip a generation, I read. And things like this, they were very much qualities that my grandfather had. They've told me stories, which are the only things of his that survive.

In one, Daniel is caught by the Border Patrol while he's ferrying a raft full of people over to America, and this bunch, they're caught red-handed, all have their hands in the air, under guard from the agents, and he leans down as they're pulling him ashore, saying, "Don't shoot; my boots are caught in the wire here," and all the while he's pulling them off, and then when they come off he slips right into the water before they realize he's fucked off. The agents fire into the water, trying to kill him. but Daniel can hold his breath for two minutes and he's so far downstream in his river, they can't do a thing, and he gets away.

That's my grandfather for you.

In another story, he's riding near the river when his horse steps on a hive of yellow jackets and he and his horse are suddenly swarmed. The horse goes completely insane from the ensuing stings and he charges uncontrollably through the bracken and eventually spills over a cliff and into the river twenty feet below.

Daniel doesn't panic, though he is sinking like a rock because his boots are filling with water. And while he's underwater he removes them as he's swept away in the current—boots tend to suck you down to your death—and he manages to swim to the river bank, though he never sees his best horse again. He lost a lot of boots in that river, too, apparently.

Daniel was exalted around these parts because of escapes like this. He was peasant royalty in the making, and his people loved him. And when he suddenly proposed to Gramma, whom he saw one day playing nanny to a truly horrible assortment of children, she was swept away from this existence in what was considered on the dusty borders of the Rio Grande River in the 1940s to be a Cinderella wedding. It completed his fairy-tale image.

Gramma, of course, accepted this proposal to marry Daniel Martinez and delighted at the envy of her family and cousins, and she was carrying his child within weeks. This child would be my father, and the only child they would have together. When she carried him to term, they decided to name him Domingo. Domingo Campos Martinez, at the vehement insistence of one of Gramma's female cousins, who said the name was dignified and macho because she had a crush on another local cowboy also named Domingo, a relationship that did not last long and existed primarily in her head, and in the woods behind the horse barn.

"*Estába albórrotada,*" Gramma remembers about her cousin, when I asked her why she named her son "Sunday," and why I was now burdened with it. *The girl was in heat.*

This is how I got my name.

Before the birth of my father, Gramma and Daniel got married hurriedly in a small church in Matamoros. She was sixteen years old in her wedding photograph and I have it, the only image I have of my real grandfather, and they both look frightened and corpse-like already, similar to those photographs taken of dead outlaws in the Old West, and with good reason, because Daniel . . . well, Daniel . . . my grandfather by blood . . . he never quite made it to grandfatherhood.

My own father, or Dad, as I know and recount him here, he was about ten months old where we pick up the story. In one year's time, Gramma had already been rendered infertile by a number of Venusian troubles, so we can surmise that an uxorious saint, my dear departed grandfather was very much not. He was twenty, had a young family at home, which was a farm on the Mexican side of the border, but he had got some ideas of property on the American side of his river, and that was all coming together. But I'm sure that death was whispering from every corner of their newlywed house. You would have had to have been deaf not to hear it, just looking at him. He was aware that the American authorities were on his trail, so he was keeping a low profile, not actively engaging or putting himself in a position to be caught. This infuriated the white law on the American side of the border. The *reínches*, they were these corn-fed white boys from Kansas, maybe Jesufied Okies, from other starving illiterate farm states to the north who simply could not come to meet the area on its terms, so they decide to flood it with warrants, arrests, and bounties, some legal, some not so much. Law kinda changes down here. Things get blurry when you can't do what you want, what you *know* is right. Border Justice.

Eventually these thick-necked yokels, the Texas Rangers— because they could not catch him—they put a large underground bounty on my grandfather, one they'd knew would pay out but that they would never have to pay.

So one final dusty afternoon my grandfather Daniel walks into the last Mexican bar he would ever walk into, sits down, and asks for the last *cerveza* he would ever ask for from the last fat bartender that would ever serve him—this was April 17, 1952, around three in the afternoon (every important story in

Mexico happens at three in the afternoon, I think because that's when Jesus died). The fat bartender reaches into a cooler and grabs a Corona, then pulls a .45 caliber pistol he was keeping under the bar for just this moment—and serves Daniel both the beer and his sentence.

My father is on my couch—this is fifty-something years later, and we're in Seattle, I've been out of work for nearly a year, Dan has had his left knee destroyed in a fight, and Dad is visiting and it is a strange thing for every one of us—just moments before one of his usual narcoleptic fits, and he is telling me this story, about his own father. This is the first time I ever hear the detail, the moments, like I'm watching it for the first time on Dan's high-definition TV, and I am . . . what? Thirty-one? Thirty-two? Thirty-two.

Daniel sees the gun, pushes the beer forward, leans back away from the gape of the gun, and puts up his hands, this story goes, and he says: "*Hombre, piénsale lo qué estás haciendo.*" Think about what you're doing, man. And here is where whole lives change.

The bartender shoots Daniel through his raised hands, into his chest, and he destroys a generation of people.

He fires four times, the first one blows apart Daniel's right hand, rips through the palm, and opens up his lower neck at the collar bone in an aortic splurt, tearing out Daniel's shoulder at the back. The three other shots hit Daniel center mass, ripping his torso apart in the back like a large erupting blossom, and thus my grandfather's warrant is served, at age twenty, at the hands of a nonevent, enterprising Mexican bartender servile to the Texas Rangers, who did not quite think about what he was doing, who else he would kill, and mar.

Because, you see, it didn't end there.

The next we hear of the story, Daniel has been carted to a hospital. His family has been alerted, and people are running off and closing their doors, attempting to avoid trouble. Children are running home to tell of this new massacre in the border town. Daniel's father, my great-grandfather—my father's grandfather, if you can follow this, and the only person who could step in and rear the ten-month-old child as family—rushes to the hospital after being told that his son was shot, but not told he was eviscerated, and so when he gets to the morgue and sees an emptied, exploded carcass, the old man has a heart attack and dies in the same room. Here, the Martinez family becomes unmoored.

That's the story that's been told, but never in detail. It existed around us, growing up, and we knew never to ask the sort of questions other people would, of our origins, because we would get this grim fairy tale told broadly, quickly, to shut us children up, so it hung around our family like a grotesque bedtime mist, or a nightmarish nursery rhyme hummed by our mother to fell us asleep. It permeated everything I knew, answered any question I could have about our past and our future, yet I never fully experienced, never comprehended the horror of it, until that afternoon.

This horror of my grandfather's death. A twenty-year-old kid with no future. His chest opened up like a clumsy autopsy in a Mexican bar. The death of his father, upon witnessing. These images were poured into our cereal bowls and left on our pillows, but the barbarity of it never really nestled itself in my heart, until I asked my father, heard the story as an adult.

I have this dream.

There's this unruly kid, and I'm trying to get away from him because he just seems like trouble, and when I turn my back, he's suddenly shot by some unseen gunman, and then in my hand I am carrying a part of his liver, purple and globuled wet, and instead of being afraid or repulsed, I find myself wondering where I should put it, if I should try to drop it back in his body, or leave it on the ground, but I'm reluctant because the earth is so dusty . . . and then I wake up, thinking I could use a drink, or a valium.

And I have this memory.

My father and I are driving around downtown Brownsville, and I'm not 100 percent certain as to the accuracy of this recounting, but I could swear to you—and I hope that I'm wrong, that my memory is faulty—that when we drive through Elizabeth Street, I could swear—in my memory, mind you—that he says, "That's the man that shot your grandfather," and with his chin he points to a fat man, an utterly nondescript Mexican with a mustache who looks like a hundred other Mexicans, wearing a soiled white pentafold, standing in the back alley doorway of a derelict restaurant. Now, I say that I hope I'm making this up because I wonder at the torture it would be to know that the man who shot your father lived, and lived right over there, scratching out a living, and then to say this to your own son, and not want to rip that man's face from his skull with your fingers, put a brick through his brain.

In my memory, Dad looks at that man the way a forty-year-old Hamlet would look at a very fat and Mexican Claudius, ridiculous in his cook's outfit, smoking a cigarette in a doorway and looking like a man who's carrying very grim things. Dad looks at him like a man who knows he should do something, anything, but also knows that he won't.

But again, I cannot guarantee the accuracy of this memory, and probably could not ask Dad if it ever happened. I just don't think I'm that cruel. And yet I have it.

�֍

Gramma was widowed with a ten-month-old child before she turned eighteen.

For three years, Gramma was grateful to be picking cotton and tomatoes for a living with her son strapped to her waist when she met Pablo Rubio Junior, my Grampa, about the time she was twenty-one. She was accustomed to hard work, and she could keep up with the men working the field. Pablo Rubio Junior drove the delivery trucks, had just come back from the Korean War where he had been a private in the trucking pool.

This was a rough time for Gramma. She was the very definition of butch, though they didn't have time for fancy things like "definitions" in the tomato fields. She felt tougher than the young men, and far superior to the women who were expected to pick less and carry smaller burdens. She was competitive and mean, and would proudly get into fistfights with the young bucks who'd be surprised at how hard she could hit, hit like a man. And young Mingo, at age four, could do nothing but watch while his mother got into dusty, dirty entanglements with teenage boys who would initially humor her in a slap fight but would then realize she meant business, and that she could punch and kick and scratch like the rest of them, and they'd end up sprawled on the dirt, in a real fight, and she'd hold her own.

Apparently, Pablo Rubio Junior found this enchanting. He was bewitched by this siren of the tomato fields (bet you didn't know there was such a thing, did you?) and he paid her court in a manner worthy of their station. They had more than their share of romps behind the truck, when no one was looking, or sometimes when people were. You take love where you can get it, in the tomato fields.

When Pablo Rubio Junior asked her to marry him, Gramma had immediately consented: An opportunity like this comes only twice in a young widow's lifetime. Plus, he was another sort of royalty in the area: He was an American; he could give her citizenship. Gramma was lucky that way.

And so he did. Grampa brought her over from Matamoros to live in the barrio he and his brothers were carving out of a useable piece of farmland, a flat loamish landscape by the port, near the dump. For Gramma, it was a long way from the threadbare farm on the Matamoros side of the river to a Mexican-American barrio on the Brownsville tide flats, though topographically it might have been less than twenty-five miles removed, and it was a long way for her to go before her twenty-first birthday with a child in tow, both geographically and psychologically.

Grampa's brothers' wives were horrified that he had married a widow with a child, married below his station as head of their clan, and they made Gramma feel accordingly when she moved in, the gold digger and her son by another man. They immediately treated her the way the cousins of old had treated her before she was swept up into the soap opera of Daniel Martinez, and the feelings of inferiority she thought she had left behind began to take shape once again.

When she had been on her own, and working the fields, she had some feeling of control, could fight the fuckers if they got too uppity . . . but here, she was expected to be a fucking lady, be all classy-like and shit, but she had this damned kid from the previous marriage, and that dead bastard Daniel—God rest and bless his soul—had frenchified her and *good* so that she knew damn well she couldn't bear *Weeto* a son (that was his nickname, "Pablo" becoming "Pablíto" becoming "Weeto." Don't ask). And that's what these barrio bitches respected, Gramma knew: child-bearing and shit. She was in trouble, she felt. In the meantime she had this goddamned kid to deal with.

I suppose at this point, my father should have thanked his stars that he was not traded for a new axle or a set of brake pads. Perhaps he was too old, his genealogy too uncertain. Whatever his shortcomings at age four, Dad was stuck with Gramma, and Grampa stuck with Dad.

I should also note here that Grampa, Pablo Rubio Junior, was never the sort of man that Dad remembers now. That Gramma, with her motivations to impress Grampa and swim in this new "upscale" neighborhood in America, these things did not at all register on Grampa. Grampa was, and I will take this to my grave, a genuine saint. A drunken saint. He was saintly to me. He was saintly to my brothers and sisters. I wish he would have stuck around to meet my younger brother Derek. Grampa would have wet himself, he would have loved Derek so much. The way he loved me, and I loved him. Grampa—and this brings me to tears—Grampa was a really good person, even if a bit of a drunk. But who among us isn't?

I'm drunk now, as I'm writing this. And I'm tearing up, remembering him. Grampa was love. A big, brown Buddha of grandfatherly love.

Grampa was the only male member of his tribe to have served in the US Army. He drove trucks through the conflict, was "in the shit" in the Korean War, and when he came back home he had his future mapped out like a Manchurian hillside. The first thing he did was buy a stretch of property for his brothers and himself, about five acres of land right smack in the center of a large field that grew sorghum, corn, and cotton on rotating years.

This was the Rubio barrio, though we didn't know it growing up. (I'm sure it would have horrified my sisters and my mother to know that we were living in a barrio, but from the safety of distance and time, the patterns are much more clear, and I can say, without complication, that we lived in *their* barrio, that we lived in a barrio, the Rubio barrio. It fits the definition. That I am, after all, a "barrio boy.")

The barrio was rectangular and surrounded on three sides by farmland, and it ran immediately parallel to Oklahoma Avenue, an unremarkable dirt road off State Road 511, just four miles from the Rio Grande, which by this point had become a broken, feeble thing hardly worth mentioning, full of pesticides and heavy metals from American manufacturing that moved south after NAFTA, and a ghost of the natural phenomenon of ages past when my other grandfather worked its boundaries.

But our livelihood still depended on it, or on its fertile soil and sand that Grampa was now selling at $180 a truckload, which he had his brothers hauling. Oklahoma was our personal "promised land." Our own private Israel.

Oklahoma Avenue was in the hinterlands east of the township of Brownsville, further rural to an already rural area. It was twenty-eight miles from Boca Chica Beach, or the Gulf Coast, and one mile from the Port of Brownsville to the immediate north, about a mile from the city landfill.

During the growing season, we'd awaken every morning at six o'clock sharp to the sound of a small yellow crop duster, flying overhead and disregarding the fact that a whole series of families lived in its path. It would make an attempt to cut its pesticide spraying short while over the barrio, then engage it once again while it was immediately over Gramma and Grampa's house so that it didn't miss the first few rows of cotton or corn.

"Growing up, we ate polio for breakfast," I would tell my friends, when I had them. "We had malaria sandwiches for lunch, with a side of the pox." Because we were sprayed with DDT, you see. It was kind of the truth; such was my resistance to pestilence in my youth. Now, if someone sneezes on a bus, I'm sure to catch cold. Such is my resistance to pestilence in my maturity. I'm fairly sure I'm infertile, as is my older brother. We've never knocked anyone up, though we've had plenty of misadventures. My sisters have had difficulty bringing their children to term, struggle in their legitimate attempts. Personally I'm now just waiting for the first signals of cancer. I'll probably go willingly. Likely go willingly. I don't want a fuss. But as a kid, I always wanted to shoot that plane down with a .22 rifle I had handy, just on impulse. Now, knowing what I do, I wish I had. It would have been fair dinkum. Border justice.

But back to Gramma. For the first few years, she beat her son in front of her new husband to make herself seem like she was totally on board with the new program, the whole new family plan over here in America, goddamn it. She treated Dad like veal. I would imagine Weeto tried to stop it, but he would also respect the fact that because it was her son, he figured she knew what she was doing, since he had no kids of his own, so maybe making the boy crawl home on his knees until they were bloody wasn't *too* horrible, or maybe when she made him hold a brick over his head while kneeling for two hours wasn't . . . I dunno. Maybe I say this because he never struck me as the sort of man who would strike children, didn't know what was right and wrong with them. I do know that for the first year, when they lived in a small one room farmhouse off that Oklahoma Avenue, that—at least from Dad's reports—Weeto and Gramma had no problem rutting like elk on a bed not ten feet from the box that Dad had to sleep in.

This I can believe. Grampa was always a bit priapic, but who among us. . . . Ah, well.

Anyhow, Grampa really wanted a son, but Gramma could no longer conceive, it has been whispered, suggested. Most everything to do with female reproduction is kept secret from men, avoided conversationally, shamefully, then celebrated when conception occurs, perhaps to keep up a sublimated version of the virgin birth.

In her intimidation and infertility, Gramma turned to her first cousin Lydia, and begged for her son, Ricardo, freshly minted from her prodigious and overflowing womb.

"Please," Gramma begged. "I will help you become Americans."

"And what else?"

⚜

This is how Gramma gave Grampa a son, Richard, as a new-born, birthed by her cousin, Lydia, and Dad had met his cuckoo bird, the brood parasite that would eventually kick Dad free of the nest, but not so very far.

His cuckolding would come much later, but that's another story.

Chapter 7

GRAMMA AND THE SNAKES

Dan and I are helping some long-forgotten Mexican mechanic replace a radiator in one of the older trucks when we hear shouting and loud metallic cracks coming from behind Gramma's garage, near her pigsty, early one Saturday morning. It sounds like a war cry, thick and high, as if signaling a Viking charge and it pierces the too-bright morning like an ice pick.

Immediately, all three of us are on high alert, and the mechanic struggles to get out of the innards of the truck, his eyes wide and white. Dan and I look at each other sideways, and for a moment, I see him thinking, *Now what?*

Another shout, another series of loud cracks, and we're all off, running to the source of the clatter, our tools and hats falling off us in our wake.

Being the smallest and lightest, I'm also the fastest, and I round the corner of the garage first, leap over an upturned five-gallon can and stop short when I see my grandmother pummeling the concrete slab she uses as a sidewalk from her porch to the gate of the sty.

In her hands held high over her head is a shovel, and she's using the flat side of it as a hammer and keeps bringing it down again and again, hollering a loud Indian battle cry and I think for a moment she's lost her mind, because there doesn't seem to be anything at the end of her blows, but dirt.

She's standing there, in full battle mode, rude trousers cut short just above the knee, her loose shirt flying open at the waist so that each time she lifts her weapon you catch sight of pale flab, and she reminds me briefly of the Incredible Hulk in transformation. Or a runtish, hallucinating barbarian braining an imaginary opponent.

Dan runs into me and holds me by the shoulder, and he too is caught short, paralyzed in confusion as well, but the mechanic charges by us, runs around the large silver propane tank that sits outside Gramma's house and immediately understands what's happening. He grabs an old rusty hoe leaning against the garage and joins in the attack: rattlesnakes.

Gramma has killed one already, smashed its head flat on the white concrete slab and it is still coiling itself around itself, turning around and around in a death spasm while she continued to smash at the living one again and again.

Gramma had been surprised by the mate, the female who very nearly bit Gramma as she killed the first one, and the mechanic tries to join in on the fray but as he lifts the hoe to swing it down hard, it is caught by the laundry line—it's close quarters combat in that yard—but he adjusts and catches the second snake in the mid-section and nearly cuts it in two. It turns and strikes back at the mechanic, who is well beyond reach, just as me and Dan finally come to, look around for some sort of weapon to join in on the fracas—where's a goddamned machete? That would be cool!—but we can't find anything except the bucket and an ax handle, so Dan throws the bucket on the snake making more noise than concussion, and though the snake is stunned, unravels itself and then attempts to run, and I pick up the ax handle and Gramma pushes me away, says I'd get too close to it trying to hit it with that, was I stupid? and the snake tries to slip away and Gramma gives it the *coup de grâce*, flattening its head against a particularly hard bit of earth, and the snake begins the same coiling thing that the other one did, rolling around and around on its back, in a final seizure.

Gramma doesn't let up though. She then turns the shovel into a large, edged spear and begins to divide the snake into sections, and the mechanic joins in with the hoe: halves, thirds, fourths, fifths, et cetera. They turn on the original snake, too, and leave a large, bloody smear on the concrete slab.

When she's done she leans on the shovel and breathes heavily, looks at the mechanic, who's also feeling a bit of that victorious bloodlust, and they smile at each other.

"*No sábien con quien estában chingándo,*" she says to him. They did not know who they were fucking with.

"*La Señora Rubio, chingádo,*" says the mechanic, laughing and shaking his head in amused disbelief. He's heard the stories, has been warned: "Don't fuck with Mrs. Rubio."

Gramma's reputation preceded her all over South Texas. Growing up on that farm in the 1930s, in Tamaulipas, Mexico, it was not uncommon for the Mexican government to encourage squatters to set up camp on the land of indigenous farmers, then by some stroke of bureaucratic maliciousness, serve the illiterate owners some documents claiming that their land was now forfeit, that it belonged to the squatters. They were called *curceríos*, the "men of diarrhea." One had set up camp on Gramma's father's property, and was slowly attempting to stake his claim. He had the annoying habit of putting his saddle and saddle blanket on a tree that was of particular value on that farm, since there was little else on it, and one that Gramma's family had asked him repeatedly to desist from using to dry his saddle, as it was killing the tree. After ignoring them for the third time, Gramma, who was fifteen, had had enough and took her father's .45 caliber revolver and woke the man up with the pistol in his mouth. She led him to a field near their house with the whole family watching, and she made him kneel in his underwear, beg for his life in the dust. "Tell me why I shouldn't shoot you right here," she asks him.

"Because I'll leave right now and you'll never see me again," was his reply, and this time, he was as good as his word.

Before that, when she was thirteen, she and her little brother Robé, who was always her wingman during this time, were out checking the traps put out on their land that their father would use to catch small game, rabbits and such. This particular day, he'd caught a thirty pound male ocelot. No shit. They were mesmerized by the cat, a *tigríllo*.

They'd heard of them, but had never seen one. This wasn't a bobcat: This was an actual fuck-off ocelot, about a third the size of a leopard, and similarly mottled, and it was pissed. Gramma was not about to let this opportunity pass her by. She was armed with a machete, and a ten-year-old brother. She could do this, she thought to herself. She had enough time to cut down a sizeable branch and whack it into something resembling a club, handed the machete to Robé, who was terrified, and she set upon bludgeoning the cat, who was not cooperating. The ocelot fought back and got in a few scratches before Gramma brought the wood down on its head. A week later, when she came by to check the traps after the first ocelot, the traps had caught the mate, the female, and Gramma brought the club down on her as well and took down *two* ocelots, took two pelts, got fifty pesos for the male and thirty for the female (that one was damaged a bit more, because she put up more of a fight). Gramma fed her family for months. That was my grandmother. That was her reputation in South Texas.

This morning, after the snakes, I believed everything I'd ever heard about her. Watching her go into a frenzied attack, when she felt threatened at a primitive, life-and-death level with another animal, watching her ego leave her and her reptile brain take over completely as she pummeled those rattlesnakes?

Yeah, I was a believer.

Gramma warns me to step back, since I am barefoot. The snakes could have lost their teeth in the grass or on the concrete walkway, she says, and I could still get stuck and poisoned. This frightens me, and I stay on the porch while she gets the hose and washes away the snake blood, and the parts. The mechanic cuts off both rattles and gives them to Gramma to keep as souvenirs. She eventually hangs them in her garage over her car. Rattlesnakes grow a section each year, and this pair was about nine years old, a year younger than me.

I take the hose from her and continue to water down the area, feeling that it needed a good cleansing and that spraying water would cool off the morning anyway, and it reminds me of the time I was four and being stalked by a particularly dominating rooster, right here, in the same spot, near Gramma's hen house. The rooster immediately saw me as a sissy and would attack me on sight, so that going from Gramma's house to our house became something of a game of cat and mouse. My legs were riddled with small, bloody pecks from the fucking thing.

I had told Gramma about this, but she didn't believe me until the day the concrete slab was being poured. This was a sign of wealth in the barrio, that you had wealth enough to avoid mud, and I remember most of the day was spent in making a large singular concrete mold out of wood planks that led from the final step of her porch to the gate of the hen house.

I had been helping gather nails, pouring water for the cement, patting it down—it was one single large pour that would break into pieces over the next ten years—when Gramma unexpectedly opened the chicken coop and suddenly the rooster ran out, flailing its bony wings and on the attack. I turned and screamed in the mostly cowardly, girly way possible, with this demon chicken swooping down behind me like an F-16, and I ran right past Gramma who, without missing a beat, grabbed the rooster by its neck and using the rooster's own momentum swung it in a high wide arc that snapped its neck at the apex. We had a nice chicken soup for dinner that night, and while I felt quite avenged, I was also thoroughly humiliated.

Don't fuck with Mrs. Rubio, indeed.

Chapter 8

POO AND PIGLETS

Gramma was never at her cruelest as when she tried to be at her kindest.

She was in the habit of buying a young pig at the start of every year, sometime in January, and raising it all year long, fattening it for the Christmas tamales.

It wasn't until I was older that I would come to appreciate the foresight involved in such a tradition, and I can say with a fair degree of certainty that this was about as far ahead as our planning for the future went—the Christmas tamales.

One particular year, she came home with two piglets: a healthy robust one that was guaranteed an afternoon on a dirty plywood slaughtering table in eleven months, and then a tiny, defenseless pink piglet that had not even opened its eyes.

Gramma's older brother, Felípe, who'd sold her the larger piglet, had thrown in the smaller one for free, to sweeten the deal, so to speak, because—as the runt of the litter—it had no chance of surviving pigletness.

She was excited when she got home, called me over to her huge fuckoff dark blue LTD before she had come to a complete stop and ground the transmission noisily into park.

"*¡Bien paca! ¡Bien míra!*" she called to me like an excited teenager, bubbling with girlishness. ("Come here! Come look!")

I waddled over, a toddler freshly relieved of swaddles. Or maybe I was ten. I dunno. Memory overlaps over itself sometimes.

She grabbed the squirming, struggling Christmas dinner under one arm, tucking him wriggling against her hip, and with her other hand, she gingerly pulled back a dirty cloth to reveal a sleeping, pink piglet. "*Mira*," she cooed. "*¡Tán precioso!*" she continued in a moment of uncharacteristic tenderness. ("So precious!")

Gramma had decided that the runt would make a perfect pet for me, even though the chances of it dying in a day's time were nearly certain. Actually, they were guaranteed.

Still, she saw an opportunity to teach me a few Catholic lessons, without her realizing it superconsciously. The first was to expect crushing disappointment in life, the second was the absolute reliability of loss, and finally, the utter futility of faith.

That might be a bit unfair, actually.

I don't really believe, now, that Gramma had intended for events to unfold in the manner that they did, but these incomprehensibly large and looming lessons were precisely what this piglet brought to my toddler's door. Or ten year-old's door.

Gramma believed much more in the healing power of her faith and prayer and in odd adaptive measures mixed with traditional remedies, rather than in anything that might have been mistaken as "scientific" or "modern," or, more sinister than that, "white." (Gramma distrusted anything "white," in fact. For a very long period after Dad and Mom were first married, Gramma referred to Mom as *la vivora blanca*, or "the white viper.") In regard to trauma care, though, Gramma steadfastly ignored even basic medical assumptions; it was not unusual for her to treat our minor burns and scrapes with toothpaste (it was the "cooling" power of toothpaste that helped you heal). And once, when the skin had burned off my right hand in a natural-gas explosion while trying to light her water heater, she said a quick prayer to Jesus and then halved a tomato and placed it splat on the back of my hand, which was now missing the top two layers of skin. I nearly punched her from the agony. (As she got older, someone once told her that WD-40 was good for arthritic pain, in her joints. She told me this one Sunday afternoon, on my rare calls home when I could muster enough Spanish to communicate with her. I responded incredulously: "What are you, a robot?"

But back to the piglet.

Gramma gave me a crate and an old blanket for my new pet, even made room for it in a corner of an old room we called *la oficina* ("the office"), which was mostly used to warehouse bits and parts of the trucks, and a checkbook.

She folded the blanket so that the piglet was kept overheated in the sweltering room and we carved a corner out of the mess and settled the piglet down. She gave me a baby bottle full of milk from the refrigerator and showed me how to warm it up, hold it to the tiny snout, and wait for the animal's instincts to kick in. They never did.

His eyes never opened, and really the only way I knew it was still alive was because it was consistently secreting a small trickle of urine and a thin, smelly excremental leakage.

This, of course, deterred Gramma nothing. She had faith it would live. She found a small portrait of "Burning Heart" Jesus, the one where he looks you straight in the eye while holding his own heart in his hands, engulfed in flame—you remember the one—and she put it over the piglet's head, then told me to pray with all my might, to squeeze my eyes shut and put all my faith into Jesus's healing power, and that if I prayed hard enough, the piglet would get better. Just you wait and see. Pray your little fucking heart out, she said to me in Spanish, and it will live.

Of course, I had no idea what the hell she was talking about, as a toddler (or a ten-year-old) when she went on and on about her *fé*, ("faith"), but I knew to repeat whatever she said, when she was praying, so I did, and after she left, I kept praying to Jesus in a long, uninterrupted conversation about how well I'd treat the piggy if it got better, how I'd feed it and hold it and take it home with me so it could sleep in the bed with me and Mom and Dad (either as a toddler, or ten-year-old) and I fell asleep after a while, with that list of what I'd compromise in exchange for the piglet to live growing and growing in that stifling oversize closet Grampa had used for an office. It was really just a catchall windowless room of greasy truck parts, oil cans, half-working tools, unbreathable air, and now, a dying piglet.

I woke up sweating a few hours later, with the sweet acrid smell of poop in the room, sugary and innocent, the faultless excretions of newborns that will not provoke revulsion.

The room was still, so hot that even the molecules had stopped moving because they were afraid of heat exhaustion.

I pulled back the cover slowly to see how the piglet was doing and saw that it was no longer breathing. Its tiny nether region had swollen, looked purple and watery to the touch, and since it wasn't even leaking pee anymore, I knew that it was finally dead.

I started praying again, hard as I could, and whimpering, begging Jesus to undo it, to bring it back, and Gramma heard me from the next room, came in to see how effective the power of Jesus had been—and I think she had actually expected the pig to recover, because we'd called in her faith card, and she was also sincerely disappointed to find out that the piglet had expired that afternoon. "Why didn't Jesus save him?" I asked her, through my tears.

"It's not Jesus's fault," she said to me. "God had other plans for him," she intoned, repeating a hollow stock answer from the church, as she'd heard told to her many times before. I was thinking, *What sort of plans? Make him into tiny tamales?*

"No, that doesn't sound right," I said. "We asked for his help. We prayed to Jesus. If Jesus can't help, why don't we pray to God instead?" Why go through the overburdened hippie public defender when you can talk to the judge directly?

¡Aye, mijo! she yelled, genuinely frightened, "Don't talk like that!" She crossed herself. I forget the Spanish word for *heresy,* or if Gramma even knew what it meant, but she stopped short of leveling the charge, putting on her *auto da fé* headdress. I don't think she ever trusted me fully again, after that comment, because of my natural Lutheran sensibility, outminding her Catholic chain of command.

Anyhow, I cried for that pig. And I never forgot that smell, in that room, either, and I still get fleeting phantom instances of it a few times every year, when I'm in some deep introspection, thinking back down that far, picking at the wounds, under the armor.

And I never prayed like that again, until the night we thought my little brother Derek died (you'll meet him later). It wasn't until some point around four or five o'clock in the morning on the West Coast, about two hours after I got the call from Robert, Mom's second husband, that Derek was in the hospital in Austin, with the back of his head crushed, that I felt that I didn't have a choice, that I had to go to that door, to God's door, and ring that doorbell after all this time. I had an image of myself standing in a downpour, my hat in my hand, in the middle of the night, asking to be let back in. God's porch light turning on. Me swallowing hard, about to say something, when the door knob turns. . . .

But I can't get into that right now.

Chapter 9

CHRISTMAS WITH GRAMMA

Having grown up destitute on a dead Mexican farm during the Great Depression, Gramma had developed the survivor's ability to draw profit from circumstances other people would find debilitating. If there had been a "Great Depression" in the 1930s, she hadn't noticed it. She was depressed, sure; but what can you or anyone else do about it? You're a starving twelve-year-old Mexican girl on a dying farm; you deal with it, find a way to cope. You don't have a choice.

This is how Gramma learned to live during her entire adolescence and into her first marriage: coping with circumstances others would find crushing, terminal.

She was like a labor boss in this regard, able to secretly earn a fairly good living while presumably doing nothing, and maintaining a status in the barrio as the chief moneylender. She always dressed like a normal, widowed Mexican peasant woman, holding on for dear life to a bulging black imitation leather purse and she kept her gold Catholic idolatry to a minimum. She wouldn't wear the cheap floral perfume popular in the barrio at that time that covered the garlic and cumin spice smells of a recently cooked, meat-heavy dish. And she would never wash away the blood red stains of a freshly slaughtered animal on her hands that *truly*—in Gramma's cosmology—defined wealth.

Jewelry, electronics, perfume, real estate, travel—none of this mattered to Gramma. It was hollow wealth. You can't eat a diamond ring. You can't eat a Ford. You can't eat a trip to San Antonio. Gramma knew where she was going to keep her money: under her mattress, and in guns.

Guns never depreciate on the border, in Texas.

Everyone in the barrio owed her money, even me, since I was about twelve years old and wanted that Indiana Jones action figure Mom wouldn't buy for me.

It also helped that Gramma had the reprehensible habit of putting *sub-rosa* life insurance policies on all the males of the barrio, betting the odds that at some point, some bit of malfeasance would befall us and she'd be able to tuck away a nice bit of change, maybe kicking in a couple thousand to the grieving family for the funeral. By the mid-1980s, she'd cashed in on Grampa's policy, after having "accidentally" dispatched him when he came home from that three-day binge he'd blindly spent at the home of his mistress. (In his defense—and knowing my Grampa—he probably thought he was actually at home with Gramma, since both women looked and screeched identically in pidgin Spanish; it was not outside the realm of possibility that he had, mistakenly, spent the three drunken days with the wrong woman and then, when he realized his mistake, wandered home to the appropriate house for his diabetes medicine, which Gramma is rumored to have switched on him, as punishment.)

I should mention here that this was a conclusion most of the barrio had reached, and that after Grampa's death, Gramma and Mom had taken what was left of Grampa's diabetes medication back to his Mexican pharmacy and were told by the pharmacist that it wasn't, in fact, diabetes medication, but some sort of vitamin. Mom swears Gramma's reaction was honest when she yelled and cried and threatened to kill everyone in the pharmacy, anyone responsible for the error.

Dan and I did not know what to believe, so we believed the worst. It was safer that way.

Writing this, it's actually kind of funny, in a twisted sort of way, to think that Grampa survived the retreat at the Chosin Reservoir, in Korea, but he didn't survive Gramma. She did what the Chinese Army could not do, in killing him, either accidentally or intentionally. That's how tough Gramma was.

Anyhow, the rest of the family, we weren't doing so well in the early 1980s, after losing Grampa.

Belts that had long gone out of fashion were tightened, gas-guzzling luxury cars had long lost any sense of luxury and were just guzzling gas, and we kids, well, we didn't really know much about any of this because we were just kids involved with our own kid stuff, going to school and humiliating each other as best we could.

When Christmas would swing around, it was always unexpected, like a relative getting out of prison. There was only one season in South Texas, and that was Hot, the Hot season, with a capital "H." Christmas landed in the Hot season, as did Easter (boy, did Easter ever), as did Thanksgiving, my birthday, the Victory at the Alamo, summer, Charro Days, winter, and . . . come to think of it, so did my siblings' birthdays, and well, most of the rest of the year. Every now and again it would rain, and the rain would be a bit cooler than usual, and then we knew it was winter. Winter, when it made an appearance, was usually just a succession of rainy mornings, which was a shame, really, because we had an odd tendency to overspend money on sweaters and fancy clothes meant for the cold, though it was cold in Brownsville for maybe one week out of every year.

On these days, Dan and I were allowed to sleep in, and I would lie in bed and watch the water make shapes on the screened window by my bed, and it would sometimes sprinkle through and land on my face, or on the book I was reading. These quiet mornings were the best moments I had growing up, and eventually, would become the reason I moved to Seattle, to follow the rain, and find more of those moments.

Moving away was also the reason I was convinced people in Texas didn't age: There are no seasons there, so there's no time to measure. Also, when I would go back to visit, everyone remained exactly the same, while I grew older. I aged about five years the first summer I spent in Seattle.

But, in return, I finally understood all the hubbub around the death of fall and the rebirth in spring, and what all those heathen, Devil-worshiping vegan wiccans go on and on about, but I had yet to identify autumn.

"Is this autumn?" I would ask people with whom I worked, in Seattle. How they *loved* educating the ex-pat Texan.

"No," they'd say. "It's late summer. If it goes on too long, then it'll be an Indian summer, and *then* it'll be autumn. After that, it'll be fall."

"Ah," I'd say, pretending to understand. "But I thought there are only four seasons?"

"There are only four seasons," they'd said. "Fall, winter, spring, summer, but autumn kinda falls in between summer and fall."

"Hunh," I said. "Like sometimes 'y' for the vowels."

Then they would look at me funny.

Another reason I was seasonally deficient was because of the trucking business Dad owned while I was growing up, where he worked primarily for the Loop Farms, hauling cotton, grain, corn, oranges, grapefruit, sunflower seeds, and other things, and so our business—his business—had a different calendar, a different set of moons and suns, and we set our clocks by those, like Hindus and Hebrews. We never celebrated Halloween because we were busy hauling onions that day. We never celebrated Independence Day because, well, we were in Texas; that's America's Independence Day, not ours. And there was sorghum to haul on that day.

But come Christmas, well, you can't keep the promise of Christmas from anyone. Even Dan and I— forced labor that we were—had been allowed to look forward to Christmas, like all good Catholic boys should, even the ones with the really good 1970s porn hidden in Gramma's bathroom, under the loose plywood in the towel drawer. No; not that one; the next one up. That one. Oh, *yeah*: That's hot stuff.

Gramma, though, Gramma had her own rules around Christmas, made it pay out like a slot machine on tilt.

See, Gramma had a yearlong con involving that pig she bought in January, which culminated on Christmas Day.

It was an easy con, made even more sinister because of how transparent and on the level she went about it.

At the beginning of every year, she'd buy a piglet—cute as a bug's ear, those piglets were. She'd bring one home after paying about ten dollars for the healthiest of the litter from her brother Felípe, and she'd make a big noise about how damnably cute the thing was, and Dan and I would get suckered into playing with it, feeding it with a bottle of milk, and holding it like it was a baby, and we'd take care of it while Gramma made a theatrical attempt at building a pigsty from the dried up and bacterially infested pen that had only recently been vacated from the dead pig before. She'd make a pathetic show of throwing plywood and rotten two-by-fours around for a few minutes, and then she'd stop, pant breathily, and clutch at her chest, at a spot where her heart would have been, if she had one, and that was our cue to step in and take over. Gramma had a crowbar made out of passive aggression that she would bring down on our heads if she couldn't get it under our hearts, for leverage.

You see, Dan and I were dumb; we had no sense of history, not even our own. We fell for this trick for fourteen, maybe sixteen years in a row. Somehow we never put it together: It was up we go and off we went whenever she'd do this, finishing any project Gramma had only to pretend to start. And it worked every single time, on anything Gramma wanted done.

So Dan and I finished building the confinement with whatever rotted lumber was at our disposal, and we let the pig loose inside, and then it became our pig, and we imitated Gramma imitating the pig and called it, *"Coche! Coche! Coche!"* I'm still not sure if that was an affectionate name for the pig—every pig—or if Gramma actually spoke "pig," the language somehow kept intact from her Aztecan bloodline. But, miraculously, the damned pig would respond every time she called it, like it understood her, and she'd pour out a five-gallon bucket of swill, never really bothering to hit the trough that Dan and I had built for it.

The swill Gramma would bring home was made out of leftovers she purchased from a local *tortilleria*, effluvium from the tortilla-making business, made up of dough and grease and lard and other sundry proteinaceous crap that she bought on a weekly arrangement, and when she poured it over the side of the sty—never bothering to aim for the trough, and how this would vex me!—the swill would spill out, spill over and blend into the pig's own filth and mud, and the *Coche! Coche!* would stick its snout into the pour and suck and chew and bite and . . . well, it was actually very charming and cute. Pigs *are* really damned cute, even when they're wallowing in their own filth. There's something almost enviable about that absolute lack of self-consciousness, which is something I probably need to discuss with my therapist. But don't be fooled: They'll take your hand right off and eat it calmly while looking at you with that dead shark eye stare of theirs.

This is why I have no compunction in eating a ham sandwich.

Anyhow, so that was our pet.

And Gramma would con us into taking care of it all year-round, going to the *tortilleria*, bringing back the swill in an open five-gallon bucket that would slop and spill in her car, and the pig would turn into a hog that would just explode in size, like a scale-model thermonuclear mushroom cloud made out of mud and shit and fat with all that it would eat, all year long, so that come December, our little two-pound piglet was nightmarishly big, big enough to eat an average person in a few minutes. In short, we'd grow a monster in Gramma's backyard and consider it a pet, lovingly calling it *coche*.

Then Christmas would come, and Gramma would kill it, right in front of us, as we all stood watching.

Back then, in the 1980s, she would do it herself—take the single shot .22 caliber rifle my Grampa left behind and just put a small bullet dead center in the pig's forehead, as soon as it kept its enormous skull still. It got to where I could tell when she was going to do it, from a very early age. The pig would be led into a garage with a rope by two or three strong Mexican men, cousins and uncles, and it would be made to stand next to a fire that had been going all morning, with a blackened tin tub set upon it with water boiling, very appropriately looking like a witch's cauldron. The pig would just somehow know its ticket was up, and it would not enjoy this moment, knew at some animal level that the assembly—the fire, the water, the burning washtub—was all meant for death, and if you've ever had elective surgery, you might know this particular reaction, when you enter the operating theater, and see the table, and the lights, and the people standing there . . . and you very nearly chicken out. That's what the pig knew, at this point: That this is all for him or her, and so it pulls this way and that way, its eyes alive like they've never been before, and then Gramma says, *"Coche! Coche! Coche!"* in a way that says, "Look here! Look here! Over here!" and when the pig looks, that's when I would say to myself, *Now,* and that's when Gramma would pull the trigger, sometimes not even looking down the sights, holding the rifle off in a straight line that ended at the pig's forehead, and the rifle would jump, and the pig's weight would first fall straight down, vertically, onto its haunches, all electrical impulse generated from its brain at that very second stopped, and it would fall securely into its legs, and then over, heavily onto its side, and then everyone would be still, for just a moment.

Then it was time to party. The pig, in that second, had made the quick transition from animal to food, and was treated as such.

It was hoisted onto a wobbly handmade table of used and scrounged-up two-by-fours and plywood, mostly from its own sty and usually constructed that very morning, and the boiling water was poured over the carcass by the women, like they were dressing a body for ritualized burial. The boiling water would make the hair and outer skin easier to shave, and they'd take to it with sharpened knives, and the hair from our year's *coche* would come easy, in a weird, satisfying scrape, and then they'd move the pig to the end of the table so that its head would dangle lifelessly off the end, and then they'd cut the pig's throat so that a huge bowl would catch as much blood as possible, and they'd let it drain at length, then remove the head altogether with a large butcher knife, while kicking at the dogs who'd sneak underfoot, attempting to lick up any blood spills in the dirt. The morning would then be spent in reducing the pig to its more profitable resources.

And there was one ceremonial moment, every Christmas during this stage of our lives, that made Dan and me feel very special and singled out, though it might—retelling it here— seem totally twisted. There's this particular cut of pork—and I have no idea where it is on the anatomy of a hog, except that it is close to the heart—that was considered the finest and most delicate cut of meat on a pig, and early in the reduction, that part was cut out, put on wooden stakes cut from tree branches and cooked right there in the fire, and then handed to me and Dan and Dad and Gramma, which was horribly conflicting, because we raised this pig, and the salt of our tears made the meat even that much more delicious.

Kidding. Anyhow, they called it *lomo,* and I have never tasted anything like it ever in General America. The closest thing I can compare it to, in mouth feel, is foie gras (again: with apologies to the vegans). It was barbarically rich, crisped on the outside and delicately soft, melting with blood on the inside. It's almost like a childhood dream. I've never had anything resembling it in my travels since.

❖

OK, so that was the worst part of the story.

What followed next can only be described as Gramma's own little tribute to Henry Ford, and I don't mean that she was anti-Semitic, because, well, we never knew what Jews were when we were growing up in Texas, except that they were some sort of people in the Bible, like the Canaanites, which is a great word. (World War II? Dan and I didn't figure that one out until *Band of Brothers.* I couldn't understand the distinction the Nazis were drawing. To me, everyone in Europe—which I still couldn't distinguish from America back then—was "white." They certainly weren't Mexican, or Texans.)

Gramma had everyone in the barrio working for her on Christmas, and conned them all into thinking it was a holiday. Her people would show up at six in the morning for the preparations of the slaughter, and then they'd *really* get to work, reducing the animal into parcels and negotiable goods. People would arrive in our driveway all day long and buy fresh cuts of pork for their Christmas dinner. It was tradition.

Gramma must have cleared one thousand dollars that day, from her ten dollar piglet, which is a phenomenal amount, when you consider the income for an average family at the time in Brownsville was roughly fifteen thousand dollars a year.

Our own family—and I should mention here that my mother, who wasn't a native of the barrio and found all this *very* disturbing, well, she kept her daughters from it. Her sons were a different story. Me and Dan: We were Dad's property, so we could go as *injun* as necessary. But for Christmas? We went all out, after the slaughter was done. We were all under Gramma's dominion.

By midafternoon, it would have taken a forensics team to determine that there had been a complete pig in Gramma's garage earlier that morning. The skin and adipose tissue had been boiled in oil to make *chicharonnes*, the head baked whole in tinfoil and dismantled to make *barbacoa*, the hooves thrown to the hounds, the blood boiled down into a fantastic gravy, the better cuts of proper meat auctioned off, the globular organs made into sweetmeats and the intestines boiled down into *trípas*. Total reduction.

By three in the afternoon, the drunk cousins and uncles had all made off with hefty portions of the meat for their own families' dinners, and the women who had helped as much as they could would either stick around to help make the sauces and meats and beans for the tamales, or they would fuck off to their own families for the afternoon, and this is when the real work would begin for the rest of us.

In preparation for the slaughter, Gramma had already purchased a huge vat of *masa*, or corn dough, from the *tortillerias* that she'd been in cahoots with all year long to fatten up *coche,* and she'd also bought plenty of the corn husks that were used to bake the tamales and were freely available anywhere in the endless geometry of farms that surrounded us, but Gramma—who had a status to uphold in the barrio—had them store-bought, because that's how she rolled. Actually, I think they were simply more hygienic, being store-bought. If Gramma could have collected the free-range corn husks for free—or had us do it—I'm sure she would have.

Anyhow, we kids did the actual rolling. We were set up in the backyard next to the now-vacant pigsty in the open yard and were set to the task: One kid would grab a good handful of dough, roll it into a ball, and put it down. Repeat, ad nauseam, to eventual nausea.

The next kid would pick up that ball of dough, plop it into the center of a store-bought corn husk he held in his left hand, and then smooth out the dough onto the corn husk with the rounded back part of a spoon, and lay it on the table for the next kid. Repeat, ad nauseam.

The kid next to him or her would then pick up the corn husk with the dough already spread on it, and then add whatever ingredient was next, or was plentiful. We normally had two to choose from: refried beans, or a fantastic meat catastrophe with raisins that had been made from the minced brains, eyes, lips, and cheeks of the pig. Delicious. My favorite part was when the knife of the person dicing the brain would suddenly "clink" on the lead bullet, and we'd yell out, fascinated. Good times.

So this was how Christmas afternoon went: an endless procession of dough, ball, smooth, beans or meat, fold, and then pile.

We'd make a raw pyramid of a dozen tamales, then the kid at the end would be charged with packaging them in aluminum foil, and they would be carted off by one of the old crones who would be in charge of the fire and the tin washtub and the steaming. These were Gramma's female cousins or neighbors. All day long they would huddle around a tin washtub, burned to charcoal by an open fire, and they'd leave a small level of water readily at the boil on the bottom quarter of the washtub, and a sort of grill would be set above the waterline, and the tamales would then be placed there in dozens and left to steam for an hour. If the Catholic Church could have seen this, they would have burned us all at the stake, because it looked like textbook witchcraft.

This was the tamale-manufacturing business. I made such a big deal about describing that bit only because when I told this story to my friend, Andy, he wanted to know everything about making tamales and found each stage absolutely interesting. He loves native cuisine. I, personally, do not, and was surprised, in fact, to find out that I was, indeed, "native." What Andy found the funniest was that I had finally seen through Gramma's scheme and realized the weak point in her operation: She had only a limited amount of *masa*, the dough. That had been her dearest investment in this. When I realized this, I developed a cunning plan of my own to get this operation in arrears by six o'clock that night, because there were some *Star Wars* action figures and play sets that needed tending to, even if I did owe Gramma another fifty bucks with a three-point vig due by the following Saturday or she would have someone break my knees.

So, when no one was looking, I started throwing every second dough ball over my shoulder onto the roof of her house. Every fifth or so dough ball would go to the dogs, already happily stuffed with the viscera that happened to spill off the autopsy table but more than happy to eat until they purged.

No one would notice as I'd roll another clump and then just toss it high over my shoulder, where it would land on the blistering tarred roof, because the sun was out in full force as it was—you know—Christmas Day. It kind of made her whole house into one giant tamale. (Hmm. Maybe that's why the roof over her bathroom rotted. Gee; now I feel kind of bad. . . .)

See, we couldn't *possibly* eat a third of the tamales that day would generate, even if we froze them. We would have been eating tamales until June. The rest would be sold at about seven to ten dollars a dozen, and it would be *Gramma* who kept the money. So we kids couldn't care less: The dough had to go. Eventually, when my brother and sisters realized what I was doing, they started laughing and participating.

So up the roof they went, and it was all going according to plan until the crows came and started swarming around her roof. But by then we were very nearly done, and she would yell, "*¡Yunior! Traeme la veintedos!*"

A true border widow, she was calling out for a rifle, Grampa's old .22 single shot. And as a Texan, I love the sound of gunplay, so I dropped what I was doing and brought her Grampa's rifle, and she shot at the crows until they left, swarmed, and returned unharmed, because Gramma was kinda drunk by this time, and so I shot and killed a few of them, to make her feel better, and she never found out that I had been the one to bring the crows in the first place, so we could finish early.

And besides, it was always safest to be on her good side, while she was drunk and armed.

Chapter 10

THE MIMIS

Before they started junior high, my sisters Mare and Margie had preemptively developed the fantasy of "the Mimis" between themselves as a means to cope with any feelings of inferiority they might have otherwise experienced by moving into the sinister world of teenage fashionistas, which, in Brownsville, was always tinged with border-town racism.

First, they dyed their brown-black hair blonde until it turned the color and brittleness of hay, then they began dressing in Sergio Valente and Gloria Vanderbilt fashions, and then finally, in further escalation, decided to call each other, simply, Mimi. They had secretly reinvented themselves for the adolescent phase of their lives, and then decided to let the rest of us in on the secret on an "as-needed" basis.

At the time, the rest of the family had not consciously realized that our job, as new Americans—and worse yet, as Texans—was to be as white as possible, and we honestly didn't see their delusion as anything other than another bewildering strata to our sisters' quest for a higher level of superior fashion, as teenage girls do.

A typical conversation between them went like this:

"Mimi, do you like my new Jordache jeans?"

"Yes, Mimi, I do. Do I look rich in my new Nikes, Mimi?"

"Mimi, you look like a tennis player, Mimi."

"I know, Mimi. Maybe I should make Mom buy me a racquet."

To help reinforce this pathological delusion, Marge had enlisted the help of Rex, a small gray terrier mix she had found rummaging in an overturned garbage can on a street near the Matamoros Bridge. She cornered the poor beast in an alley and caught it, lifting the matted, dreadlocked mutt by the armpits and deciding, right there, that the dog was a poodle and that it needed saving, naming it Rex. No one disagreed, or questioned why.

Rex was introduced to our family as the Mimis' fugue was buzzing at its fever pitch, intoxicating everyone who came near and caught a whiff of the Mimis' *Anais Anais* perfume. (We had all seen the commercials on network television while watching *Dallas* or *Knots Landing*, and it was a forbidden fragrance for rain-depressed English women with secret muscular boyfriends who drove Jaguars dangerously through one-lane unpaved Scottish roads, so the Mimis had to have it, and so they found it at the local JC Penney, and had Mom pay for it.) Dan and Syl and me, we just kind of stank from the heat and dealt with it.

Anyhow, Rex's right hind leg had a malformed kneecap that made his leg jut stiffly at a forty-five-degree angle, so it looked as if Rex was in a constant state of micturation, even when he was walking or sprinting forward, like he had been distracted by some urgent event that demanded immediate investigation while he'd been peeing and had forgotten to lower his leg in charging forward.

The older Mimi, my sister formerly known as Marge, just overlooked this because she wasn't deathly allergic to furry animals like the younger Mimi, my sister formerly known as Mare.

The older Mimi convinced our mother to adopt the dog and have his hair carved into poodle fashion, had even bought it colorful striped sweaters that made the near toothless dog pant wetly in the year-round South Texas heat.

With his fancy haircut and new powdery smell, Rex found himself terrifically misplaced on our property, about five miles outside of the Brownsville city limits. The other feral dogs that happened to be kept around didn't know what to make of him when he'd limp up to them and start barking, with his odd jutting leg, but thankfully they didn't kill him, just kind of got this look of annoyance on their dog faces and decided to avoid this new poofter that might be competing for the late afternoon dog swill Gramma would reluctantly put out at sundown.

Out there, among the outhouse and Gramma's pigsty, Rex looked as tragically displaced as his kneecap. But, in full appreciation and retrospect, perhaps that was the sort of companionship the older Mimi (Marge) had really been seeking out there, subconsciously, and had found in Rex someone as confused and dislocated as the Mimis felt in their designer jeans and trendy tennis shoes, but lacking access to an indoor toilet.

The shift to junior high had exposed the Mimis to new ideas of glamour and status, and for the first time they were really experiencing the sub- and superconscious derision that exists when cultures and races collide against one another in geopolitical reassignment, like you find in border towns, and they were smart enough to understand that which was never spoken about: None of this was ever, *ever,* pointed out. You created a polite fiction, and encouraged everyone to participate. Which is what the Mimis did.

And so the rest of us followed.

Marge and Mare, as the Mimis, had decided to align themselves with their more American—more European—genetics, even if it was through bad hair dyes and pretending not to understand Spanish.

Dad's genetic line was mostly of the Spaniard conquistador: He, like them, was tall, light skinned, and prone to fits of pork. Mom was light skinned, reddish in tint, and spoke English, so she was considered "white." We were—genetically—predominantly European. Gramma was the Indian; Gramma was the Aztec in the family. And since she had the balls in the family, we identified—culturally—as Mexican. Gramma had been made an American by Grampa, and Dad had been "naturalized" as an American when he was six years old. Mom, we would later come to understand, had a secret and very old American history.

And yet we all felt so terribly *untermensch* that Marge and Mare had to have a psychotic episode in which we all participated to help them through junior high. We all helped in creating the Mimis.

It was really that simple: Fed up and humiliated with their circumstances, the Mimis decided to change them, retroactively.

They made a conscious decision and agreement that they would be—and act—rich and white, even if their family wasn't.

Grampa's death had plunged the barrio into a rivalry between his next younger brothers and Dad, who was seen as the illegitimate inheritor of the trucking business. They clearly felt that Gramma and Dad did not belong in the barrio and were certainly unworthy of inheriting the only viable business in that barrio, the trucking business Grampa built after he returned home from Korea. They wouldn't come right out and say it or do anything overt to draw business away from Dad, but after Grampa died the regular and paying customers who had been Grampa's were no longer Dad's and were now suspiciously doing business three houses to our west, with Grampa's brothers.

The trucking business began to disintegrate around Dad within the first few years, and he was started on his slow road toward desperation and religion.

Meanwhile, the Mimis had made their decision to be two blue-blooded, trust-funded tennis bunnies from Connecticut, accidentally living in Brownsville, Texas, with us, a poor Mexican family they had somehow befriended while undergoing some Dickensian series of misfortunes.

For those of us watching, the whole "Mimi" thing took on a momentum of its own, though we seriously didn't think it would last. But at some point it took hold, and by then no one thought it peculiar, especially those in the family who didn't speak English or could not understand the Mimis when they showed up at family gatherings.

"*Yo no puedo-o hablar-o Español-o,*" one of the Mimis would say to an uncle or cousin, who more often than not would linger lasciviously around them, at first conflicted by the idea of being turned on by so young a relative and then mentally calculating just how distantly related they were and tabulating his odds at scoring with this new white chick who just happened to show up at this barrio party.

But only after two or three beers.

"Mimi, how did you like my Spanish?"

"Oh, Mimi, it's getting really good."

"Mimi, do you think they understood me?"

"Oh, Mimi, who cares?"

Mom developed a fascination with the Mimis, too, like she couldn't believe her luck, now that she was related to royalty.

Feeding into their fantasy gave her one of her own, so she was always ready for an air-conditioned trip to the mall.

She took the little clothes budget reserved for us boys, my brother and me, and patched it into the Mimis' wardrobe, because it was a sign of status for the family that the Mimis look their best; it is important for families of little wealth to have their daughters be as attractive as possible for means of social elevation.

In this way, it became acceptable for the Mimis to take the lion's share of the children's clothing budget, and none of the rest of us could question it, even though at the time, we didn't exactly know why.

But it still felt wrong.

Clothes would come in and out of fashion so quickly that I was often left with the Mimis' recently stylish hand-me-downs. No one else in my grade school was remotely label conscious, or capable of reading in English, really, so it passed unnoticed that most of my clothes were made for glamorous junior high school girls. Almost every child at my school came from recently immigrated families—kids so poor they'd save half their free lunch to share with their younger siblings at home, their heads shaved to rid them of lice.

My best friend, Arthur, he noticed, though. He was part black and part Mexican and had just moved to Brownsville from some big city slum in Michigan, where his mother's boyfriend had been employed at a GM factory, and he read labels.

"Hey, Dom," he said in that lilting, sort of inner-urban street funk, "Yo, man; you're wearing a girl's shirt. Or is Esprit making baggy boy's shirts now, too?"

I loved Arthur dearly and was totally embarrassed. So to change the subject I slugged him high in the chest and ran away crying, him in his bald head chasing me down to punch me back in my girl's blouse.

If she had any guilt, I imagine the justification my mother probably used was that my older brother and I would just ruin our clothes, working with Dad in the sandpit and under the greasy trucks. It made better sense for the Mimis to be in high fashion than for the feral boys to ruin their clothes.

"Mimi, you look just like Jennifer Beals in *Flashdance*. You should join the dance team at school."

"I know, Mimi, I think so, too."

"Mimi, I think you should dye your hair back to its original color, 'Ash.'"

"I know, Mimi, I'm trying."

"Mimi, is your dog OK? He just spit out another tooth."

During this time, Dan's eyesight was so poor, people thought he was Asian, so often did he squint. He couldn't read the blackboard in school and constantly ran into corners or short, skinny people. In every photo he took in junior high, he looked like he was trying to see into the photographer's eyes, through the camera's lens. This, of course, went entirely unnoticed, and it was the younger Mimi (Mare), with 20/20 vision, who got vanity glasses with her name etched in gold script in the corner. Dan wouldn't get glasses until he was in the military, when he was seventeen, some four years later.

"Mimi, you don't need those glasses, Mimi."

"Mimi, I do need them, Mimi. They make me look rich. They say my name in the corner, 'Mary' Mimi."

"Mimi, I think there's something wrong with Rex."

"Yes, Mimi, your dog doesn't have any teeth."

"No, Mimi, it's not that. He smells like pee all the time now."

Always a bit incontinent, Rex would not mind if, when he was attempting to pee, he'd just spray the underside of his own twisted leg during the larger part of the activity, because he could hardly lift it out of the way of the hot stream anyhow. Now, he didn't even attempt to move his bad leg out of the way, he just kind of let it have it where he stood, looking around like a confused Alzheimer's patient, panting breathily all the while. Our indoor plant pots, usually a collected oasis of old stinky dog urine, were now suspiciously micturation free. This had to mean he was pissing elsewhere, and freely.

Rex was definitely circling the dog drain.

After a few months of studying the toothless, stinky gray dog, I finally checked out a book on dogs from the school library. I read that people who have allergies to dogs are not allergic to poodles because poodle hair is almost identical to human hair. The younger Mimi (Mare) still could not get within a few feet of Rex without lapsing into violent sneezing fits, fits we were afraid could trigger asthma attacks. For me this clearly illustrated that the dog was not a poodle, but the older Mimi (Marge) would not hear of it. "You're just jealous of Rex," she said. And she was right.

❖

Eventually, Dad's failure at navigating the business left to him—and usurped by Gramma—crept into the Mimis' fantasy. Dad made a decision that would make his family as Mexican as his mother. He decided that as soon as school ended, Mom would take the Mimis and Syl and drive them to California to partici-pate in the seasonal grape harvest with the migrant workers, to meet up with Dad's cousins who did this periodically, since the

Mimis were now fourteen and fifteen and Syl was sixteen, and they could all, with Mom, collect a full salary. They would be treated like adults there, paid the same as everyone else.

Mom, I remember, was horrified at the implications, at the shame of having to send her virginal and royal daughters out to the fields. Plus, Dad's extended family out in California were very different from us, wild and frightening and . . . well, Californian. (Texas Mexicans and California Mexicans are very different from each other, like the Scottish and the Irish—fundamentally the same genetic code, but completely different in accent and habits.)

The Mimis, though, were undaunted. They did not understand the implications.

"Mimi, we're going to California!"

"Oh my God, Mimi! We're going to be 'Valley Girls!'"

"Mimi, gag me with a spoon, Mimi!"

"Mimi, your roots are showing."

We packed up Mom, the Mimis, Rex, and Syl in the beige 1980 Pontiac Bonneville, already an antique on its second engine and failing transmission, and they drove out of Brownsville and the Rio Grande Valley, eventually took I-10 to Indio, California, and into the Coachella Valley where they would pick grapes for three months like Steinbeck's Okies, way back when. Dan and I were left seething with envy.

Although, the year after the Mimis went to California, I would take this ride as well and also ended up picking grapes for the summer, and I would realize that all my envy was utterly unfounded. That we had been "migrant workers" for that period didn't occur to me, or to anyone else. That label would never stick. Could never stick. We couldn't descend to that level. We just had to do it to help out Dad; that was all. Desperate circumstances calling for desperate measures and all that. This is actually one of the few positive lessons I learned from my father: Sometimes you need to do humiliating things for work, to get through bad times. And it actually taught me quite a bit, that summer I spent there.

When it was my turn to go to California and pick grapes, I was stuck with Dad a lot of the time, which I heavily resented, but in retrospect, I realize now that he taught me more during that summer than he had taught me in the thirteen or so years previous. In the deep early morning, when the vineyards were still damp with the morning dew, and the hordes of pickers were lining up and splitting into work groups and preparing for a difficult day, Dad held me back, had me blend in with him toward the back of whatever mob we were assigned.

"*Cálmate, cálmate,*" he'd say to me, when the whistle blew at five o'clock in the morning and everyone was off to work, one person on one side of the vine row, and his partner on the other. Every bunch was sure to get picked this way. Dad, instead, was asking me to stay back, slow down. Keep still.

I kept still. He went to his side of the row, and I started to clip the grapes. Slowly. Making sure not to lose a digit. I clipped the bunch, held it up in the morning light, looking for rotten grapes, and then artistically clipped those free. I was making a still-life. This kept me preoccupied and I didn't hear from Dad for a while, and my attention was suddenly seized by the family clipping away next to us. They were insane: clipping left and right, high and low, competitively throwing bunches into boxes and having their children cart the boxes to the front, where they'd be picked up, assessed, registered, and transported to the flatbed truck, where strong toughs were in charge of loading the back. They were filling up six, seven, eight boxes to my one. But mine was prettier.

Eventually, I looked through the vines on my row and saw that Dad had found himself a nice shady spot and had cozied himself up against a post, was taking a snooze, looking very much the picture of the Mexican-taking-a-siesta thing, but without the sombrero. Just a baseball cap and a mustache. So I slowed down, too.

Asking him about it later, he said, "What the hell was the point? Those other people are going to win that bonus for the most boxes because they had nothing else except for this, and we get paid the same anyway."

Don't get me wrong: We would eventually get to work and make a notable showing of progress by the end of the day, but not until we were good and ready, when the sun had warmed up a little and we had had breakfast.

Anyhow, the Mimis' little excursion as migrant workers was quite different. When they were at their peak, the Mimis had been capable of creating a real sort of magic around them, enchanting both people and places, in such a way that you could be looking at the same dreary landscape as them, the same terrible and hopeless event, and while you might be miserable and bitter, they would be beaming, enthralled, and enthusiastically hopeful. And then, if you got near them, or were blessed enough to maybe talk to them, you would walk away feeling the same way they felt, too.

They were a gift to everyone who was lucky enough to get caught in their Anais Anais, the Mimis. They made all of us Americans.

But it was too much for even them, the reality of this trip. Sadly, I think it was childhood's end for the Mimis; the vineyards had somehow inverted their secret garden, and the low door in the wall had closed shut behind them.

The year previous, when they had made the first trip to California, the Mimis had indeed become Valley Girls: the hippest, cutest, best-dressed migrant workers of that year, and very likely for many years to come. I would imagine those migrant workers had had every quiet, onanistic nighttime wish come true, working alongside girls with movie-star looks, picking grapes at the vineyards.

The older Mimi (Marge) continued to dress like Jennifer Beals in *Flashdance* out in the fields, where the sun would sizzle any inch of exposed skin. She wore a spaghetti-strapped, red and white–striped Esprit top, white cotton shorts, and a matching headband with her red and white leather Nike tennis shoes, and took pictures of the vineyards and the workers with her Canon AE-1. Her headband kept a white division of skin on her forehead from tanning along with the rest of her face, and as a result, she was forced to wear headbands for a few months afterward, way after headbands were out of fashion.

Eventually, though, even she started dressing like the rest of the migrant workers, or else she would have died of heat stroke. There were no photos taken of that.

The younger Mimi (Mare) did not fare any better. Her vanity glasses with the fake lenses were scratched well beyond recovery, even blighting out her name etched in the gold cursive. Her roots grew out eventually, except this time, her hair turned a lighter brown as a result of the heat and the pesticides of the grape fields of Southern California.

The hard work went on all summer, and eventually it became bitter enough to breach even the walls of the Mimis' perfectly constructed fantasy, which had once withstood the ugly reality that had been screaming at the door of the Mimis' magic garden: their father's failures in keeping his family together. The wolf was now breaking through, with each snip of the clippers, and each box of grapes they had to fill, Mom and the Mimis. Oh, and Syl.

And so sadly, eventually even they were humiliated, and the delusion of wealth that had kept the family's idea of itself buoyant was deflated and left buried in a Californian vineyard, because when they returned to Brownsville—the Bonneville limping in on its second transmission—no one ever mentioned the Mimis again. They had been left behind in the grape fields, and it was Marge and Mare who returned in their place.

As it happened even Rex was finally able to break out of the fantasy of the Mimis. He found his own low door in the garden, before it disappeared.

He wasn't among the returning party, though we were left with enough fleas in the carpet and the vague smell of urine to remember him for many, many years after.

He died unexpectedly one night, when they were still in California. Mare found him first, awoken by her allergies, and stumbled across Rex's still body on the floor on her way to the bathroom.

"Hey, Marge, wake up," she growled back to her sleeping sister. "Your dog's dead. It's four fifteen; time to go."

In his dying spasms, Rex's deformed leg had rigored stiffly into a 90-degree angle away from his body in a final salute and "thank you," I'm sure, for the hospitality of his final days. He was that kind of dog, always minding his manners. He was buried with the help of some unknown migrant in an unmarked grave out in the grape fields, but regally, in a quiet funeral fit for a dog king, a very long way from the Matamoros Bridge where he had started with the Mimis.

Chapter 11

DAN'S FIRST FIGHT

The summer he turned thirteen, Dan took up the role of his father's keeper. It was dusk, sometime after the Fourth of July, and we were still working at the grain fields, bringing in the final trailer load of the day and Dad's wiring was, as usual, faulty.

Every year we'd have to rebuild one or two of the thirty-five-foot trailers using cheap interlocking paneling intended for home construction as siding for the trailer, two-by-fours for support, and a chain and winch assembly to keep the integrity of the sides intact, across the iron bed. Into here would be poured cubic tons of grain and corn throughout the summer until school started again. We always worked through the Fourth of July, so it was never much of a holiday for us, and as an adult with work that was nonagriculturally based, I puzzled at the big deal others made of it.

Mom was also there some nights as the work wound down, as she would drive up with dinner sometimes and I loved it when she stayed, because she'd sit in the air-conditioned Bonneville and watch from a safe distance as the hopper would unload its fill into the trailer bed. Inside the car was the only place I could get away from the grain dust—this tiny, flaky allergen that would stick to you like itching powder, adhere to any exposed sweat-soaked flesh and irritate, just fucking irritate, you to insanity. Cornstarch and long sleeves were the only folksy preventive measures against this, but it was too hot to wear long sleeves. And the grain dust was invasive, viral, and I think responsible for all my allergies today.

Tradition had it that work ended at nightfall, but sometimes the Loops brothers—the farmers who contracted Dad to deliver their grain to the elevator—would insist on one or two more loads in the dark, using their "crazy white man big medicine," this thing called "electricity." Dad didn't like this because then it would be clearly evident that the lights on his trucks were on the blink, and besides, he'd usually go out after work when he was flush, and quite often, he had already been drinking during the later part of the day.

As night is falling this particular evening, he decides to do a preliminary check on the running lights down the length of the trailer and on its end. He's tired, has had a long day, and it is not likely over yet, so with some sense of resolve he lights it up and sure enough the lights blink, go out, blink back on, stay on, then go out, and then blink again. This means a short, and means he'll have to travel the length of the wiring with a flashlight for an exposed breach in the connections.

He takes one side of the trailer and Dan takes the other, just after one of the Loop boys, who is fourteen and one of Dan's friends, finishes loading the trailer and drives off in the dark to get refilled from the combine.

Dad then decides to pull out onto the state highway and onto the shoulder, the wisdom being that it might be too heavy to pull out of the muddy road with a full load. (I'm actually making that part up, in the retelling. I don't remember why he decided to do that.)

We are on a field immediately off of Highway 511, just a few miles from our house on Oklahoma Avenue, one of the more accessible and less remote farms that the Loop Brothers own. The dirt road intersects the state highway, and Mom and I are on the dirt road opposite, watching comfortably from the Bonneville as Dad pulls the trailer out and onto the pavement, and then lines it up on the shoulder, parallel to the field.

In the distance to the south, a tiny speck of light signals the rare oncoming car, heading in our direction. The trailer would be well off the road before there was any danger, it seemed. But the car, or truck as it turns out, is speeding and comes on very quickly, seems to slam on the brakes and skid to a halt, nearly ending in the ditch behind the trailer.

Neither Dad nor Dan hear any of this because they're back in search of the electrical short under the trailer, and the tractor is idling, but Mom and I watch this happen from the opposite side of the road, don't react or respond because we're not sure what it means, sitting safely in the Bonneville, listening to outlaw country music on the radio.

This is during my "Rambo" period, when I carried homemade knives with me everywhere I went and would incessantly whittle sticks into points, because I wasn't more creative. Mom wouldn't let me do that in the car, so I would just sit there with my blade *du jour* while we watched the combine doing its work, counting the turns on the rows of grain until that unending field was finished. I wasn't allowed to leave or go home, and if Dad needed me to help him, he'd signal, but until then, I could just sit in the car without inciting his ire. I was on call. I was eleven.

Mom and I watch as the guy driving the truck jams his transmission into park and throws open the driver side door, then plants his heavy frame onto the ground with both boots at once like someone intent on starting some shit. He's shortish, about five foot eight, and dressed in the Mexi-cowboy thing with his shirt opened down the front and wearing a cowboy hat. Pear-shaped, like our uncle Richard, like a fat Mexican bully with that thick, solid fat on his upper torso that could be shoved around to make his point.

He stomps up the length of the trailer and finds Dad, starts yelling at him. I can barely make out what he's saying, from the car. "What the fuck's your problem, you asshole?" he screams at Dad in Spanish.

Dad is not comprehending. He hasn't seen anything, nor heard anything, and this guy just appeared out of nowhere to him.

"You came out of that road right in front of me with no lights!" the guy yells. He's clearly drunk, and did not see the trailer pull out until the last minute. Granted, the lights may have been flickering.

Dad is in between the rear axle of the tractor, working on the male plug that goes into the electronics housing of the trailer. He's caught, defenseless, and the guy reaches up and punches Dad hard, right on the cheek. Dad gets hit, is surprised, but doesn't drop anything he has in his hands. He looks at the guy and yells back, *"¡Pendéjo!"* ("Asshole!")

Out of nowhere, Dan, thirteen and big for his age, steps out from behind the guy and grabs him roughly by the shoulders, plants himself, and swings the short, fat guy around into the trailer, a concussion that makes the fat guy bounce back hard, and Dan gives him a three-punch combination to the head and chest, which makes the Mexi-cowboy think twice about what he wants to do next.

Dan and him square off, but the fat guy is stunned from the impact and has his hands down, while Dan has his fists up and wide, loud. Dan is clearly frightened. He's a thirteen-year-old boy. Our father, on the other hand, has not moved from his position or dropped the electronics in his hand, still not understanding he's in a fight, but he's at the very least in a position to the guy's back and rear so the guy doesn't know where the next threat is coming from when Leonard Loop comes down off the combine with a shovel and slaps it into the ground, making a loud cracking noise, like he's trying to separate fighting dogs.

The fat guy looks around him, spits out some blood from where Dan hit him and then turns and walks quickly back to his truck, gets in, and squeals off. The whole thing lasts about eight seconds.

Years later when we talk about this, even Dan admits that he would have been in trouble if the guy had more heart and fought back after that initial exchange. Dan was, after all, only thirteen.

My father is of course immensely proud of Dan at this point. When it's safe to come out, he does so, and for some time they stand around exchanging war stories with Leonard, who is also proud of himself for grabbing the shovel and slapping it on the ground. The last hopper load gets dumped into the trailer and Dad lets Dan drive it all the way to the elevator, as per usual.

At the grain elevator, Dad is ecstatic, telling the story over and over again about his brave, strong, fighting son.

I am there for the last retelling, and he turns on me and says in Spanish, "And what happened to you, Rambo, with your knives?"

I blush a deep crimson, my fingers gripping the handle of the homemade knife in my pocket, feeling a mixture of shame and anger, the basic bartending blend of *verhuenza*, a besmirching of honor.

This is in front of all his cousins and friends, who, by the looks upon their faces, are thinking thoughts similar to mine, that Dad should not be making fun of anyone who was not recently saved from an ass-kicking by their thirteen-year-old son.

But Mingo, on a roll, pressing his own unintended humiliation, says, "He was probably hiding behind one of the tires, with his knife, like this!" He makes a frightened pouty face, and crouches back, oddly similar to the very posture he had taken during the brief scuffle, after he'd been punched, but I don't point this out because I didn't actually notice it then in my shame, but only now, these years later, in the recounting. The bastard.

When he gets home that night, Dad is still very excited, on that post-fistfight high that can be very intoxicating. He pulls the trailer into its spot and turns it off—a sound I still, to this day, love to hear, the winding down of an engine—and he immediately showers and changes into his pressed blue jeans and a fresh shirt, while Mom shakes her head in disbelief and obvious disgust as he splashes on cologne and leaves, the rest of us too tired to care or wonder where he's off to.

Dan is also very pleased with himself, secretly, I can tell that night. He's always been something of the tough guy at school and is pleasantly surprised he could carry it off outside school, in the land of men. He can't help it. He wants his father's admiration. What boy child doesn't? He is the caretaker now, the family keeper. He is now a man, according to his father.

Chapter 12

THE OKLAHOMA JONESES

Our neighbor, Lúpe, died of liver cancer around the time I was twelve. Maybe it was later. Everything that happened back then felt like it happened when I was twelve, after I was ten.

For two full years, his deathbed maintenance had been attended by both Gramma and her sister, his wife, Lupíta, both at home and in the same hospital in Matamoros in which Grampa had died.

During this time, the whole of Gramma's and Lupíta's routine revolved around his drain circling: trips to Matamoros, trips to medical supply stores, trips to the family witch doctor, trips to unfamiliar witch doctors, and sometimes, even reluctant trips to medical doctors in Brownsville.

Lúpe and Lupíta were raising five children, coincidentally arranged in exact chronological gender order as our family, before Derek was born. They had three older girls and then two boys, an odd predetermined symmetry that guaranteed a high level of competition among us. They were our *Juanses*, our Mexican Joneses.

Their oldest, Lupíta Chiquita, had been dropped on her head as a baby and was developmentally disabled, which was a merciful turn for our oldest sibling, Syl, because it meant she had no one to compete against, like a cross-town rival who shows up late and retarded for a scrimmage.

My particular doppelganger was José, or Joe. He was four years my junior and had a lazy eye and even lazier habits, which also precluded me from any real sort of competitive comparison. He was small, round, and dull witted, and was never really all that much into role-playing Indiana Jones, probably because I was always Indiana Jones and he was always . . . well, someone else. Someone slower. Someone fatter. Someone who walked around dressed only in his father's briefs. It just worked out that way. Always.

The Mimis hadn't fared so well with their same-age competitors, though; their competition was healthy and attractive by the standards of the barrio, and as a result, the competition at times became ferocious, feral. Fashionable.

Even the final issue of the Martinez clan, Derek Allen (named, obviously, by the Mimis), would eventually encounter his own dark shadow across the way. Derek snuck up on us, as an "Oops!" baby Mom delivered in her early thirties, when I was around thirteen or fourteen years old, and he became the object of everyone's affection, as a family. Not to be outdone, the Ramirezes next door had one of their waitress-daughters get knocked up by a trucker, and within a year she had a son named "Juan." Or Jay. Or something. Anyhow, he couldn't pronounce Derek's name. In fact neither could Gramma.

I mentioned this recently to my friend, Sarah, when I was reading her a letter that Gramma had written me years ago, and I pointed out how Gramma could neither spell nor pronounce *Derek*.

"Well, that was the point, wasn't it?" she said.

Anyhow, Lúpe, the father, was a bastard. He was a mean, tyrannical farmhand who had married into Gramma's family by knocking up her younger sister, Lupíta (again: the names were coincidental), and they set up shop next door to us and eyed everything that went on at our house with carcinogenic envy. Perhaps they felt the same way about us.

Martín, the oldest boy—Dan's competitor—was a pederast, something he very likely learned at the knee of his father, if the soft sciences are correct. When I was younger, about seven years old, he used a purloined skin magazine to lure me and his three-year-old little brother into their laundry shack, a rickety, mold-ridden and musty one-room storage shed that had been amateurishly plumbed to house their most prized of possessions, a 1970s Maytag. As a result, the concrete slab floor was in a perpetual state of slipperiness.

Once inside the shack, Martín pulled out the magazine and zipped down his cheap trousers, produced his brown, rough-hardened penis, uncircumcised and calloused. He flipped through the mildewed copy of *Oui* to a page that would satisfy his emergency and secret farmer's kid kink, and then grabbed my seven-year-old hand and urgently shoved his cock into it, telling me to rub it, back and forth, while his narrow brown hips bucked forward and he whispered a steady "*Shhhhhhhh*" as he flipped to a better photograph.

Joe just kind of sat there, watched through his one good eye. "Motherfucker," he said.

That was his first word, and he was good at it.

I remember the day he first learned it, his dad proudly stepping back from the alley between our houses and encouraging him, thrust the little round boy forward and said, in Spanish, "OK: Go."

Joe, three years old and duly prompted, narrowed his eyes and said, "Motha-FUCK. MOTHA-FUCK."

Lúpe beamed. He had a three-year-old man.

And that's what Joe said now, but a bit more clearly: *Motherfucker.*

No more than a minute had passed as Martín found another photograph of a naked, provocative woman to incite the fire in his peasant's desire —and making do with what he had, or, more to the point, what I had, in hand —when we heard my father calling out from the back door of our house.

His dick in my hand—hard, young, malevolent, startled— he clutched me by the shoulders. He put his hand over my mouth and said again, urgently, "*Shhhhhhhhhhh* ...."

I had no desire to call out to my father. As far as I knew, we were doing nothing wrong besides being in possession of the magazine, which would bring down the wrath of severe, hypo- critical Catholic piety upon all of us, and this was far from the first time I'd been in possession of such goods, so I was not exactly sure why Martín was behaving this way.

I was about to tell him that I could just walk out and own up to telling Dad that Joe and I were playing in the laundry shack, and it would be over, but Martín was insistent, bordering on violent.

Even at this age, I had learned how to talk people down from escalation, learned when not to press. It would come in handy later, too.

So I didn't press. I let him feel he was in control by keep- ing still, keeping quiet, and watched as, through the crack of the loosely hinged plank door, we saw Dad retreat inside the back door to our house. I saw my chance and yanked myself free when Martín stopped to zip up his trousers. I wandered out into the yard and—realizing I wasn't being pursued, walked back across the grassy unused separation between our house and the Ramirezes' house, painted an awful electric green color with shit brown trimming.

I walked into our house through the same door Dad had just backed into, through our own laundry room—also personally plumbed—and pretended nothing was wrong.

My father immediately seized upon me in a most surprising way. It was as if he knew exactly what had happened, and what Martín had done to me, had had me do, just a minute ago.

I wailed horribly, like a stricken thing, collapsed at his feet and struggled against his pulling arms, and he lifted me like I was a shifting sack of flour and he struck at me, demanding me to tell him where I'd been, already disgusted at my victimhood.

He pulled me by the arm across the gravel drive to Gramma's house, banged open the door and demanded of her to determine right there, on her bedroom floor, whether I'd been buggered within the last hour. Gramma, who had been kneeling at her corner altar praying, calmly looked over from her Bible and pulled down my underwear while Dad held me prone, and she studied my asshole for a second and then quite reasonably declared that, no; no, your son has not been corn-holed. Dad, satisfied with this proclamation, left quickly, stormed out while I lay there cowering, sniffling, uncertain of what had just played out.

Mom finally caught wind of what had been happening and rushed over to Gramma's house, saw me laid out on her floor with my shorts and underwear askew, and said nothing. She picked me up from the crumple I had turned myself into at the foot of the bed that Grampa would nearly die in within the next year, and I sobbed into her neck.

I don't remember what Mom was like then, but I think she tried to comfort me. I don't know what she felt. It must have been horrible, though, being a stranger in this family, with them treating her child like this. But Gramma chuckled lightly. "His underwear was dirty," she said in Spanish, and reached up to kiss my hot, teary cheeks.

I didn't resist. I wasn't there anymore. Anyway, I'm not sure whether she meant that as a shot to the limitations of my personal hygiene or Mom's ability to keep a house.

Years later, while talking with Dan, I finally got around to admitting that this had happened. I started to tell him the story and he stopped me. "He tried the same thing with me," Dan said, and then there was a dark, low silence between us. That part frightened me.

Years after even *that*, when this finally came up in therapy and I told both elements to Sally, my therapist, she asked, "Do you think that's why your father knew what happened so quickly?"

"Hunh," was my response.

That's why she's the therapist.

Back to Dad: Sometime later, I remember being back in that alley.

Martín is shirtless, walking by their house, visibly pretending nothing is wrong, a pink towel hanging on his shoulder, leading Joe by the hand to their backyard.

Dad yelling at them.

Them stopping. Martín turning around, frightened.

Lúpe coming to see what was wrong.

Dad yelling some more at both Martín and Lúpe.

Lúpe and Martín responding, looking back defiantly.

Lúpe scoffing.

Prove my son fucked your son.

Another exchange.

Me now sitting at Dad's feet, and him gesturing down at me, at his youngest boy, his despoiled, feminized boy.

Them dismissing my father, and turning to go.

Their door slamming shut behind them.

Dad standing there for a second longer, then turning to go back inside, leaving me to cry on the back porch step.

I sit there sniffling, waiting for someone to come get me, waiting until it's safe to go back inside, but no one comes out, except the mosquitoes.

Chapter 13

IN WHICH MOM IS INTRODUCED TO THE BARRIO

After Lúpe died, his family was left rudderless, frightened. Martín took the helm and abruptly assumed his father's duty as patriarch and chief pederast-in-charge. He dropped out of high school and began working a night shift at the new windshield-wiper factory near the airport, giving his mother his entire paycheck at the end of every second week like a dutiful peasant. If this arrangement was to his disliking, he told no one; he seemed happier for the unburdening of education and the chance to get his hands where they belonged: manufacturing goods. Kept them from roaming elsewhere.

We were long expecting Lúpe to expire, but still, when it happened, it came as a surprise. We, as kids, had the good sense to go by our own clock, preoccupy ourselves with the chores and desires of our adolescence, and on that Monday, when Lúpe finally lapsed, Dad had taken Dan and me out of school and had us working the sand pit, with Dan on the backhoe loading sand into the beds of the rare few trucks that showed.

Lúpe's death had become a sort of a holiday in the barrio, and no one was really working that day, but Dan and I were oblivious. We did what we were told unquestioningly and waited patiently for the next truck to show, though on that day, it would be hours between loads, when it was usually just a few minutes.

And so we sat in the swelter, keeping ourselves preoccupied with what we could, when eventually no one else showed, after lunch. My job was to be in the bed of the dump truck while Dan maneuvered the boom and bucket of the backhoe. He loaded the truck with scoop after scoop of river sand, and I was to avoid getting killed if I could, or buried under the sand, while removing all errant roots and matter that was decidedly not sand, or unsandlike. Dan and I had a game where he would bring the boom over, and I'd stand still, and he'd try to bury my shoes, and then not hit me with the bucket as it unfurled, inches from my head and chest. I had complete trust in him, and he never once did touch me, though the hydraulic machine could have crushed me in a matter of seconds. Dan, even at age twelve, was that good at the backhoe.

We were baking in the cab of a loaded truck—our one driver doing tandem runs—listening to the local classic rock station, when Dan inexplicably slipped out of the driver's side, not saying a word. About fifteen minutes later, I became curious and lifted my head from the sweaty crook in my arm and looked over to where Dan should be, and in the side-view mirror, I saw his head bobbing in the collected brown yuck pool that had appeared there some days before, after a particularly hard rain and flooding of the Rio Grande, which was now resting peacefully back within its banks. I saw his head come out of the water like a tiny round Loch Ness Monster, spitting out water and thought, *Oh, bliss.*

I was down to my Y-fronts and in the water in half a minute, chasing after Dan and splashing. It was only a few feet deep, and terribly disgusting, probably frothing with heavy metals and bases from the manufacturing plants, but we didn't care: It was a pardon from the sun.

Dan had emerged from the pool and was on the shore, about to jump on me from a muddy outcrop, when we heard a car turn the corner into the sand pit. Both Dan and I instinctively charged out of the water and grabbed our clothes, determined to pretend we were working so as not to incur the wrath of Dad. Then we both just sort of stopped, understood we were caught red-handed, put on gritty, dampened jeans over our murky wet legs, and waited for our feet to dry in order to wear our shoes again. The car slowly pulled up parallel to the truck, and we came around the other side. We noticed that it was not just Dad, but Mom, too, and Joe, my eight-year-old neighbor proxy, in the backseat, which was terribly unusual.

I think I can speak for Dan when I say that while we were standing there, waiting to get reamed by Dad, we were sur-prised that rather than violent and full of rage, Dad was instead distracted, quiet, not even out of the car yet. This was quite unusual as well. I called through the back window to Joe, who looked like he wanted nothing more in the world but to jump out of the car and join us in the water. I said, "Hey, Joe; how's your dad doing?"

"He's dead," said Joe, his wandering eye wandering further, looking uncomfortably at my Mom, like he was about to ask permission from her to join me and Dan.

Dad had come by to park the backhoe and close down shop for the day, take us back home to clean up for the wake, which would be held later that Monday night, and we did it slowly, automatically, and . . . well, funereally, because no one wanted to be in the car with Joe.

Lúpe's impending death had created a stranglehold on the barrio, had kept everyone in a sort of holding pattern for the better part of a year, because Gramma had become the midwife of his expiration—nothing excited her more at this point than a visit from the Angel of Death—and Dad, beholden to Gramma all his life, had gotten locked into her rhythms, and subsequently, so had the trucking business. Attending to the dying man had filled her days, fulfilled her completely, perhaps allowed her to pay penance for Grampa's death, and now that her sister's husband was dead, it wasn't only her that felt like her direction had been lost, it was Lupíta as well, and also Dad now, who lost his way for a few days.

That had been my initial conclusion, back then, as a kid. I thought Dad had lost his steering because Gramma would now have nothing to preoccupy her days, and would then reinsert herself in the day-to-day management of the trucking business. Not that she had ever disengaged entirely; she just kind of did it from the reeking, cancerous bedside two doors down. But things were changing again.

Looking back now, though, I think there had been much more to this dispatching of a scourge from the planet of the acceptable than we were capable of understanding as kids.

You see, sometime back, I heard a fantastical tale of family lore, many years later when we were much older, sometime in late 2007, and it forced me to reevaluate that day, and those moments of watching Joe, watching Dad, and watching Lupé's daughters cry out like they did at the side of his casket, as he lay shrunken, green.

About three days before, I had flown into Texas and had made a complete ass of myself after drinking way too much on the extended flight back home, and had then continued knocking back drinks rather enjoyably at Syl's fortieth birthday party, when suddenly the traveling, the lack of food, and the inordinate amount of booze I had been drinking sort of locked in and I became an insufferable boob at her party, and had to be helped to bed. It was awful, terribly humiliating, and I was gathering the emotional capital to apologize to Syl and her husband, and eat a crow buffet, with crow juice and crow dessert, while I was staying with Marge.

Marge had waved the incident away, said I should probably be apologizing to Syl and Ruben, but emphasized more the damage to my health, which I then subsequently waved away. If life doesn't in fact get any better, I reasoned, I don't want *more* of it; I want *less.*

Marge is a research scientist, a PhD living in Sugarland, the city within the city of Houston, with her husband, Corwin. I can't really claim to know what it is she does. It's research, I know that much, but if she's ever given me the elevator speech as to what it is she researches, I must have gotten off at a previous floor, because I don't know what it is. But I get Marge now, as an adult, if that makes any sense. She's civil and well-adjusted, understands schedules and calendars and planning in advance. I still can't get Dan to commit to a string of vacation days when I visit. When I fly in to see him, he continues to work and has me wait for him until he gets done with his day. Terribly frustrating. Plus, she didn't judge me from what she had seen that other night.

Anyhow, that morning, it was me and Marge and her two kids, and strangely, how life works, Marge is the person in the family to whom I feel closest now. Twenty years ago, after the Mimis episode, she was the one I despised most. Simply could not get along with her. Marge was establishment, I was rebellion. The foibles of youth.

It was when I was staying at her house when I remembered something that Dad had said, about Lúpe, that Dad suspected that Lúpe was actually Syl's father. He said he remembered a day, early in his marriage to my mother, when Mom had been upset with him, had wandered off, and Lúpe had told him to sit still, in Gramma's mother's kitchen (Dad's *abuelita*), while he fetched her. *Buelita* kept looking out the window and shaking her head, ominously. Finally, Dad said, when they returned, he had noticed bruises on Mom's slender, white legs.

I remember that my first reaction to this story, when I heard it, had been indescribable. It was a mixture of things. I remembered feeling a vengeful revulsion and the memory of the old sexual assault wound at the hands of Martín and the horrible, more humiliating events that followed at the hands of Gramma and Dad—followed by an overwhelming feeling of helplessness that no one in our family was ever able to escape the hostile advances from that Ramirez family, and a deep, sincere desire for vengeance, if it was true.

But then, suddenly, during that weekend at Marge's house, I was feeling relief that I would not have to apologize to Syl and her family for my terrible behavior at her fortieth birthday party, because it just so happened she wasn't really related, like a disgusting *deus ex machina,* which I knew was just horrible of me, and I fought hard not to feel it. But it kept popping up.

✤

Dad had difficulty adjusting when his family dispersed to the north without him, when the kids left for college and Mom fled with Derek. He would still attempt to exert his sense of *patria-*

familias by barging in, uninvited, to my sisters' apartments and then settling himself down to watch cable (he found the nature shows erotic) and then have a snooze until dinner time. He even tried doing this with Mom, at her new apartment, while she was filing for divorce. Eventually everyone started locking their doors and telling him to get lost, beginning with Syl. Syl was never shy about yelling at Dad, and this had hurt his feelings. So much so that he was now wondering if, in fact, she was really his daughter.

Here's the problem, though: It would be just like Dad to choose to believe that his young bride had been raped so many years prior rather than have to accept his oldest daughter's unwillingness to put up with his unannounced visits and regularly boorish personality. It's the only thing that made sense to him.

But it was absolutely ridiculous. Syl had always been the strongest of the kids, the most able with confrontation. She had forged borders in a family that had none, created boundaries behind her when Dad—especially Dad—was at his most repulsive, or belligerent. And that is why he would rather believe she wasn't his than learn to cope with her boundaries.

"You have to promise never to repeat this story to your mother," Dad had asked of me and Dan.

"Of course not," I said, already calculating when I could get a moment alone with Mom to ask her the truth of the statement.

"So why do you think it happened?"

"Well, because we couldn't have kids when we first started out," he said.

This was an issue with my sisters, conception. Marge and Mare had had a difficult time of it. Marge's husband wanted to name their daughter, the second child, Porsche, because she cost as much to conceive. Mare struggled through her pregnancy as well. But Syl was like India: Too many people to keep track of, so that her kids would eventually develop a class system.

Listening to this story, I had a martini of a reaction: revulsion, revenge, and pity for Mom, being thrown into the den of wolves like that, a poor half-white city girl thrust into a hive of stinging locusts . . . and then uncertainty: This was, after all, Dad's story.

"So then what?" I asked.

"Well, then she was pregnant with Syl," he said.

The revulsion came back, with the image of this field tramp, his groin green with the virulent fertility of machismo, his ugly, ferocious seed on a seek-and-destroy mission. It was a putrid, disgusting fecundity, turning my stomach, imagining what my mother could have suffered from that fieldhand, who obviously intimidated my father.

This had been my mother's position in the barrio of my grand-mother: If Gramma and Dad were reviled as outsiders, Dad's new, unMexican wife was absolutely detested, a source of fear, distrust, and highly sexualized fantasy. She was America come knocking, next door. So the rape would have been acceptable.

Dan and I talked about this later, over beers.

"Dad said he always had a suspicion about Syl," Dan had said.

"And everyone else ... ?" I said. "I mean, six kids; that's not exactly barren."

"That's what he said," he responded.

I don't remember the further explanation about the prolific stream of children that followed. I usually make fun of Mom by telling her that she needed an Excel spreadsheet to keep track of all her kids, and that she kept forgetting to scroll all the way to the last column, where my information was kept, and that's why she forgot about me so often.

"Aye, June!" Mom would say. "You're so crazy."

Indeed.

A couple of days later, after my awful behavior at Syl's party, Mom and I were in a car traveling to Austin to visit Derek, who was pretending to be in college there, and I had some personal business besides. If it's one thing the roads in Texas are good for, it's for putting distance between bad memories.

We had two hours or so to talk, and, of course, I asked her about Lúpe, even though Dad had asked me to keep silent. I'm sure Dad knew I couldn't possibly keep this to myself.

Mom's face deflated in a kind of sadness, tensed in another response I couldn't read.

"That never, never happened," she said quietly, after I finished relaying the story I got.

"Your father, he's just . . . I . . . " and then she couldn't say anything. Her face hardened.

And I believed her, believed the body language more than the language she couldn't evoke.

The car was quiet as we drove the complicated east to west route. These trips are unusual in Texas; normally you're either driving up or down, north or south, I mean. Hardly ever does one have reason to drive left and right on the map. Texas, in my mind, is long, not wide. Texas is deep, not . . . broad.

I was reminded of the drives of our youth, all the time I was forced to ride with Mom for company, when I was incapable of escape. Things were different now. I usually had a drink or two before I got in the same car with anyone in this state, which made the unfathomable distances tolerable.

"So he made it up?"

Mom slowly shook her head from side to side, looked like she was about to tear up, but she didn't.

"That poor man," she said. I'm sure she meant Dad.

Nothing else was said for a while. The thrum of the highway played under the carriage of the car, the usual background sound to Mom's and my relationship. Our relationship was a travelogue. Once, in a magazine contest where you had to write your life story in six words or less, I came up with, "Mom said, Leave before you're left." I never heard back from them. The wankers. A little too much truth, probably.

Anyhow, I was much relieved to hear it from her, that she had never been sexually brutalized in that manner. Not like Dan and me.

But, on the very heels of that, I have to admit I was also a little disappointed because it meant that I had to, at some point or another, apologize to my oldest sister and her husband for ruining her fortieth birthday party.

I am, after all, my father's son, selfish and cowardly.

Chapter 14

FAITH

By 1986 Dad had become a truck driver with nothing left to haul but marijuana.

Through his early thirties, he could do little with the trucking business he had inherited from Grampa except watch as it crumbled around him and his step-uncles usurped what few dirt-hauling contracts came the way of our barrio.

As a result Dad could no longer sleep at night and would pace the length of the new addition to our house incessantly. Every three or four hours, Dan and I would hear his muffled footfalls on the carpet, which increasingly lost its ability to absorb the concussion of his steps year after year, so that by the time we were in our teens, we could feel him plant his feet in his bedroom, even though that part of the house was built on concrete.

Then he would stomp his way to our room and throw open the door in total disrespect of our privacy, at any hour of the night, but especially at daybreak.

I think he did this at first to catch either one of us masturbating, in an attempt to humiliate us. But then it just became his habit, thrusting open the door to wake us up, get us on some small task before we dressed for school on school days, or get set to work proper on weekends.

He would stand there in his Y-fronts, looking like a lean, tall, diapered child with his curly black locks backlit and haloed from the overhead light in the kitchen. He'd scratch at his belly quietly and turn something over in his mind and in his mouth, and then he'd say in a small, heavy baritone, "*Levántensen.*" You two get up.

That's how our days invariably started back then.

How they ended, for him, was just as unvaried. After some perfunctory attempt at keeping shop, Dad would normally repair to one of the makeshift bars that dotted the poorer subdivisions just outside the Port of Brownsville and drink many of the dollar-fifty Budweisers, increasingly dreading the wobbly two-mile drive home in the dark as the night wore on, because the lights in his trucks were unreliable.

Dad felt at home among the dispossessed at this time, I think maybe even superior, and for five years he listened as his meager inheritance spilled out of the unplumbed urinals in the piss rooms of those bars, splashing a clear yellow onto the baked earth just on the other side of the plywood walls.

It was in those bars, on soiled and untreated planks of plywood flooring, that I spent much of my time away from school as a child, watching and listening from the safety of the floor, facing the people in the tavern as my father put in marathon hours on barstools. The men at the bar talked of nothing to one another, spoke in a vague and cryptic *lingua hispanica,* a pidgin code that insinuated more than clarified.

As a child listening in, I figured there was much being left to allusion or circumspection, and that as an adult, I would eventually be allowed in on the big secret, but I have come to realize this has never been the case: Men in bars have nothing to say.

When I'd grow sleepy, I'd curl up in the cab of his dump truck, parked just outside, and wait for him to finish drinking and drive us home.

Dad drank lengthily and with intention, so I would tire and retreat, giving him the freedom to overtly ply the unremarkable bar whores without fatherhood weighing in on his conscience.

Later, when I was in my teens, he'd come to confide in ugly detail these secretive instances. "See that bar over there?" he'd say, in abhorrent and gleeful English as we drove by some ramshackle building. "I fuck a lot of women in that bar. . . ."

I would wince when I remembered the long hours I spent there with him, sleeping in the cab of his truck.

At home Mom kept sentinel over the bookkeeping. She watched the flow of money slow to a trickle and then stop outright when I was in junior high. She tried to keep her desperation to herself, but there was no way for her to hide her worry.

For anyone listening, there were rumblings all around of our deeper declension into poverty. My sisters, brother, and I knew things had turned outright dire when our mother stopped shopping at El Centro Supermarket and had to shop at Lopez Superstores, which catered to the people on welfare in Brownsville.

Shopping at El Centro had been a badge of honor for Mom, a status for the family. She taught me this at a young age, and I thought everyone knew it, too. Once, at a barrio party at some neighbor's house, someone mentioned a sale on milk at Lopez.

"We don't shop at Lopez," erupted from my five-year-old mouth, in Spanish. "That's where poor people shop," I said with authority. This was immediately met with nervous laughter, and later with a sound beating on the way home.

To see my mother come home with Lopez Supermarket on her grocery bags when I was in the seventh grade was a watershed in my life. It was then that I realized we were in real trouble.

One morning Mom surprised me by showing up at my seventh-grade homeroom algebra class and removing me, getting us on the road out of Brownsville, heading north. There was no explanation.

"Are we going to Kingsville?" I asked. Sylvia was in school there, at what was then Texas A&I University, and I could think of no other reason for us to drive that way. Syl, as the oldest, was the first of the girls to attend the local farming university, in Kingsville, Texas, about an hour outside of Corpus Christi. She'd qualified for a number of federal grants and loans in her bid for freedom, all of this done in something nearing secrecy from Dan and me: One day, Syl was just gone, and I had no idea where she was off to. I had no idea what "college" was.

"*Sientáte y lla cállete,*" she snapped at me in irritation. Sit down and shut up.

While she was growing up, Mom spoke English, though she knew Spanish. Everyone in Brownsville knows Spanish. But after years of living with my father and Gramma, she'd forgotten most of her English and spoke only Spanish now. She'd gone native.

I don't know why it didn't occur to me what we were doing that morning, that Mom and I were driving shotgun for Dad, who was on the road somewhere behind us in one of his flat-nosed tractor trailers, carrying a large load of marijuana and headed north. I had heard the stories, knew some of the tactics of smuggling by this point, but I didn't make the connection. Mom and I were driving ahead of him to ensure the customs station was closed, and if it happened to be open, we were charged with turning back and warning him.

We headed north on Highway 281, one of two highways out of the Rio Grande Valley. This is an unkempt, sun-roasted, and broken-up tarmac with its northernmost terminus just outside of San Antonio. It cuts right up the center of the Rio Grande Valley, the southernmost spit of the geopolitical border of Texas with Mexico. The only other escape out of the area, Highway 77, is equally dismal in vistas, but parallels the coastline of the Gulf of Mexico. That route slices through the largest nonfunctioning ranch in Texas, the King Ranch, one of the oldest ranches in Texas and with the bloodiest history. It's been out of full operation for years, producing only a dismal percentage of what it did in its heyday, but its continued existence has little to do with cattle ranching.

The King Ranch provides the real border between Mexico and Texas: 200 miles of uncrossable, wretched, and sun-drenched land.

Before the Patriot Act, back in the 1980s, there were two U.S. Customs checkpoints blocking the migration of drugs, fruit, people, reptiles, and parrots on the roads between the United States and Mexico—both about one hundred miles north of the Mexican border at highway choke points.

The station on Highway 77, in Sarita, is the busier and better financed. It boasts the newest in anti-immigrant technology, full staffing, and a huge billboard with a creepy propagandist image of "The Good Border Patrol Agent" and his militant German shepherd asking you to drive safe and be sure to turn in them wetbacks if you see them.

The checkpoint in Hebronville, back then, was an Airstream trailer with an attached carport to protect the agents from the sun, and it would often be closed for breakfast or lunch, so we were headed toward that one.

Mom is driving on 281, headed north that hot summer morning. I'm accustomed to this. Outside in all directions, the farmland throbs in a liquid, mundane mirage, like every other morning. Brown asthmatic plants and stunted trees sizzle during the hot hours of the day, which is most of every day. Drivers become hypnotized by the redundancy of the farms, the hum of the tires, the visible and predatory heat. Under the spell of the third-world sun, imagination and reality eventually begin to slide back and forth seamlessly, soporifically, so that you're hypnotized into an uncaring, unquestioning stupor in order to let the time move on without punishing your mind further.

Mom and I drive through this scenery like we have a hundred times before. We say nothing to one another. By now, we have each decided that the other is unworthy of conversation. We stare out the windows and think very different things.

The old Bonneville struggles along at top speed, sputtering through its third engine in its ten years with us. Air-conditioning is a luxury long lost, so my window remains half open, drying out our sinuses and sucking the moisture from our skin.

Inside the Bonneville, I am stupefied to near unconsciousness by the drive. The torpor lulls me into a hypnagogic state, a dreamlike trance of fantasy and escape, so I really don't mind these drives anymore.

Mom, on the other hand, is electric. She sits upright, hands clenching the beige Pontiac steering wheel. An hour into the drive and she has not yet told me where we're driving.

She plays the radio unbearably low, keeping the music just under audial reach, making each country song sound like a memory.

Mom is thinking about the hundred dollars she and Dad had spent before six o'clock that morning—one hundred dollars that would help them make two thousand dollars, if things went right.

Their first stop on this morning felony excursion was to Dad's *cúrandera*, whom we knew as *La Señora,* Dad's personal witch doctor, for an emergency session. They were let right through at five in the morning, and they had only one burning question: *Will the checkpoint on Highway 281 be open?*

After years of sitting through them with Gramma, I didn't have to be there to know exactly how the session in the *cúrandera's* office went.

La Señora is older, matronly, dresses in a thin frock with her hair pulled back in a bun. She has them sit across from her desk, in a black leather love seat with chrome handles. A panorama of photos hangs around her office, some wallet-sized, others larger and in portrait. A pencil sketch of a Camaro by one of her grandsons hangs next to a window. It's really not very good.

She listens closely to their question, nodding sleepily at their preoccupation. Sympathizing. Understanding. They've reached a decision and they can't turn back, they tell her; they need to do it; no other choice anymore.

She stands up abruptly and walks behind her desk, which is cluttered with sheets of notebook paper crawling with ink: illegible notes, names of people, sets of cryptic numbers, home addresses of saints. She closes her eyes and scribbles something on her yellow legal pad, nonsense to anyone else reading it.

Then she walks over to a chest of drawers. On top of it is a cluster of saintly action figures, candles, incense, and photos of her own grandchildren, each bearing a remarkable similarity to all the other photos. In the center of her Sears-Roebuck chiffonier sit two cheap leaded crystal bottles, both filled with clear liquid. She gently finds a matching shot glass and lifts it to the light, making it sparkle.

She places the glass on the surface before her and into it pours out one bottle's contents, then the other. When the two clear liquids mix, they turn a deep crimson and thicken like plasma. She nods her head, as if her suspicions have been confirmed.

She turns back to her desk, plops her large figure back into her chair, and then turns to face them on the love seat.

Before her, on the desk, sits a glass orb filled with water resting on a black plastic ring. No shit. She sits up straight, closes her eyes, and regulates her breathing into a loud rhythmic, slipping, flowing stream of in-out, in-out breathing that unconsciously forces Mom and Dad to do the same thing. After a few seconds, when they've moved into their own theta waves, she opens her eyes suddenly and strikes the glass orb sharply with a metal wand, making it ring loudly in the clear morning air.

Then she lifts the orb between her two pudgy hands and stares deeply into the inverted image of the room around it. She holds it up to her face and peers intently—and they, sitting opposite, can't help it either: They also peer deeply into that inverted image of the room, too, though they try not to.

Sitting opposite this chicanery and watching everything she does, attempting to apply meaning to it, and watching what your money has bought you, you're drawn into the ritual and you can't help but try to figure it out, I always felt, even as a kid, when I was in there with Gramma.

What *does* she see in the orb? Did it move? Did something just move? Look deeper; it's upside down. That's me there, that's her, that's JFK behind me, there's the Camaro in pencil . . . was that a flash of color? Does that mean something to her? Does it mean something to me? Does that mean anything at all? What the fuck does it all *mean?*

Does it mean anything at all?

"No," she says with certainty. "The checkpoint will not be open this morning. Go in peace. God be with you. You can pay Maria, who is just now getting up and feeding the chickens."

✤

When Mom and I reach the checkpoint at 11:45 that morning, it is very much open for business. A line of cars five deep stretches back from the Airstream trailer. Our job now is to go through and then turn back around and report to Dad that his doom is indeed imminent.

Mom is visibly shaken. She turns off the radio with a hard click and considers this, considers her options. She goes over her instructions in her head, the "if/then" variables. Though she never said it or asked, I think she assumed I had figured the whole thing out by this point, though I really had not.

From the car, we can see a skinny middle-age white guy in green border patrol garb sitting on a reclining chair in the open doorway of the Airstream trailer facing the cars as they pass under the tin roof. It must have been 110 degrees inside the trailer, 100 in the shade.

From his position, never bothering to get up, he sits fanning himself with a newspaper and sleepily peers into the cars, asking if everyone is an American citizen, waiting for an accented answer, smiling, and then waving them through, like a sympathetic priest granting absolution to his untidy native and newly Catholic horde.

There is a very specific profile of mule that border patrolmen look for. Mom and me, we don't fit any of these profiles, but we feel visibly guilty just the same. She turns the radio back on, and rolls up her window.

Suddenly, she turns her head sharply to face me and I automatically shift my body away from her, pressing myself against the passenger door because I've been slapped too many times from the driver's seat and I've learned to protect myself. There is venom in her eyes but no blow headed my way.

"Don't you *dare* do anything stupid here," she spits at me in English. This catches me by surprise. Never before had I seen this amount of hatred from her. Well, just once before, that time in the third grade. Her eyes rip into me with an accusation of possibilities, and then they turn back to the bumper of the car in front of us. Her hand nervously turns the radio off, then back on again, but she rolls the volume back to nothing.

That's when I figure out what we're doing here.

"Hi, where y'all goin'ta today?" asks the skinny little man in the swelter. Mom's window is now only halfway open, and in her nervousness she rolls it all the way up.

"Hi, sorry. I mean, San Antonio," as she opens the window.

"Y'all American citizens?" he asks, disinterested.

"Yes," she says, and she leans back so he can get a clear look at me, nodding my head. I don't say anything except a quiet "Yep" when I nod, but he has not heard me.

There is an uncomfortable pause, I think because they're supposed to hear your accent. There is an anxious beat and he still hasn't let us go when I say, "Yes, I am," a bit too enthusiastically, and that doesn't go over very well either.

Mom laughs nervously. She had been hoping our light skin would exonerate us, without problem.

"Y'all have a nice day," he says, like he hasn't noticed anything awkward.

We drive through, and I feel her seethe for the next few miles.

That was about noon.

Somewhere behind us, at a roadside rest stop, Dad and my older brother Dan are waiting near Raymondville in Dad's tractor-trailer, which is attached to the trailer with the marijuana. In the argot of the smuggler, these trailers are said to have a *clavo*, which translates to "nail" in English.

The two center I beams that run the length of the trailer make perfect housing once you weld metal plates all along the underside and at the tail end. It creates a long rectangular box sealed at the rear end with the axle of the rig.

Ten fifty-pound square blocks of marijuana can be slid down the length of the rig, which can carry up to five hundred pounds' worth of pot, enclosed at the end with a plate, creating the image of, well, a "nail." This is what Dad and Dan are carrying.

I wonder dimly if Dan has figured out what he's doing out here, on the road north when he should be in high school, but Dan has always been more streetwise, much savvier than me.

I figure that if I've figured it out, he'd have figured it out long before.

It turned out that Dan was actually doing most of the driving, because Dad was too frightened, too panicked, but this was not unusual. Dan was sixteen at the time, but he had been driving trucks since he was ten. The thirteen-gear diesel trailer was not foreign to him. Every day after school and weekends, he'd have most of Dad's obligations to fulfill because Dad would give up sometime during the day, or during a hangover, and rely on Dan to finish up for him. Dan was expected to be something of an indentured servant as firstborn son.

Me, I was a late bloomer, the runt. I learned to drive automatic at ten, and standard around thirteen, which is considered unacceptable on the Mexican farm, and I could sense my father's disappointment.

I resisted learning because I did not want my brother's responsibilities. I resisted learning because, unconsciously, I understood that this was a point of macho pride with my father, and I wanted to avoid this despicable association with the peasant-minded friends of his, even at that age.

"Chuyíto lla máneja con Chúy," he'd say to me as we'd drive around the outskirts of Brownsville, avoiding sheriffs and cops because his truck had no working turn signals or brake lights, let alone insurance, or reliable brakes. He was referring to some cousins of his, saying how young Chuyíto was now driving with his father, older Chúy.

This was meant as a direct challenge to me. (*Chúy* is pronounced "chewy," and is somehow a nickname for the name Jésus. *Chuyíto,* a diminutive of *Chúy*, was Jésus Jr. Beyond that, I have no explanation.)

They lived in a cluster of mud-soaked hovels behind our barrio, vaguely related to Grampa or Gramma. Don't remember which.

Chuyíto was my age, about fourteen, and his skin was the gray color of the mud puddles that eternally surrounded his ramshackle clapboard house, even in drought, a result of the absent plumbing.

Planks of lumber sometimes led from the doorstep to dry ground, you could see from the dirt road. His sisters were loud, prenatally obese girls who had every quality of unlikable spinsters or single baby mamas from age six. My only contact with them was on the school bus, which we had to share because there was no "short bus" for their trip to the remedial school, and their whole family, it seemed, was too proud and thick to learn English, so they went to different schools, until they were old enough to quit.

Chuyíto, the boy my father was comparing me with, rarely wore shirts, like his own father. They simply didn't see a need for them. Elder Chúy sported a huge swollen brown belly that spilled laterally over the front of his trousers, which were usually a brown polyester relic that never seemed to cover the elastic bands of his underwear, and neither one of them ever seemed to wear shoes. Any sort of shoes.

Sometimes, elder Chúy would pull into our driveway very late at night and hock a pistol from Gramma for five dollars so he could get a final six-pack of Budweiser while he had a gang of children hanging on for dear life to the back of his pickup truck, as he drunkenly maneuvered through the dark and dirt roads, dreading the finality of an evening when he had to report home, brood in tow.

Chuyíto was a direct facsimile of his father, except molecularly condensed by about two-thirds. His fourteen-year-old belly protruded with parasites and his nose perpetually ran with an electric green infection. He had quit junior high and was now driving his own dump truck, earning a man's wage, and this was a sign of virility in the barrio, for both him as a preteen and for his father. Soon Chuyíto would have a wife and child and live in the same hovel or hovel complex with Chúy.

Now, to be compared with this crude germ of a boy, to be asked to compete with him for the sake of my father's pride— this just repulsed me to no end.

Once more I saw that there would never, ever, be an understanding between my father and me. We were alien to one another, and he could not understand why.

"*Cúando yo era tú edad, yo era una vérga con ójos!*" ("When I was your age, I was an erect cock with eyeballs!") Dad liked to boast to me when he was feeling good about something he'd done. This apparently was a very good thing. Something virile, cocklike. Dad had lots of colorful quips like that.

When he was dissatisfied with me or Dan, he'd violently exclaim, "*No valés tres tajádas de vérga!*" which roughly translates into "Your net worth is equal to or less than that of three slices of cock!" Mexican men have an unusual fascination with cocks.

Anyhow, this phrase was apparently a bad thing, and I was supposed to feel shame, though I simply could not, try as I might, because it just made me giggle at the image. And wince, of course: Three slices of cock? Man, that just sounds painful.

No, there would never be an understanding between myself and this stranger who called himself my father, this man whom I disliked more and more every day I knew him. And I outright refused to let him take any pride from what I did.

This is why I was ever the shotgun rider at this time, ever the passenger accompanying the women on errands, which was supposed to feminize me, humiliate me, and that is why Dan was "privileged" to drive him around—and not me—and why Dan was stupidly risking the rest of his life and good name for Dad today.

✢

Mom and I drive on to Hebronville. I'm dehydrated. I want to stop at a store.

"We can't," she says to me. "We have to turn back; I think we're behind."

She is obviously on a schedule of a sort, one she doesn't impart to me—you can't undertake something of this magnitude without a plan, right? You have to have contingency plans, things mapped out, timed out, choreographed. . . .

Still, I'm hungry and really thirsty. So I persist. Certainly we have time to get to a convenience store. They can't have scheduled this thing to hinge on a few minutes. Certainly they've devised this thing more cleverly than that.

"Please," I plead. "Just stop at the 7-Eleven."

Begrudgingly, she pilots the noisy car around the small town and finds a small convenience store. I get out with a couple of dollars and come up short when I try paying for some donuts and a chocolate milk. I return to the car for more money.

"Just get in!" she yells, and I do, leaving the food at the counter.

Mom whips the car around and I'm in trouble. Used to it by now.

She drives forcefully and loudly through side streets and gets back on Highway 281 heading south. It's about twenty minutes back to the checkpoint, but it will be on the opposite highway, the one headed south so hopefully we won't arouse suspicion, slipping through there twice in one day in our noisy car.

She turns off the radio with a snap. Really annoyed with me. The windows are up, but somehow it isn't so hot anymore. I look out my window and try to think of other things.

We travel like that for a few minutes and when the checkpoint is in sight, we hold our breath so the guy won't see us and right then we see Dad and Dan and the trailer heading right for the checkpoint.

Dad had become nervous, or maybe brave, though very likely he was blinded by his $100 faith in his *cúrandera* and had charged forth without waiting for Mom's report.

"Oh, God," my mother says, and I felt all the blood drain from my face from just the tone in her voice. I had never heard her voice so charged with fear.

"Oh, God," she says again. With her left hand, she grabs the knob that controls the headlights and flashes at Dad, who is only a few hundred feet from the checkpoint. She flashes four times, in clear view of anyone who is paying attention. I wonder if that is their signal that the checkpoint is open, but question the wisdom of doing it while he is next in line, in full view of the guy at the checkpoint, were he to look over his shoulder through the window at the noisy southbound car he has just seen drive through his checkpoint.

She slows down, slows terrifically down, the noisy car going less than twenty miles per hour on the highway, and for a moment, I can see Dad is driving. I can see that the blood has drained from his face, too, making his eyebrows stand out a rich black on his pallid, deathly white forehead, his face a grotesque mask of someone pretending desperately to act like everything is A-OK, but doing it horrifically badly.

I see Dan in the passenger seat, holding onto the handrail above the door as a means to steady himself through this craziness, through this stupid, unnecessary risk, and he looks calm, collected, uncaring. Like he isn't there. Does he even know what they are carrying? Am I reading into the look on his face?

There are no cars ahead of them now. The trailer is next in line. It slows to a crawl, and I can see Dad desperately trying to ignore the crazy flashing noisy Bonneville rattling through the southbound lane, keeping his eyes fixed to the road, pretending like he isn't smuggling anything in the empty trailer behind him. This empty, useless trailer with the I beams all sealed up, with the two Mexican men driving it, with no obvious destination, no paperwork, no affiliation with any hauling or trucking company. No, sir. Not trafficking in drugs. Just driving through. To Houston, probably. Circuitously. Looking for work. Oh, yes; we're American citizens—that's not why we're nervous. We can prove *that;* that's nothing. We're nervous because it's the pot we're hiding. And because we're only getting $2K for risking ten years. Isn't that funny? Isn't that just fucking hysterical?

But the skinny white guy is having lunch and can't be bothered.

In one of the weirder moments of this whole debacle, the Bonneville, the Airstream trailer, and Dad's tractor are all lined up like some cosmic event and we see the skinny border patrol agent with a white napkin tucked in his chin and Dad's bloodless face up in the trailer through the window of the Airstream as the agent waves them through with a fork, like he's conducting an orchestra: "Go on through. Go on through. Go on through."

Mom continues driving south, stunned by what has just happened, and I am careful not to say a word. We almost reach Raymondville and stop at a Whataburger to get a quick, wordless lunch, then spend some time sitting in a parking lot, waiting. When she feels it is safe to return, she turns the car around and heads back north, back through the same checkpoint.

"Are you sure this is safe?" I ask. She doesn't answer.

When we pull up again to the checkpoint headed back to Hebronville around three o'clock in afternoon, there is a different border patrol agent at the trailer. He is a small, clean-cut militant Mexican with a southern drawl, and he does not like others who remind him of himself.

"Y'all American citizens?" he demands instantly, leaning into the car through the window, smelling for marijuana smoke. You can never be sure who is Mexican these days.

"Oh, yes," says my mother, who is probably quite relieved the hard part is over and it looks like we are getting away with it.

"How 'bout you, son? You a 'Merican citizen?" He gave me a direct glare through reflective sunglasses.

There is nothing more potentially hostile than the indigenous ego interpreting the laws of his conqueror upon his own people.

"Yes, sir." I say, careful not to move or fidget or look away, like I've learned.

He reminds me of something Dad used to say, when he was feeling clever. "Never give a Mexican a pencil," he'd say. "They're better with shovels and machetes."

The sunglasses give away nothing, sitting on his nose in stark contrast to the deep, coffee color of his face. He looks back at my mother, then at me, like he smells the nervousness of earlier. Something tugs at his intuition. He is very good at his job, even if horribly loathing of self. By watching him, you wonder what itches him more: his red neck or his wet back.

"Where ya'll headed?" the sunglasses finally ask.

This catches Mom off guard. Her subterfuge had ended when Dad had driven through the checkpoint. She left all her answers back in Raymondville.

"We're going to Hebronville," she says unconvincingly.

Had he asked one more question, had he pressed it, we would have been in some sort of trouble. But he doesn't, and he backs off and motions us through. We drive off, but we aren't exactly relieved. That instance showed us that at any minute, it could have been all over. Crossing the checkpoint was only the superficial point of relief: When you're this far on the side of wrong, everything is a threat, every moment a reason to panic, and we were just not good at it.

Mom drives the Bonneville through Hebronville, and we are about to hit the open highway again—281 turns into the "business district" in all those tiny Texas towns—when we notice Dad's trailer in the parking lot of a cheap motel by the side of the road. Dan is lodged between the rear-most tires, working on the brake lights. I am very nearly surprised that they aren't working.

Mom is as alarmed to find them there as I am. This confirms my suspicions that there had been no planning beyond the consultation at the *cúrandera's*. This whole debacle had been based on nothing more than $100 worth of faith.

Mom pulls up next to the trailer, and I think she expects a victorious reunion. She gets out of the car and almost runs up to Dad with her arms out, who turns to her and suddenly looks like he's about to punch her.

"Pínche vieja pendéja!" he erupts when he sees her. ("Stupid fucking woman!")

Mom stops cold.

"Que chingádos estábas pensándo?" ("What the fuck were you thinking?")

Her face is a cocktail of misunderstanding. Then we both suddenly realize what he is upset about: the flashing of the headlights.

"If they would have just turned around for a moment, it would all be over and *it would all be your fault*," he spits at her in Spanish.

His words continue to snap and hiss around her like bullets in a firefight, like he's been trained to do, mercilessly, and she follows him forward to the cab of the truck, kowtowing to her ongoing punishment.

I have a moment alone with my older brother, both of us keeping out of the fray. We'd both learned to ignore the invective when it was directed at someone else, but especially when it was directed at us.

"Hey, shithead," he says to me in typical blithe and brotherly greeting, not looking up from under the trailer in the failing light. Squinting.

"Do you know what's going on?" I ask.

"You mean about the pot?"

"So you know?"

"Dad said Mom was not going to tell you cuz you're a fag."

"So where is it?"

"I don't fuckin' know," he says, continuing on the wiring. "Probably under here somewhere," he says as he bangs at the side of the I beam with a pair of pliers, which make a dull *clunk*. He stops looping the black electrical tape on the brake lights, curious now too, and knocks again under the I beam. It's more a *thud* than a *clunk* this time.

He dislodges himself and walks over to where I stand. We both stare at the trailer. From where we stand, it looks like every other piece of near-broken down equipment we've ever owned. Rusting, miserable, and totally criminal.

There is a cluster of pallets loaded at the fore of the trailer, over the fifth wheel, but it is otherwise barren. Then, as if in answer to our question, it hits us like a punch in the nostrils: the unmistakable smell of moist marijuana. Sweet, sweet heavenly marijuana.

"So where do you think it is?" he asks me.

"Fuck if I know," I answer truthfully. I was two years away from even smoking my first joint; I didn't know the calculus of smuggling.

Later on, when I do learn the metrics of it all from my Uncle Richard, I learned a few other things Dad had done wrong. The most important of which was that he traveled in the middle of the day, in the heat. When you're carrying pot through the checkpoints, Richard said, you travel really early in the morning or late in the evening, when it can't be smelled and when the agents are changing their twelve-hour shifts. The more dominant smugglers paid drivers to go through repeatedly, like Mom and I had done to observe shift changes, and had the best hours down to a science. But most important: never late at night, and never, ever under the heat of the sun. Had Dad been stopped, even for a minute, the whiff would have certainly given them away.

The other thing, Richard said, was to carry a load of mechanical farming junk on the trailer like you're driving somewhere with an obvious purpose. And have a story about the destination, written paperwork and shit. White man magic. Dad had done none of this.

"Lucky for us, *La Señora* was right!" Dad said, walking back with Mom, excited and seemingly over his histrionics. "She made them blind and we were let through like they were closed!"

I thought, *Oh, for fuck's sake,* and was about to say something when my brother swatted me on the back of the head, to save me from further abuse and to protect me from my mouth.

When we left them, Dan was doing the driving. They pulled out of the parking lot and headed off to Houston and their payoff. Mom and I turned south, back to Brownsville. Mom was her usual quiet self, except this time she played the radio louder. This meant she was thinking. It was getting dark and I was sleepy, so I slept. She would get us home. She knew the way.

For that, I could trust her.

Maybe this day was what cemented her decision to leave him, though it would not happen for some years more. Maybe she had made the decision before and had convinced herself to stay longer, for the sake of the children, like a good Catholic martyr. Then again, maybe Mom just swallowed the abuse that day and put it away to process later. I never knew and have not yet asked; perhaps eventually I will. She never talked to me about these things, and by this time I knew better than to tell her anything because she told my sisters—whom she felt were her real family, freshly hatched and safe—anything we discussed. She kept none of my secrets from them, and all were open to humiliation.

For that, I could not trust her.

She turned a blind eye to the nights he came home late, stinking of some new whore, I knew that. Or figured as much. But now that he was risking the lives and futures of his sons—her sons, ignored and feral—would she do something now? Now that her children were in jeopardy, would she seek the divorce that lurked in every corner of the house?

I'd like to think that, would like to think that she was looking out for us, that it was for our benefit she would eventually pursue that divorce. But I know better than to believe it because when she did get the divorce, it was well after all of us were gone, all of us except for Derek, and she's still paying for that guilt.

And so is he.

When I was in high school and college, I read books about concentration camps—J.G. Ballard, Viktor E. Frankl, some bad Vietnam memoirs—and I didn't quite understand why I identified so readily with them, the grind of that low, tough gear that gets you through an impossible experience, seemingly without end. How you just keep on. And on. Hope disappears. And you still go on. Then suddenly it's over. And hope doesn't surprise you again, once it's gone. It has a different name. Different face. And you're not happy to see it, or surprised. It's like a long-forgotten agreement. Sort of a, "Oh, there you are. I've been expecting you, I think."

That's what we experienced. Mom, Dan, and I lived in an emotional concentration camp, held captive by a petty tyrant and his mother. There was no hope of escape, which is also why we were so foreign to each other, for years and years after.

When you live in a concentration camp, it's every man for himself, I felt back then.

Not that Frankl would agree. But maybe he would have agreed with my mother, who was hoping—always hoping—for Dad's better self to emerge, to make better choices for his family, and not put them in harm's way.

It never would, so Dan and I had to shift our faith to Mom, and hope that her better self would emerge, to save us.

It did, eventually, but that would take time, and I was long gone by then.

Chapter 15

FOOTBALL

My God, did I hate football.

For years the punishment, the ritual drilling in dirt, the concussions, the running and jumping and ill-fitting equipment—I didn't get the draw. I had no idea what the hell I was doing there. I did it because Dan made me do it. Not Dad, but Dan. Dan made me play football.

Perhaps I should thank him here. I won't. I'm not sure that I should. How I hate it even now.

Dan still charts his entire year by it, like a farmer scheduling his harvest. I won't talk to him for most of the NFL season, because he's just an emotional wreck, and when I need to discuss something important, I wait until the Super Bowl is over.

For months, it seemed, our football team would practice in order to schedule a game against an equally inadequate and unprepared South Texas high school team full of kids who were terribly similar to ourselves, only to expose our inadequacies and incompetence at their feet, and then one side would soundly beat the other by scoring hundreds of points, this way or that, while cheerleaders blandly encouraged the team and their families, with meaningless chants, boring and terribly unsexy cheers.

That was football, for me. I would study the other kids playing it, wondering what the hell would possess them to give up so much of their time for this. I knew why I had to; what the fuck was *their* problem?

But I still managed to make friends there, like you do in prison movies. Like you have to. And enemies. I made lots of those.

Primarily, I made an enemy of my coach. I was in the ninth grade when our varsity team (my brother included) lost 21-0 to the worst football program in the state, a school in an even poorer district than our own: Gladys Porter High School, and a friend of mine gave me a paper bag complete with eye holes and a frown to wear over my head, which I thought was hysterical, and the coach saw me.

He was a runty little guy, Coach Chavez, who always asked if my mother was coming to our games. He gave me the creeps, because he'd seen her at my brother's games and leched over her. Mom was pretty cute in the 1980s. Chavez was about five feet, five inches tall and had a habit of picking his nose and smearing the enormous yield across the bottom of his cleats while he was talking to sweaty, inattentive boys. He was a disgusting little man in brown polyester shorts, and portentous in my inability to get along with short men as an adult.

He was my first-period coach, and he drew me out immediately after he saw me in the paper-bag hat-thing, and told me to dress in full gear and run around the track until he said stop. Something inside me clicked, and I thought, *How dare you? How fucking dare you try and punish me? My father is twice the coward you are!* I figured I could take *double* anything this little fucker could dish out.

It just stood to logic.

So I ran in full gear, in the furious August sun, and after half an hour he tried to flag me down and tell me to stop. I said, "No." I kept going, my helmet amplifying my breathing around my sticky, slimy mouthpiece. Forty-five minutes and the whole team stopped to watch, disquieted at my passive hostility. I wouldn't give him the benefit. Made him uncomfortable in the face of his superiors, who were now suddenly watching, suddenly worried about liability. I kept running. The whole program stopped to watch me jog at the end of the class, knew that something was not right. I had jogged thirty-six laps in less than an hour, eight and a half miles, and I would have kept going, because I wanted to drop from heat exhaustion, but the bell rang and I was already in Dutch for my second period algebra II class, for being late.

That oughta show him, I thought, as I showered and nearly collapsed. He never spoke to me again, and I got a bear claw and a juice out of it from the trainer, who almost called an ambulance.

But I also had friends in the program, one or two. Friends who just disappeared, it seemed like.

Like Albert, who had a lighthearted exuberance about him, especially in his inability to play ball. That's why we were both B-team quarterbacks: We both stank at it, we were both less consequential than the plastic gear we were wearing, and we could both speak English, so there was no other position for us.

The primary difference between us was that I didn't want to be there. Albert did, though I think it was more for the glamour of being a B-team quarterback: It worked well on his ladies. Anyhow, he was always hurt, so he never really got to play. He broke his collarbone the first week of practice and then there was something with a thigh muscle, making me play out all the B-team games by myself, and we'd get annihilated.

I remember the first time we traveled elsewhere to get the shit kicked out of us by an opposing team. Albert was there at the Athletics Building when we returned late that night, around eight o'clock or so, and he stood outside the door of the Bluebird bus and I was the first one to answer him, when he asked, "So what happened, Chicken-man?" (There's a story behind that nickname.)

I said, "We lost, man. Fifty-six to zero."

A complicated look came over his face. He said, "What happened?"

I said, "They were fucking bigger than us, better. I couldn't get a hand off to anyone. I got my ass kicked every single play. No one was blocking, from the line. I'd get the snap and before I could turn around, I was tackled. They were just better than us."

It was the truth: As a scheduling error, we ended up playing their varsity team, in front of their whole school, who suddenly thought these guys had a shot at state. However, it was quickly answered a few weeks later when their varsity team played our real varsity team and they realized they had played the practice dummies a couple weeks before. They lost, 86-0.

Anyhow, I never forgot the way he looked at me right then, and asked him about it later, when I was driving him to his girl-friend's house one afternoon in my sister's Volkswagen Rabbit.

"You thought it was my fault, didn't you? That we had lost like that?" I asked him.

He grinned sheepishly, in a very likeable and friendly way.

"Yeah," he said. "I thought you fucked up, Chicken-man. After all we practiced, I thought you lost your balls in the game." It was certainly not the case. I just kept getting my balls stomped.

❖

All right, about "Chicken-man": I got that nickname in the football program at Hanna because of a *quinceañera* I was forced to participate in. (These are the coming-out parties for fifteen-year-old girls. They're so popular, they drive the local economy.)

How this begins is, one night, my father comes home drunk and we'd just somehow bought an electric clipper, and Dad decides I need a hair cut (I was looking like Lyle Lovett would, a couple years later). He manhandles me into the bathroom, puts my head in the sink, and just starts clipping away at the sides of my head, sort of jokingly.

Now, I'm in my odd adolescent stage here and my head is out of whack, proportionally. I've been getting bad haircuts that enhance my large Aztecan nose, or, at this point, overgrown ears. Dad somehow clips at the sides of my head and makes my hair complement the shape of my head, totally. Suddenly, I cannot tear myself away from mirrors. I look like an Ashkenazi Elvis: I'm in love.

A few months later, my hair is shaggy again, and so I ask my dad to do the same thing. He says, in Spanish, "Are you retarded? I was drunk that night and didn't know what I was doing. You could have ended up bald. Here's five dollars; go get a haircut."

The only thing I could figure out that he had done that no one else had done before was cut my hair to Marine Corps regulation, almost. So when I get to the trailer of the woman who would cut hair for five bucks over by the sandpit, I ask her to go short.

"Just short," I say.

"Short?" she asks, kicking her toddler daughter away from the chair I'm in.

"Short," I say.

"Shorter?" She asks, after she has cut it really short.

I look in the mirror. It doesn't look right.

"Go shorter," I say.

"Shorter?" she asks, after a couple minutes.

"Shorter," I say, and barely wince when she switches to scissors and clips off a part of my ear.

"Oh, my God! I'm so sorry! I've never done that before!" she says as the blood runs down the back of my neck, crimson against the white cotton bedsheet she is using as a barber's bib.

Over tears, she tells me she cannot accept payment for maiming my ear, which, I understand in some cultures means that I can't marry again, but I'm perfectly all right with it because it gets me a free haircut. Though, again, something is not quite right with it.

"*¿Que chingádos te paso con tu pinche pelo?*" ("What the fuck happened to your fucking hair?") Dad asks, as soon as I get home.

"She cut it," I reply.

"*Te miras pelon,*" he says. ("You look like a convict," or rather, "You look bald, like a convict.")

The *quinceañera* event was awful, as to be expected. I still have some photos, and I look like a survivor from a Russian labor camp. That wasn't the worst part, though.

That next Monday, at first-period football, I'm out on the field doing stretches and one of the smaller, tubbier mustachioed coaches with a sense of humor walks by me and says, "Martinez! Did they catch you stealing chickens? What the fuck happened to your hair? We used to shave people's heads like that, when they were caught stealing chickens."

And it stuck. What's interesting is that it never quite got up to Dan's sphere, and he never heard my nickname in football practice. In my own group I was known to be able to take a good hit. I'd grown up with Dan and Richard, after all, and these guys here were pikers, had plastic, and rules, and were not going to kill you, which were the rules I grew up with. So when they'd come at me, I'd stand my ground. Take my hits. But then suddenly my nickname was "Chicken-man," and "Chicken," in the same way that a huge guy is called "Tiny." I'd like to think.

However, the first time I was called "Chicken-man" in front of Dan, he gave me a look, and I couldn't explain it, so I just kind of sat there, saddled with it, in his eyes, and it hurt. I don't think I ever explained that to him.

✦

Anyhow, Albert and I had become fairly good friends. He liked my British Knights so much that one day he asked to borrow them. I said, Um, sure, and he gave me his leather boots, very ala Lando Calrissian, I thought. They were popular at the time, that style of boots (sort of Ugg Boots, for boys, a kind of farmer chav), but as the school day was ending, I realized I couldn't go home with them, so I searched him out, found out his last period class, and tracked him there, found he wasn't actually in there, and then got his home address from a mutual friend and had to skip the last period of school to find him at home, where he was outside on a patio, doing homework. He looked very happy, and not at all surprised to see me. He made shrimp from the freezer, and we hung out and talked about what was going on with him.

Albert had an eye for the cutesy Mexican girls of the area, and they certainly had one for him. In Brownsville, the drug dealers have a severe "madonna versus whore" issue, which is really quite dangerous. Mexican girls with angelic faces are revered as dainty princesses and auctioned off to the most virile and competent dealer, known by the flashiest truck and the bloodiest sinus, even at, say, fifteen years of age.

As a young man, if you had any sense of self-preservation, you would stay far away from these girls, because they were considered untouchable and reserved for the next available son of a drug dealer who would fall in desperate love upon laying eyes on her, and then beat them in public for talking to another boy, later. These were not people accustomed to rational resolution of grievances.

Because, even if you listened to the cries for help from atop the pedestals where these girls were kept, and even if your motives were pure—and, let's be honest, they never were—the lionized male children of drug dealers were totally incapable of understanding how to treat their women with the respect of an equal, that they might have something of interest to share, (and in full disclosure, they very likely didn't, beyond what they saw in fashion magazines and on Univision) so these pretty girls were left lonely, isolated in their dangerous native beauty. No, they were the image of the holy mother, and the drug-dealing boys couldn't wait to fuck them, and any man talking to their objects of affection was someone who challenged their virility, someone to be shot. Which is what is widely speculated to have happened to my friend, Albert.

Albert was said to have a girlfriend in her early twenties, and when you're seventeen, that's a considerable bragging commodity. The trick was, she was married to one of those import/export people in Matamoros, the sister city to Brownsville. The woman was unhappy, and she sought out Albert.

After a few weeks of this, her husband sought him out as well.

Albert was at a friend's house down the street from his own when he noticed four men in suits, sitting in a Mercedes on their street. The neighborhood was terribly working class and rapidly going downhill, so a Mercedes really stood out. According to gossip, he knew they meant business, and Albert would not leave his friend's house. Finally, after nightfall, he summoned the courage to sneak out the back, barefoot and in shorts, making his way to his house when the car lit up and roared into his family's driveway.

The four men rushed out of the car brandishing Uzis, and his mother was in the doorway yelling, "Hey, what do you think you're doing?!" They flashed her some bunk badges, saying they were with the FBI and that Albert was being taken in for questioning and they stuffed him in the trunk and drove away. Cops were called, Albert's father's past iniquities were researched, and the legal interpretation was that because Albert's father was caught smuggling marijuana some ten years before, he had something else to hide, and it cost him his son's life.

Albert's father swore it wasn't the case, that his shrimping business was now legitimate, and having shared lunch with Albert a few times, visited his home, I can agree. His house was modest, and Albert had no more money than any other of us kids. He was diddling the wrong Mexican princess, and he paid with his life. He just disappeared that night.

His case was on *America's Most Wanted*. It was made national, very public, but it left a big hole in a lot of people's lives. That poor kid. My friend, Albert. Just gone.

He wasn't the only one.

Another kid from football, Arnold, was shot in the chest by a double-barreled 12-gauge shotgun, in a case of mistaken identity. He had been sitting on the trunk of his car, an old Mustang LX that he was rebuilding, late one Saturday night while watching the drag races on Billy Mitchell, which were impromptu and haphazard, and these two Mexican guys drove up and shot him in the chest, point blank, out of the passenger window. The people scattered, left Arnold on the ground asking for help.

The next day, the kid who pulled the trigger turned himself in, said it had been a mistake; they had been looking for a rival gang member.

Arnold's locker was cleaned out over the weekend, and no one ever talked about him again. He just disappeared, too.

And another: Alvaro, the first kid to get pubes, two lockers down. He was the first guy to have the courage to take a shower, because his pubes had come in early—what had he to hide now? He was killed during spring break, on the highway from South Padre Island. There was an image of the car wreck on the news that evening, and I saw his sneakers, covered in blood, still on his feet.

His locker was never cleaned out, like everyone had forgotten he had been in football, and I would look at it every day, remember those bloodied tennis shoes on the news.

It was hard not to think you were going to be next.

Chapter 16

THE ARTLESS DODGER

I played hooky for the very first time at fourteen, from Central Junior High, and it would be a constant, recurring theme in my life, and happens often, even now. It's what I want to do.

I was in the eighth grade then, and Carl was in the seventh and Anthony had been hovering somewhere in between for two years. We needed to see a BB gun at the Montgomery Ward in Amigoland Mall about two miles from the junior high and we skipped the second half of school to do it, after lunch. Something about a camping trip the next day and guns were necessary. We paid for it though, frightened as we were to return that subsequent Monday. But we got away with it.

Carl and Anthony lived out on the undeveloped developments in the eastern fringe of Brownsville near me, about a mile in either direction from my own house. They were my only friends because of their own dislocation.

Carl's dad was an ex–border patrol officer who hurt his back sometime in the early 1980s chasing after Mexicans crossing the Rio Grande and now exacted a pension and wouldn't allow himself to speak to either Anthony or me, avoided us when we were over at Carl's place. They were one of about five non-farming white families who lived that far out of town, in an enclave three miles from the nearest paved road. Still, they had central air-conditioning and indoor plumbing, clearly civilized, so they were the envy of the rest of us, who drove by and leched equally at Carl's sexy twin sisters, who were both very sweet and very kind, and their comfy indoor toilets.

Anthony was mostly Vietnamese, generated from that spate of dislocated Viet fishermen who were moved to South Texas in the 1960s and then moved elsewhere in Texas under nefarious circumstances. However, Anthony's father seemed more like a smuggler than a fisherman. His mother was Mexican, and the mix somehow made Anthony tall, but slender and darkly wolfish. He had teeth like a young Martin Amis and hardly spoke as a result of it, even kept his upper lip hung tersely over the lower in order to keep his teeth from showing when he laughed. He had long, thin, muscular arms and legs that come with hard hours of labor, the sort of build I came to fear later because of the quiet resentment that produces it. He had a sister the same age as my sister Mare, named Janie. Janie had perfect, bouncy tits and Dan and I would go very quiet when she was around.

Anyhow, Anthony and his family lived in the other direction from Carl's house, farther away it seemed, in a classically Mexican overdeveloped hacienda made of pink, very tactile stone that, when first built, knew no financial limits, but was quickly left to ruin. It had a swimming pool—complete with winding slide—and *that* was the source of a lot of envy, until it, too, was abandoned a year after it was built. Anthony's father was a drug dealer, we all decided.

Carl, on the other hand, was a perfectly white suburban kid. Baptist, nappy headed, member of the 4-H club, and used the phrase *fixinta*. Once, while camping in the bed of one of my father's trailers, for privacy, I produced some pornography from my uncle's collection and Carl jacked off in front of me and

Anthony, making us really uncomfortable. "I'm fixinta come," he said, motivated by a bland *Playboy* centerfold, and then he did as promised.

Carl and Anthony were better friends between themselves than I was with either of them. They liked being the same kind of stupid, and I raced to develop further. Games of "pinch-a-buggy" and punching one another in the upper arm for sport didn't appeal to me so much. Plus, I also saw the looks Carl's mother would give Anthony when Anthony wasn't looking, the same looks I was certain were aimed at me when I wasn't looking.

So it wasn't with too much sentimentality that I left Carl behind for a whole new set of friends in high school, and he started hanging out with more FFA types, passionately discussing things like butter and animal husbands. Husbandry. Whatever.

Anthony I sorta missed, but mostly because he quit school and drifted farther and farther into obscurity and drug dealing with his father. I'd see him occasionally as I drove by his house, and I would honk and wave and he'd wave back. I suppose that was as much as I could ask.

❖

High school did not offer anything more promising in the way of socializing.

In the mornings before school, kids congregated around the low stone benches that lined the front of the high school like birds at a feeder. The kids who drove their own vehicles would assemble in the student parking lot, but it was much more social in the front, away from the classic rock and stolen cigarettes.

During the fall and winter, the temperature would dip into the mid-seventies in the mornings before the sun could recover and bake the planet brown around noon, and these cool mornings are among the few things I remember about high school, shivering in my over-sized shirts. I'd bus the seven or so miles and get to school an hour before classes started and socialize as I could not at any other time, living way out in the middle of nothing. School had become my only available means of socializing and I began to dislike the interference of classes and teachers and bells.

After school it was the same thing. I hated that people had to leave because I liked them hanging around. I couldn't understand why they would want to go home, to leave such an enjoyable atmosphere. I wanted them all to participate in my John Hughes fantasies, godammit.

When I was forced to get home, I had to deal with Dad or Gramma. I'd be met with verbal assaults and demands that I change into my mechanic's clothes and get to doing something, anything, outside on the trucks or in the yard. "I didn't spend all day in the air-conditioning looking at women's asses like you!" Gramma would yell at me, in Spanish. While there was daylight left, I'd have to crawl under the dump trucks and check fluid levels, grease the joints, change flat tires, do some sort of maintenance, or maybe help whatever mechanic *du jour* was attempting to revive our decrepit equipment. Other days, I'd have to drive the backhoe someplace. Or the trucks. No concern or mention ever of homework. Not that I would argue; I just knew it was a lost cause.

Gramma had these horrific manias, these extensive manic bouts about working, about making oneself as useful as possible. It stemmed from her years picking crops and priding herself from picking the most crates of tomatoes, bales of cotton, or whatever vegetable she happened to be working, but now, when she couldn't be producing, she would explode in psychotic episodes for others to do *MORE!* and *MORE!* and *MORE!* There was always a panic, always a reason to burn white hot with deadline: You just needed to figure out what it was, *so DO EVERYTHING, DO IT ALL, AND NOW!*

This is how we grew up with her, and Dad, too. "*Ándale!*" she or he screamed when I'd walk up the drive after the bus would drop me off. "Come on!" she'd yell at me in Spanish. "Felípe is already waiting at the field in the truck and we need you to fill him up! We've been waiting for you since three!" Felípe, her younger brother, would eventually set himself aflame and nearly die from some sort of private guilt that demanded self-immolation, in his mind. (It had been big news in the barrio, and Gramma failed at finding someone to sue for it.) Living with Gramma was making me wish I had done the same thing, and succeeded.

I absolutely hated coming home.

Weekends were the worst. Saturday mornings Gramma would start mowing her lawn around six thirty, when the sun was good and hot, and she would eventually find a reason to mow the same patch of earth beneath my bedroom window over and over again until I was up and demanding to take over the lawnmower, just to get her on her way.

This happened a lot.

When Tony found me hanging out at the front of the high school, I was ripe for the picking, quite the low-hanging fruit.

"Hey, you're Domingo, right? Dan's little brother? Yeah, I partied with your brother a few times," he lied. "Hey, come with me to buy a joint at the Wall."

I had a bad feeling about this. The Wall was not for the unini-
tiated. It was the barrier between the tennis courts and the neighborhood immediately to the school's north, creating an alley that
was largely obfuscated from all angles. Bad people hung out there.
Bad people who could not under any circumstances complete full
sentences, verbal or written. In English or Spanish.

"Uh, I dunno, man," I protested. "I don't think those people
would like me."

"Arr, that's not true, man," he insisted, kinda jittery. "Jaíme
and those guys are cool. We're just gonna buy a joint."

"What if they think I'm a narc?" I didn't dress like them, in
camouflage and jackets with Pink Floyd buttons on the lapels.
And I didn't have that lesbian haircut, the spiky thing with the
long tails in the back.

"Look, don't worry about it, man. Just come with me. I'll
talk to these guys. How much money you got?"

This was actually the reason I was recruited, I came to realize
later: I was an addition to his stable of boy-whores, able to conjure
a dollar or two more toward the purchase of beer and marijuana.

He fancied himself a con artist, but he wasn't very good at it.
I felt sorry for him, mostly, transparent as he was. I could always
see what he was doing, how he was trying to manipulate me,
and so could everyone else. We all saw right through the cajol-
ery, the logisticizing, the pleading, but he was oddly charming,
if a bit hairy, like a seductress from the Bible.

Personally, I think I played along out of sheer boredom, but
more likely because nothing else had come along.

"I got three bucks for lunch," I said. "It's supposed to last
me for today and tomorrow." We had started on our way to the
tennis courts, and the looming challenge of the Wall.

"Arr, a dollar-fifty a day? That's pathetic," he said, embarrassing me. "Here, let me have two dollars."

Tony believed himself to be the school guru of pot. By the time he invited me to go skipping, he was living in a hippie fantasy that only ended when he had to report to his parents, who knew that the only time Tony ever lied was when his mouth moved.

At the Wall, I was sniffed over with more disdain than I felt necessary, but not because I seemed a narc. It was because I was terribly uncool, in a striped collared shirt borrowed from my father, fading blue Levis, and white Reeboks. I was a dork, sure, but come on: Who isn't at fifteen?

Tony bought three joints for the two dollars and lit one up right in front of the guy from whom he bought it, giving him the ritualistic second hit before passing it to me, letting the guy know I was cool. There were a lot of unspoken rules to pot smoking. Many of them, I still don't know, and quite frankly, don't care to know anymore.

We stood there, the three of us, in that concrete alleyway and smoked the entire thing.

"'Ere," said Tony, holding in his breath and passing me the toxic little joint burned down to a nub.

"Hey, man; I can't smoke anymore. I think I'm high. I don't think I've ever been this high before. I'm afraid to go to class."

The other guy studied me for a moment, his thoughts registering clearly on his face. Suspicion, realization, ridicule.

"Ha, ha," he said slowly. "You're stoned." Pointed at me.

"A ha ha!" said Tony, studying my scared eyes. "Dude, you'll be fine," he said, and kept the remaining two joints for himself.

I wasn't fine. In my first period, I tried reading but my eyes kept jumping back every three words. I smelled of pot. The guy behind me said in the voice of a forty-year-old, "Hey man. You stink of smoke." It made me really nervous.

My cousin Dora heard this and said, "Domingo, did you start smoking?"

"Cigarettes," I said. "It was cigarettes. I gotta go." So I got up and left class without asking permission and without any excuse and walked around the campus until I came down. I wasn't missed. Our teacher was an ex-hippie and she understood my abrupt exit, I think. Mostly she was pissed off and hated her job and hated her students, but she liked me in her own acid way, so when I had to report back the next day, she didn't question it. But it wasn't an auspicious beginning to my hanging around with Tony. Or rather, it was exactly the sort of thing that he and I had imagined high school to be. Tony and I both had fantasies about what high school was supposed to be like; the only problem was that no one else played along, and they were determined to make it difficult for us, with like, grades and attendance and stuff like that. But Tony said he had a way around it. So I went with it, and my path, already bent, became properly crooked.

I don't think I ever thanked him for that.

Chapter 17

DAN'S SECOND FIGHT

Dan had been big for his age his entire life. As such, he considered himself protector of his loved ones, especially because Dad kept insisting on the idea, because Dad knew himself to be incapable of that role.

It was rare for Dan to be much of a bully, though the mood did sometimes strike when we were kids, as will happen with someone who is exploring the boundaries of his strength, of his compassion.

He was actually a really sensitive kid. I remember one year Dad had moved ten hours north to Dallas to find work, and Mom had insisted that the whole family would travel the vertical length of Texas in the 1980 Bonneville—highways 77 to 37 to 35—in order to have Christmas as a family. Dad had been fairly unconcerned with the idea of having the family together for the holidays, but Mom was obstinate. Dad had liked the new solitude, liked being functionally single. He'd go to church on Sunday morning, sure, but then he'd hit a porno movie before he had to make it back to the dismal two-room rental he was sharing with Richard. Having the family around in Dallas made him claustrophobic. Or maybe he didn't want anyone seeing how he was living, especially his family.

Anyhow, it was when we were on our way there, or on our way back at some point during those ten painful hours when we were all tired, cramped, hot, and cranky, that Mom had the radio tuned to a parochial country radio station.

All the kids were singing tunelessly along to Juice Newton's *Angel of the Morning* to pass the time, when something about the plight of the scorned woman at the center of Juice Newton's song really plucked at Dan's ten-year-old heart, and he cried for that woman's pain, looking off into the dusty, uninterrupted Texas horizon. Mare was the first to notice the tears on his cheek and she brought it mercilessly to the attention of the brood, delicious and full of tangy spite, and we all turned on him like sharks attacking one of their own.

We pointed and laughed loudly, humiliated him for what seemed like an hour, like we knew how. God it was heavenly, how we had him crying, this time out of a deep, painful shame at showing compassion. It's what passed for love in that Bonneville.

When I relayed the story in therapy years later, my therapist, Sally, asked, "Do you think maybe he was crying for your mother, in the role of that scorned woman?"

I winced, bit down hard: I preferred to hold on to the idea of humiliating Dan for being a wuss. I suppose I should ask him about that.

This isn't to say Dan was free and loose with his compassion, not to me, at least. I was his little brother, and as such, I needed a certain amount of domination, both physically and emotionally. Though Dan did have his moments, as a leader or teacher.

One day, we were left alone in the house, which was a rarity when we were kids, and Dan had been poking around in the one shared bathroom. He'd found a box of maxi-pads and decided right then that I could use a lesson in the menstrual cycle.

I should say here that all dealings with female plumbing were absolutely verboten, kept secret from us boys, so we had no idea what these things were for. Well, I had no idea: Dan had apparently received some information about their use, from somewhere outside the home. So he was going to teach me what he knew.

"They put it in their underwear, with these," he says, and begins to peel off the adhesive strips.

"For what?" I ask, confused.

"Because once a month, they bleed. They go 'on the rag,'" he tells me, like I should know what he's talking about.

"Oh," I say, completely bewildered. I'd heard the phrase, but I did not understand what it meant. "Is that the rag?" I pointed at the pad.

"Yeah," he says. "It goes like this," and he pulls down his Y-fronts and inserts the maxi-pad under his tackle with the adhesive side up, then slaps the elastic band back into place.

"See?" he says, and begins walking about, pretending he's a girl with an unusually large basket.

I'm laughing at his pantomime, and when he's done, he pulls down his underwear once again to end the lesson and suddenly realizes his mistake. He starts pulling the pad out of his underwear, and with it comes the skin of his teenaged testicles and penis, and he makes the most comic, twisted face I will ever see him make in all the years I've known him, as his penis and scrotum are stretched out to nearly the length of his arm, and I am on the floor exhausted with laughter, tears running down my cheeks and incapable of catching my breath, nearing an asthma attack.

"Boy," I said, when I could catch my breath and he was doubled over in agony, "I bet they don't have *that* problem."

Anyhow, like in all pack-animal hierarchies, Dan had a role to play, as did I. I wanted what he had, would always want what the leader had. He was my hero. Still is, in a lot of ways, actually.

He played football all his schooling, and he liked it, unlike me, who played football all my schooling and hated it. I played football because he expected it of me. In this way Dan was more influential to my upbringing than Dad ever was.

Dan was solid, had a good relationship to the earth, and had natural, bracing foot placement, always. A cock-strong kid who was also quick on his feet, he was a perfect pulling guard on the offensive line and a tackle on the defense. He would be in every single play in a game, never had a chance to sit on the bench, and made varsity when he was a sophomore. I never really left the bench, would go to games just for the trip to Whataburger we got afterward. That was my reward for five days of practice and enduring the Neanderthal coaching staff.

I grew up small, lean, intimidated. I accepted early that I could not naturally pull off alpha male aggression, that I would have to train at it, like a sport, if I was ever going to be able to defend myself. Richard had taught me that.

But that wouldn't come until a few years later.

Dan, on the other hand, was naturally burly, could hit like a mule on the field.

But Dan never had training in boxing, never really learned how to throw a punch. And in our barrio, well, no one ever really liked to admit that they didn't know how to throw a real punch, wouldn't pay or put in the repetitive hours to throw a legitimate jab/reverse combination because somehow, in the land of machismo, it seemed elitist to enter into any type of program for self-improvement. In a stressed community, any sort of elevation is looked down upon, felt as a judgment on the rest of the people.

What? They seemed to say. *We're not good enough as we are now?*

We were expected to be *chingon* in the barrio, and without any instruction. On top of that, we were also expected never to shy away from an opportunity to show our inability to do so.

"*Tirar chingásos,*" we'd call it. ("Throw down. Throw some fuckers.")

I dunno. It confuses me, too.

Anyhow, Dan, in high school, never had too many reasons to fight, or dominate any more than was necessary. He was a likeable enough kid, had gotten into one or two scraps as a younger teen, but had gone through his teenage years mostly untested. When I started high school, Dan was a senior, a varsity football player, and did what he wanted around school. He was already enlisted at seventeen, shipping out at the end of the school year. Dad was working long-haul trucking at this point, which had left my older, larger brother to enjoy a bit of unexpected independence like a regular, normal high school teenager. He was happy; he had his little forays with the blonde Baptists and Mormon fauna—the "slim-hipped gentiles" all new immigrants are unconsciously promised upon becoming an American—and he was feeling pretty good at being the boy king.

Then one day, in the halls of Hanna High—alum to the likes of Kris Kristofferson, thank you very much—I happen to walk by Dan's third-period class, as it's letting out.

One of the only two or so black students at Hanna, this guy named Ted, comes out of the classroom first, shuffling in a way that seems light, joking, as the rest of the students begin to swarm into the hallway. I notice next that Dan has emerged from the same room, slow, serious, with a strange look on his face that I've never seen before.

Dan has been challenged, threatened.

I hadn't clocked it.

Ted, halfway down the hall, turns on his heel and flicks his hands like flippers, says, "Come on, man. Come on . . . "

I suddenly realize he's saying this to Dan. I think he's joking, because he seems to be smiling, happy. I don't get there's a fight developing because I'm fourteen years old, and Dan and Ted have been, up to this point, friends.

In my innocent understanding of the world at fourteen, friends didn't fight. They argued, they said mean things about each other, and they parlayed loyalties, but they never actually fought.

Fighting came from enemies, who were marked as clearly as Draco Malfoy, Darth Vader, Alan Rickman in "Die Hard," or, closer to home, guys named "Paco" or "El Smiley." So I think they're kidding.

"Kick his ass, Ted!" I yell like a pre-teen girl squealing at a concert.

It was in good fun, right?

I turn and face Dan, who has stopped now, in the hall, the look on his face suddenly recognizable to me. It says, "You disloyal shit." It says, "I'm being called out. I'm scared. I have to do this, and I don't want to do this. I have to do this. Not for anyone else, not to prove anything, but for myself. I'm going to do this, you disloyal little fuck."

I see his face drain of blood, and he hands me the single red folder he's carrying. He's wearing black denim jeans with vertical striping (it's 1987) and a collared shirt, also with thin vertical black and red stripes. I had been with him when he had asked

Mom to buy it for him, at JC Penney. And he's wearing his contact lenses, which Mom had finally consented to buy for him, after he had enlisted in the army and had his first-ever vision test the summer before. Mom had been horrified, guilt ridden, when she realized he had long suffered with -5 vision, had gone without glasses his entire life while his sisters had bought vanity glasses. So she'd bought him the contact lenses just a few months before. They had been quite dear.

I remember all this because at the flash point of realization—that Dan is in a fight—it's like a Polaroid of that moment and all its minutiae.

Dan is in a fight, and there's no feeling in the world more isolating. He's in a fight, on his own, and backing down is just not an option. You can't, as a boy king.

See, Ted is well-known in the school, and not just because he's one of the two black kids. Well, that certainly helped, but Ted was from Chicago, the popular lore went, and had a reputation of being a gang-fighting bad ass.

He had a cult of kids in my grade who followed him around like flunkies. The only other black kid in the school, Marlon, had been the quarterback on my freshman team and had been a "friend" of mine, back in junior high school, but now he's here, cheering Ted on, in fighting my older brother.

All this helps my ideas of friendship mature instantaneously. I realize at this moment that your friends can turn into fighting enemies, and that you can never really trust anyone, ever.

I take Dan's folder and hold it, follow him dumbly as he follows Ted out to where Ted, flashy and ghetto-inspired, is making a lot of noise, drawing as much attention as possible, like Cassius Clay had done to Joe Louis before their first fight.

Thing is, the next period is my Latin class, fourth period.

Lunchtime at Hanna happened on fourth and fifth period, and I had been quite loose with the times I'd squandered my fourth period previously, with the people who'd had fourth-period lunches. I'd taken the "three martini" lunch once too often and was at the point where, should I miss one more class, I'd lose the credit and would be held back for the year. I was walking a fine, tender line.

The horde of spectators—now immense, with the noise Ted is making—is walking past my Latin class, which is held outside the school in one of those square mobile classrooms that had been established all around the campus to help with the overflow of students. Hanna was, at the time I think, the second largest high school in the nation.

My Latin teacher, Mr. Jacobs, stands at the doorway to the classroom, his interest piqued by the volume of the crowd. Mr. Jacobs is a tall, gangly blonde-haired fella who wears bowties and at the time was a ringer for Ed Begley Jr. I have no idea what he was doing in Brownsville, other than missionary work, because he often said his life's goal was to become a monk.

He stands on the doorstep and watches as the crowd of students swarms to the alley behind the Wall, behind the tennis courts, which are adjacent to his classroom. He understands what's happening immediately, and catches sight of me, becoming relentless in his higher-minded teaching:

"Domingo, you're coming to Latin class today."

"But that's my brother. I have to be there."

"I can't make the choice for you, Domingo, but you know what's at stake here."

"Mr. Jacobs, please; it's my family; I have to be there."

"Domingo, you know the situation. I can't protect you. You have to make the choice yourself. Forward or backward, Domingo. Forward or backward."

With that, he goes back inside and closes the door, as the few other students in Latin class step in behind him and the tardy bell rings.

I have never been more twisted inside, and I hate Mr. Jacobs at that moment and don't understand what he meant by "forward or backward." What kind of shit is that? Dan is fighting the unchallenged titan of Hanna High School, and I'm forced to attend my Latin class, or else I'll be held back a year and won't graduate with my class.

Glumly, I climb the steps into Mr. Jacobs's class and sit down, with absolutely no hope of absorbing what will be taught. Mr. Jacobs sees this and teaches accordingly, a light day. He drops his curriculum and decides instead to explain to us Latin students the difference between *obscenity* and *profanity,* since he himself had been recently taken to task by an associate principal for saying "a profanity."

"No," Mr. Jacobs had corrected her. "What I said to you was 'obscene,' and not 'profane.'" He had told her to go fuck herself, I think he was saying; not for God to go fuck Himself.

He didn't make many friends in Brownsville, either.

To make the time go by faster, I open Dan's notebook and flip through his academics. It isn't exactly convincing, as a student's notebook. It's more of a prop, with empty line-ruled paper and half-hearted attempts at note-taking, indiscernible scribbles and the lyrics to *Knocking at Your Back Door,* a song by Deep Purple that had much more *double entendre* than I was capable of understanding at the time.

It's a terrible fifty minutes, spent in that Latin classroom, and I don't think I ever managed to thank Mr. Jacobs for forcing me to make the choice that day. (Except by getting horribly drunk at one of his summer parties and frightening a girl I liked named Kathy, but that's another story.)

When the bell rings, I erupt from that classroom and run down anyone I can find for news, news, news of the event.

Certainly it is on everyone's mind, on everyone's lips . . . ?

And it is: The first familiar person I see is an old friend of Dan's, Israel, from way back.

"Oh, man," he tells me, "Dan got his ass *kicked*, man. You should have been there, man. They fought for like, an hour. Dan's all messed up."

This news is like telling me that Jesus had been shot, in church: just not possible, in the cosmology of how I understand the universe.

"Where is he?" I demand. "Where is everyone?"

"He went to Dennis's, I think," Israel says.

I bolt: Dennis lives near the school, around the track and over the golf course, in an apartment spread that was, I suppose, middle class, for Brownsville. I sprint the whole way, Dan's notebook developing a sweat-shaped image of my palm by the time I get there. I hit the doorway running and don't bother with the doorbell or a knock, just sorta yank it open and burst through, and am completely embarrassed to see Dennis's mother on the phone just stop midconversation and look at me, the boy who has just disrespected her house. She is on the phone with my parents, I think.

I fumble through an apology, and she nods in the direction of Dennis's bedroom, continuing with her conversation with her back turned to me.

Timidly, I make my way there, and this time, I knock on the door and immediately see Dan sitting on the bed, holding an ice pack to his eye, with Victor playing cut man, his best friend. Victor and Dan go way back.

Victor's family has a lot of money, are upper middle-class Mexican and own a chain of jewelry stores in Brownsville and Matamoros. Victor has been incredibly loyal to Dan since they were in junior high. Victor is a good friend, will eventually become my good friend.

Every Christmas since I was able to drive, I was charged with bringing four or five dozen of Gramma's freshly made tamales over to Victor's house, and they'd receive me like a state visitor, which would make me uncomfortable with the attention, and entirely bewildered at their good manners. They would call every member of their family to the dining room table and have me join them, and everyone would take a tamale and eat it, claiming they were the best thing they'd eaten that Christmas. I would blush and squirm and say, "Uh, gee, thank you?" It was just tamales, for Christ's sake; we had a warehouse full of them, back at Gramma's. I shot the pig myself, this time.

Noblesse oblige, though the class dynamics had been lost on me.

I always loved Victor's family, who were very kind to me and Dan all our teenaged lives. Things began falling apart for them after Dan had left to join the army, and I was in my senior year later on, as Victor's father had been under investigation for some anomalies in his taxes, accusations of smuggling and other federal stuff, but never did we think any less of the family, of the man. Everyone in Brownsville is dirty, works the angles. Politicians at every level are laughably crooked. Law enforcement is openly in bed with criminals—not only in bed, but in like, gay and lesbian pornos—the federal agencies are corrupt to a toxic level. It's endemic with the area, the culture. Victor's father simply managed to draw the attention of federal thugs; he did nothing any other family in Brownsville had not done at one point or another. He just managed to be good enough at whatever he did to get caught. I don't know how they managed the cheek to focus on Victor's dad.

Anyhow, it was during those troubles that Victor had phoned me, out of the blue, because he'd taken a weekend off from college to help his mother move out of their house, which had been seized by the feds, and they were desperate to get out of there because once the Feds locked the doors, they'd lose anything that was still inside, and would I please help them tomorrow?

Sure, I said. I had something planned, but no problem: I'd be there at nine. I'll bring someone to help.

The next day, I showed up with my friend Alex. We were the only people Victor had called who showed up; we worked all day and got his mother completely moved out of her house and into storage. She was so grateful that it was terribly satisfying to be able to repay her kindness after all those years, when she needed it. It was like a circuit closing, and it felt good, though she cried all day, from losing her house, and then from gratitude to me and Alex for helping her and Victor when no one else did.

Sidenote: It had been Victor's mother, actually, who had spurred me on to do something with myself in one of those throwaway moments, to promise her that I wouldn't allow myself to settle in Brownsville. I had found a pathetic job as a waiter at the newly opened Olive Garden in Harlingen, Texas, when I had first moved back to Brownsville from Seattle. (People in South Texas don't tip, and by that I mean: nothing. They simply do not tip. Once or twice an hour, a couple might be feeling worldly and leave behind a single dollar after finishing their lunch. I could work an entire ten-hour shift and make less than $5 in tips. That job lasted about a month. But the humiliation of knowing that "birthday song" lingers still.)

Anyhow, I was on a lunch shift when Victor and his mother happened to stop in at the Olive Garden, and they sat, thankfully, in someone else's section. I was on break when I noticed them, and I was putting away my pocket copy of *Cyrano de Bergerac*, when Victor's mother said, "Domingo, *niño*," in her perfect melting and lispy Galithian Spanish, "You simply do not belong here, in this area, in this job. You need to be where people will appreciate you more, or you will end up as a waiter all your life, because you're too smart for anything else here."

I was more befuddled at the fact that she had recognized *Cyrano de Bergerac* and mentioned that she had read it in the original French (it was available in French?) and had drawn her conclusions from the fact that I was reading it on my break to fully understand what she was telling me. I knew I hated South Texas, but what did *Cyrano de Bergerac* have to do with it? I just identified with the nose thing.

❖

That was Victor, and his family. It's not surprising to see him there, nursing Dan, holding the ice pack to his eye. The blood vessels in one eye had burst, from a punch that had caused the contact lens—one of the early large, hard glass models—to scrape his cornea. Dan had continued to fight, even though he had nearly been blinded, and while Dan sits there quietly sniffling, Victor proceeds to tell me how it went.

They had met in the alley behind the tennis courts, with half the school assembled to see the fight. Most of the crowd was there for the simple pleasure of watching the pugilistics, but others were there to support either Dan or Ted.

Ted had been loud and mouthy, talking shit loud and ghetto, while Dan had been quiet, reserved, angry. Frightened.

Ted's little entourage of freshmen kids had been there, too, Victor says, leaping and howling and picking fights with others in the crowd, pulling up their shirts in a threatening manner.

Ted half-pretended to talk to someone in the crowd and then tried to sucker punch Dan to start it off, but Dan had expected it and saw it coming, stepped forward into the swing and caught Ted in a grapple. It was on, and their styles couldn't have been more different.

Ted tried to keep Dan at bay, pushed off and defended himself at a distance, then charged forward throwing overhead punches. Dan would deflect and swing wide haymakers, grabbing at anything Ted threw his way, and locking them into a pinch, which Dan would win, but then he would let go.

In the tussle Ted would connect and Dan would too, and then grab or smother Ted, keep him pinned in a submission hold, and then Ted would say, "OK, OK, I'm done," then would get up, say something to the crowd, and then lunge at Dan again.

Dan would win every single exchange, would pin Ted down at the end of every scuffle, but in the end he looked like he got the worst of it, which is how teenage fights are scored.

Ted, being black, looked as if he had not bruised, had not been hit once, except for the swelling around both his eyes.

Our sister, Mare, had been there, in the crowd, and when Marlon and the rest of Ted's entourage had threatened to get involved, she came at them with her tennis racket, beating them back into the crowd. Mare wasn't alone in this; Dan's friends—both Victor and Dennis—had been behind her, and had calmed her back down, and made certain it had stayed a one-on-one fight.

And it was a one-on-one fight that Dan had won ten times over, but his sense of fair play and being a good guy allowed Ted to keep rearing up every time he'd cry uncle, and then Dan would let him up, even help him up, at times, as Victor told it. Then Ted would try something else, something dirty. The burst eye, in fact, came from the time Dan helped Ted get to his feet: Ted was sitting on the ground, beaten again, grabbed Dan's offered hand, and then used it as leverage as Ted swung to hit Dan, from the ground, after he had said it was over. This finally pissed Dan off, and he hit Ted back so hard, he didn't come back up, just rolled over on his stomach and said, "Oh, good hit, good hit . . . "

And that's how it ended. That fight lasted nearly forty-five minutes.

In the final analysis Dan did not have a hardened heart, after all that we'd been through with Dad; he would not do anything to someone else he felt was too damaging or too unfair. Like I said, Dan was a good kid. Ted, on the other hand, was trying every trick he knew to hurt Dan, right down to imitating karate movies, doing reverse mule kicks that never connected, or grabbing Dan's head and trying to slam it against the tennis court wall. Dan wouldn't fall for it, used the training he'd learned from football to keep Ted from marshalling the grapple, determining his balance. Dan was just better at it, but he wasn't a finisher; he didn't have it in him to hurt Ted. In the end, what ended the fight was exhaustion, and the lunch bell.

But Dan had survived. Not only survived, but outmatched the Titan of Hanna High, if you really knew how to score.

Though sitting in Dennis's bedroom, you wouldn't have known it, funereal as it was. Fights do that to you, make your soul feel dirty afterward. Make you feel ashamed of yourself, if your moral compass is intact.

This fight had been city versus farm, and the city had repeatedly conned its way out of a sound beating at the hands of the farm.

Dennis's mother had called Dad, had explained what happened, and Dad said he would be right over. Since both Dan and I have been the victims of Dad's explosive and illogical temper, we both expect and dread the further punishment headed our way, when he gets there. I think he'll have a fit over Dan losing the contact lenses, for not winning decisively, for the potential trouble from the school, the cops, anything that would occur to Dad, but it doesn't happen.

Dad is uncharacteristically understanding, comforting even, and he and Richard had dropped all they were doing that afternoon and drove to Dennis's to pick Dan up and take him to the emergency room.

They x-ray his nose (no fracture) and his wrist (hairline fracture) and his thumb (clearly fractured). Then they take Dan to dinner and buy him a beer.

Dan had fought, and survived, like a man. He was in the club. The club that Dad and Richard had never been able to enter. Maybe make deliveries there, through the tradesman's entrance, but certainly never enter through the front door.

An uneasy peace settled in the school after the fight.

Dan showed up to school the next day, with his red notebook stage prop intact. Ted didn't.

Ted was last seen down the alleyway, after the fight, smoking a joint with Marlon and putting a handkerchief to his nose. He dropped out of school and wasn't heard from again until we read a story in the *Brownsville Herald* about three months later, when he accidentally shot himself in the thigh, trying to remove a .357 revolver from his waistband as he sat in a car, late at night, across the street from the house of a girl he once briefly dated. That girl lived on a road that led straight to our house, out on Oklahoma Avenue, about five miles away. I didn't see the threat, until Dan pointed it out.

"He could have been coming here," he had said with a sort of sadness, looking at Mom and Derek arguing in the kitchen. His voice betrayed a complicated regret, like his feelings were hurt, with the implication.

Big hearted to the end, Dan even attended Ted's funeral, which I could not understand then, either. Ted's mother, who knew who Dan was, spotted him in the crowd and clutched Dan to her, as she broke down crying. Dan held her, and wept openly as well.

Chapter 18

DELTA CITY REPEAT

By age sixteen, my foremost ambition in attending high school was to get clear away from it before nine o'clock in the morning. Not consciously, of course, not for the first few hundred times.

School, I had noticed, was considered "my time," which meant I couldn't be pressed into labor by my father or grandmother for fear of government involvement. So I learned to take advantage of this.

Either by school bus or by my mother's Taurus, I'd make it to school before seven thirty and wait out options for escape. By my sophomore year, Tony had become my principal friend, or veteran pimp. He was by this point a grizzled imitation of the artful dodger, but with seemingly good parents and an even better little brother who was about to lap Tony at high school graduation.

Together Tony and I would find ways to while away the hours by doing anything other than attending class before we had to report home again.

We were big fans of Huckleberry Finn and Tom Sawyer, and I think we even tried believing we were continuing a long-celebrated American tradition by ditching class and getting stoned, a fantasy combination of Mark Twain by way of Hunter S. Thompson, but in full disclosure, we were just lazy and looking for a good time, not fully understanding how we were handicapping our future.

The skipping itself was not a problem, I would eventually come to learn; the problem was being allowed back into school, when we wanted to go back. Tony halfway convinced me that he had long ago mastered this obstacle, with a bit of bronze-age technology. Admittedly, I never did question why he was still held back all this time if his chicanery was so foolproof.

To his credit, Tony actually initiated me into the trade that I'd eventually pursue, graphic design. But in this early stage, it was plain and simple forgery: There was no "design" in what we were doing. It was Tony who placed the first X-Acto knife I ever held in my hands, and immediately, I felt an overwhelming sense of possibility, holding that little penknife.

He showed me how to use the X-Acto to surgically remove and rearrange grades and absences on a report card before it got to our parents. We'd intercept the report card and make our alterations, photocopy the doctored product and slip the manufactured version into the school district's envelope to cover our trespasses, and then lay it nonchalantly on the dining room table before our parents got home from work.

Tony took careful pains to explain this whole process to me, his flunky—a term that came uncomfortably close to becoming literal—over the photocopier in the library, feeding dimes into the machine like he was playing slots, in search of a copy that didn't blur or show the incisions in the original.

We were stoned and forcibly schoolbound because he couldn't get his mother's car that spring day.

"Look, man," he said through his trendy and tinted John Lennon glasses, a wanker style, even then, "You just gotta remove the 2 from in front of the 23 absences, then lighten the reproduction, and you got three absences in first period instead of twenty-three. Now take the 8 from the 48, move the 4 over and put the 8 in front of it, and now you have a B in Spanish instead of an F."

"Ho," I said, in total understanding, a big smile growing on my face, conveying how thoroughly I understood. Give a man a ride, he skips for a day. *Teach him how to forge. . . .*

Oh, it was ridiculously shortsighted, sure, but at that age, I never thought further than the immediate threat. Simply convincing my mother everything was quiet at school was enough for me; dealing with school records and the larger consequences of robbing myself of even *that* low-shelf an education—all that I would face at a later date. And certainly have.

That first year, Tony would usually borrow his mother's car, a blue Oldsmobile Delta 88, which was my own mother's dream car but totally unaffordable to us, and he would use it for our expeditions.

It was with complicated disquiet that I rode in this car on almost a daily basis to South Padre Island and back, a resort town at the end of a twenty-eight-mile highway that somehow felt much more cosmopolitan than Brownsville ever could, possibly because people from all over the United States vacationed there.

We'd drive there three or four times a day, listening to Led Zeppelin, as was Tony's unwavering musical proclivity, and I'd nod my head in unison and in rhythm with whomever else was stoned or drunk in the car.

There was a revolving cast of extras, but me, Tony, and Chris were the standards. I didn't trust Chris at the time because he reminded me too much of myself, and I felt threatened by him, somehow. But I didn't know that then.

Most of the other transient guys were idiots, even before they were stoned, so there was very little discovery or anything of interest ever said when others were in the car. Collectively, we just wanted to feel better than sobriety, not understanding that we were feeding what would become addictive personalities.

Among Chris, Tony, and me, though, we were capable of telling good stories, appreciating smart things, and Chris had really good taste in music, when he was allowed to take over the radio.

Once, Tony blew us all away by narrating a story he made up against the wordless musical theater piece, "On the Run," on the *Dark Side of the Moon* album by Pink Floyd, while we were high and parked at the country club. He just stopped the car, turned up the volume, and narrated this fantasy piece he'd written while the "song" played on the radio. We were all enraptured by this. I've always loved radio plays, and this was among some of the best I've heard.

He'd never top that, all his life. That was his crowning artistic achievement, the poor bastard.

✤

My junior year—and his third senior year—Tony's parents bought him a Dodge Laser. It was the year he would most assuredly graduate, they felt, and it was a chance for him to develop responsibility. The car was a dopey silver four-seater, about which we would eventually become quite fond.

By that year, I'd be dropped off in front of the school as early in the morning as possible because I was embarrassed to be seen in the aging Taurus. Among the poor and working class in Texas, an automobile is as telling as a tax return, and I had been taught by the Mimis long before to pretend that one was *rich* and *white*. And a 1986 Taurus in 1990, well, that wasn't quite well-to-do in Brownsville. It wasn't quite *Dallas* enough.

The minute my mother disappeared around the corner, though, Tony would drive around the other corner and park right in front of the school, in front of everybody, to pick me up in order to carry on with our naughtiness.

My man. (Or perhaps, as I came to understand it later: my pimp.)

"Dude, you gotta come skipping with me today," he'd say.

"Nah, Tony; I gotta go back to class today," I'd protest. "It's Thursday and I haven't been since last week." Some days, it'd be the other way around; I wasn't always the bottom. Plus, by this time I'd already been branded; Tony's company alone was enough to telegraph my ethical slips to any administrator watching, so they'd regard my documentation with suspicion.

"Look, I got two signed reentry slips; I can get you back in tomorrow or next week. It's not a problem," he'd say. "I found a place to get killer weed, and it's pickup day in Wood Hollow."

Since we didn't have jobs or an allowance, we had to figure out a way to finance our junkets, or "skiving" as J.K. Rowling calls it. Tony had figured out that the local grocery stores would pay back a deposit on those five-gallon plastic water bottles at six bucks a pop. He had the Oasis truck's delivery routes and schedules memorized, and we knew escape routes out of every posh neighborhood that could afford to have water delivered.

This was actually a lot of fun, walking up to houses, hoisting the bottles over your shoulder, and walking back to the car, only to drive up a few streets and do it again, utterly without interference because no one was around to stop you, or would have stopped you, if you waved at them and smiled. They'd smile and wave back and continue with what they were doing. It never failed.

The challenge was to keep from giggling, stoned as we were, in our trousers and cheap dressy shirts with wet stains growing down the front or back.

There were instances, of course, when we'd be caught red-handed, when a door would open or a home owner would unexpectedly emerge from the hedge. Then we'd sprint away as Tony, self-serving coward and bastard that he was, would drive off and leave us to fend for ourselves.

"Arr, dude! They could get my license plate!" he'd laugh as we'd breathlessly catch up to the car, many blocks later, and curse him.

He always kept the lion's share of the day's activities. Very Dickens. Most of it would go into buying five or ten dollars' worth of pot and some beer, but it would never even out. And no single dealer would ever sell to him regularly. No one really liked or trusted Tony, and with good reason.

So when he said he'd found some place to buy pot, and it wasn't the morons who hung out by the tennis courts before school, well, I have to admit I was intrigued. Besides, he was a friend, unsalvageable pariah though he was. But these things could turn out badly, so I went; I wasn't really keen to own up to a three days' AWOL at school anyway.

We first drove to the housing project east of school, where a woman sold $2 quarts of Budweiser out of her living room from a cooler to anyone with money—no questions asked—and we bought a couple of quarts, then smoked the half joint Tony had on our way to his new "supplier."

I was getting a bit high when I began to recognize the route he was taking and was then thoroughly taken aback when he drove into my maternal grandmother's driveway. I couldn't understand why he had driven here, was confused by the context. This was the same driveway my family Pontiac would regularly pull into after church on Sundays when we were growing up in the late 1970s—my mother's mother's house, in downtown Brownsville.

I was . . . I think the term is "unnerved."

My two uncles, Johnny and Abel, were working on a '79 Camaro when Tony drove up and parked, hood to hood, with their Camaro that morning.

I sat frozen in the passenger seat, uncertain what to do next.

The hood on the Camaro was up and they were both leaning into the guts of the engine when we drove up. Their heads popped up like bearded, biker prairie dogs to look at the new development. Tony, taking my noticeable start into account, told me to be cool, to chill out; these guys look mean but they're all right.

"Anyway," he said as he was getting out the door, "they're kinda dumb but they got great weed."

Didn't I know it. Abel and Johnny had a long history with local biker gangs, even a rumored affiliation with the Hell's Angels. They could get drugs nobody else could in this town, and as a result they were total burnouts hardly capable of cogent speech patterns in either English or Spanish, landing in jail as often as other people attended church.

Though what they lacked in brain they certainly made up in brawn. Not that they'd tear apart a citizen like Tony, or me, not in the daylight, anyway. They had a code about that sort of thing. But if they felt cheated, they'd take a tire iron to my head long before they would recognize me as their nephew, or that I'd been there the month before with my mother, their sister.

They were that burned out.

So I sit there, paralyzed, in the front seat, side B of *Houses of the Holy* playing on Tony's mother's cassette deck over the deafening blast of the air-conditioning, watching this terrifying pantomime play out before me.

Tony, half-shaven in his preppy clothes, closes the door and hails his greeting. Abel, already brain-dead from years of sniffing paint, narrows his eyes in suspicion at first and then noiselessly says, *Heyyyyy,* while opening his arms in a wide accepting gesture, drawing Tony into their fold. Johnny looks up from under the hood of the Camaro.

Next is the sly, silent exchange of the malefactor. Tony looks servile, trying to charm, averting his eyes, looking anywhere but directly at Abel in the eye for fear that Abel might charge, like a gorilla. Abel, suspicious and cautious, gives a sharp, quick upward jutting of the chin that says, *Did I sell to you before? Who told you I got weed?*

Tony lowers his head in quiet confidence, talks to Abel, then includes Johnny. Johnny nods his head, then motions toward me in the car with his chin. They all turn to look at me. My eyes wide. Big smile, nodding. Tony says something, and they all laugh. Led Zeppelin playing loudly in the car. Abel slaps Tony on the back and leads him around to the back of the car. Johnny looks at me and smiles, then forms his index finger and thumb into a mock roach smoke and laughs. Me mimicking him. Johnny still not recognizing me, even now. Tony and Abel come around the other side of the car, Tony's hand in his pocket, both of them laughing, like they're suddenly old friends.

Tony turns and waves; both Johnny and Abel wave back.

The door opens and Tony says, "Dude, we got a big joint for two bucks," as he gets in the driver's seat.

He puts the car in gear and we drive away. This has freaked me out to no end. Abel and Johnny are both waving, making the universal roach-smoking signal as we drive off, and it leaves me feeling really, really conflicted.

The car slips up the southernmost terminus of Highway 77 and we head north from urban Brownsville, just to drive around as we smoke the joint. Tony lights it and it starts burning purple. "Purple Haze!" he says, and then follows it with his characteristic "Aaaa!" Making the obvious pun doesn't bother him. I'm concerned that the joint is burning purple. Abel and Johnny are not known for their temperance.

"Hey, man," I say, "I'm kinda scared about smoking this. I've never seen one burn this color."

"Argh, dude!" says Tony. "Don't worry about it. Those guys got killer weed, man, they're like bikers or something. It's probably laced with something. That's why it was two bucks."

This idea sounds appealing to Tony. It freaks me out. We are both getting incredibly high.

"Hey, man," says Tony. "Wouldn't it be fucked up if like, when you were high, your hair went into like a huge orange Afro? And the higher you were, the bigger your Afro got? You couldn't go anywhere because people would be, like, 'Man! That guy's *stoned!*'"

I am busy thinking about having just bought weed from my Uncles Johnny and Abel. Johnny had been stabbed in the back with a flat-headed screwdriver about a month earlier in a street fight. His lung had been punctured, and my grandmother said you could hear whistling every time he inhaled. He wouldn't go to the hospital to get it treated for three days.

We are halfway done with the joint when I realize we're headed south again, having turned around somewhere.

"Hey, man," I say to Tony, "I don't want to get stoned anymore."

"Arr, well, put it out," says Tony. He is nodding his head back and forth to Zeppelin. Tony fancies himself a guitarist. His left hand is fingering chords into the neck of an imaginary guitar. I watch his fingers moving for a few seconds, suspended and twisting around there like an overturned king crab, and I can find no concurrence with the chords in the song.

"Man, I mean I don't want to smoke pot anymore," I say to him. "I don't want to skip class anymore. I want to get back to school. Not today, but like, in general. I don't want to feel like this anymore. Like I'm doing something bad. I feel like this all the time now. Dirty. Look at that really fucking small house over there."

We're on an overpass, and I notice a house beneath us in the Brownsville Country Club about a quarter of the size of the houses surrounding it.

Tony finds this segue in my announcement hysterical. He starts laughing so hard that I have to make him focus back on the driving, but then I laugh along with him.

"You're stoned," he tells me.

"Yeah," I say. "I'm way stoned."

"Hey, man," I say a little later. We're driving back to South Padre Island now. "You know those guys we bought weed from earlier today?"

"The bikers?" he asks.

"That was my grandmother's house, man. Those were my uncles," I say, even though I am really embarrassed by it.

Tony finds this befuddling. He can't figure out what the bikers were doing at my grandmother's house. "Those dudes were my mom's brothers, man. My uncles," I explain.

Tony laughs so hard he has to pull over to the side of the road. His laughing is infectious, and I find myself laughing right along with him, laughing harder than I've laughed in a really, really long time, but I'm feeling utterly beyond redemption on the inside, like I've done something today that I can't take back.

Like my course is now set.

Chapter 19

ROOM 124

When I was seventeen years old, I ran away to Juarez, Mexico, with about seven bucks in my pocket, five of which I had borrowed that Saturday afternoon from my retarded neighbor, Lupíta Chiquita.

No one noticed I had gone, and I don't think I ever got around to paying her back.

My friend Karsten had a father who lived down there, outside of Juarez. Karsten was a tall dorky white kid with black hair, and he would make the three-hour trip to Juarez whenever he needed to swindle his reluctant father out of "tuition" money or whatever was immediately needed in Karsten's shiftless teenaged life.

Karsten's father owned the only Holiday Inn in Brownsville and had Karsten set up to live alone in room 124 while Karsten presumably attended St. Mary's Catholic School. Room 124 was immediately next door to the industrial-size air conditioner and was unrentable because of the thrum and vibration of the overburdened machine.

Karsten was eighteen but was still in high school, when he went to school. When I met him, Karsten usually found a way to cash his tuition check and blow the money just hanging around doing anything but going to class, playing video games on a first generation Nintendo, drinking warm tequilas and Mexican rums with no chaser, and trying to have sex with unwilling girls.

He lived utterly without any adult interference. For food, the Holiday Inn kitchen was obliged to feed him two meals a day, and it produced some of the most offensive combinations of food known to humankind, but it kept him alive, though not at all grateful.

Down in Juarez, Karsten's father—who was Cuban and not Mexican—had bought a large horse ranch and was busy accumulating the adjoining land that surrounded his. Karsten's mother had left them when he was ten, and he never said why. I never thought to ask. Karsten was tall and dark haired and had sharp European features you didn't see in the white people around that part of Texas. French, almost. He also had strange, cultured manners, nearly Victorian, especially when he was around girls.

His nearly civilized manners made Karsten very awkward and lonely in Brownsville, and he was desperate for female attention. He was a very odd, very tall boy.

Karsten drove a retired mid-1980s Ford cop car painted totally white with a factory cassette-playing radio that didn't eat cassette tapes. This was a rarity among the cars driven by my friends during this time. Both the front and back seats of the car were a deep plastic blue, eternally gritty. There was a constant stratum of beer cans, newspapers, old cassette tapes, and food wrappers crumpling underfoot.

I don't remember where Karsten said he was from, originally; I think somewhere out east, and he spoke no Spanish. He was in Brownsville because it was the closest thing to a "city" in the United States, and his father had wanted him educated in America.

Karsten, on the other hand, had other ideas, and he resisted his education at every turn without consequence, which was fantastic to me. He was eighteen years old and alone.

We had a lot in common.

✦

On the night I'm first introduced to Karsten, I'm driving around with my friend Henry and his best friend, John. They are unrepentant potheads, tirelessly listening to anything recorded by Metallica and rhythmically "banging" their heads in slow motion as we drive around Brownsville and Los Fresnos and South Padre Island in utter boredom searching for some sort of underage deliverance or entertainment in Henry's 1986 Mustang LX, with his portable CD player wired into the tape player and playing very loudly but prone to skipping. I'm in the backseat, cowering from the volume surrounding me. I'm not much of a stoner anymore, not like them. I like beer. It feels more honest to be drunk, somehow. We keep the beer at the feet of the front passenger side, and I keep bugging whoever isn't driving for another.

"Turn the music down," I yell from the backseat.

"Give me another beer," I yell from the backseat.

"Roll up your fuckin' window," I yell from the backseat.

"Wah, wah, wah," says Henry, in the passenger's seat. He's letting John drive his car. John is a minister's kid and fits the stereotype perfectly. Except he isn't a slutty girl, which would be much more interesting.

"You're like a baby back there, always needing something," from Henry.

"Turn the music down; I can't hear what you said," I yell from the backseat, purposely.

They start giggling. Henry hands me a beer. I crack it open and take a long draught from it and do the *dook dook dook* imitation of a baby suckling from its bottle of baby formula and they both start laughing hysterically when John loses control of the car.

We happen to be on the Queen Isabella Causeway, coming back from South Padre Island around eight at night and eighty-five feet in the air when the Mustang cuts across three lanes of traffic and he over-corrects and we're inches from hitting the side of the bridge and dropping into ten feet of a very shallow bay. He cuts back again and miraculously the Mustang steadies itself at seventy miles per hour and we're all knuckle-white and not breathing.

Metallica is still blaring even though the moment feels totally silent. For a few seconds, I feel their fear mingling with mine, our sense of death at that moment tangible. I feel Henry and John's elevated perception like we're three soldiers on a frontline getting shelled, waiting for the next shell to hit our foxhole, and everything has suddenly gone quiet under the audial blanket of the Metallica.

I lean forward through the bucket seats and yank the power cord from the CD player. "What the fuck was that, John?" I say. I am totally sober now, riding the adrenaline into a rage.

"Nothing, man; it's cool," he says, attempting a giggle, continuing to drive.

"No, it's not, man," says Henry. "You almost lost it there. That's not cool."

"No, I didn't," says John. "I was totally in control."

"You were *not* in control," I say, now screaming like George C. Scott. I'm furious.

John has nearly managed to drive Henry's car over the side of the only elevated bridge in five hundred miles, and I want to throttle him.

"You were *not* in control and you very fucking nearly killed all of us, you stupid piece of shit! Pull over in Port Isabel and let Henry drive," I demand loudly, pointing my finger in the rear view mirror, trying to look him in the eye.

Henry is quiet. Henry is rarely quiet. Henry is small, lean and a great kid, but he's not quiet. A soccer player. From way back. One of my favorite people during this time of my life. Henry has a future, will eventually move to Austin and marry this girl he loves, Carla. She gave him his first blow job. He was so happy about that. This is his car, so he's captain.

"Hey, man," says John. "Just chill out, all right? I mean, I didn't do it on purpose, but, like, the car handled cool and I was all right and I had it together, you know? I mean, it's not like anything happened, right?"

"Just shut up right now and at the next stop, you're pulling over," I say. The bridge is over two miles long and we're coming into Port Isabel, a speed trap of a fishing town, like a pilot fish on the revenue-generating shark that is South Padre Island.

"Hey, you're not, like, the owner of the car, all right?" says John. "Right, Henry? He can't tell me what to do."

"You *fucked up,* John!" I yell. "You lost control of the fucking car and you almost fucking killed us!" I'm really mad. "Admit it. Just fucking admit it, John."

It starts to become important that he admits it.

"No," he says. "I didn't. I mean —"

This is where Henry loses it. "John, you lost control of the car, John. Admit it," he says, the rise in his voice noticeable.

"No, I —"

"Admit it!" I say. Suddenly, it becomes very, very important that the idiot owns up to it.

"No, I —"

Henry: "Admit it, John."

John: "Nah, man, I —"

Me: "John, admit it!"

Henry: "Yeah, John: Admit it."

John: "Dude, I —"

Henry: "*Pull the fucking car over!*"

This surprises the both of us; we've never seen Henry this mad. We're all startled at the outburst, I think even Henry. John instantly obeys, and he pulls into a restaurant parking lot right off the bridge.

We all exit the car in the empty parking lot, and John leaves it running. We do a sort of fire drill. He's a skinny kid at seventeen, John, with stringy blonde hair and an army jacket. I don't remember what I'm wearing but it can't be much. Cotton T-shirt with THE CURE on it and jeans and a pair of cheap British Knights, usually, at that age. Henry and John cross paths at the back of the car and when he's coming by me John says something to the effect of . . . "Hey man, I *had* control of the car . . . " and I attack him, swinging hard. I have the full can of Budweiser in my right hand and I smash it to his head, and it explodes on his head like a beer grenade, showering the three of us in the choicest hops and barley. I hit him so unexpectedly he jerks himself against the side of the car. I don't really know how to fight at this point and I also know this isn't right but I'm so mad I'm swinging at him, left right left right. He crumples, and I start to kick at him and I accidentally kick Henry's car, at which point Henry runs around and pushes me away from John, who is now on the ground covering his head, and when Henry pushes me away, John straightens up and punches me over Henry's shoulder, pops me square on the cheek. I push Henry aside and rush at John, ducking my head and I put my shoulder under his sternum like I've learned after hundreds of hours of football practice, and I shove him against the car and start punching him in the neck and face with my right hand over my head. John gets in a couple of weak, undercut punches in defense, until Henry grabs me by the waist and swings me around and throws me onto the ground.

I'm livid like I've never been in my life but I stop; I sit. Seventeen years I've lived my life in this outpost, alone, isolated and with an eroding sense of wonder about America at large. I can dream of nothing but getting out of here and exploring the rest of the country, watching leaves turn color and following the winter; I want out of this shit hole of a border town at the bottom of Texas, out of this racist, ignorant, locus-eating, lower Texas toxic hell pit. I've endured my father, my grandmother, years of pathetic education, beatings, berations, concentrations of shame, and this heat most hellish. All I have to do is graduate high school in a few weeks and I can leave, I've been told. *And I have listened.* I don't care what the means are. The military, a bus ticket, this "college" thing other people talked about, stowing away—I just want out. Out of here. Away from people like John. And he almost took that away from me tonight, on that bridge.

My mouth is salty and bloodied, and his eye is swelling from where I hit him with the Budweiser. "Just admit it, you stupid fucker," I say and spit.

Henry tries to temper the moment. "Just be quiet. Just stop it," he says to me, holding John against the car. John's body language is not in the least bit threatening. It is mostly that of a liar, uncertain how to lie next. I am sitting on the ground, disgusted.

"John, just admit you lost control of the fucking car and let's go," Henry says.

John looks down at me, his eyes wide. He's not sure why I'm as angry I am. John understands anger, lives with it from his Baptist-revival fire-eating preacher father, but there's usually some sort of Yahweh logic and a way to get out of it. He doesn't know how to get out of this one, obvious as it is. He's scared at the density of my rage and does not know how to dilute or lie his way out of it. He's frightened of me, even though we're exactly the same sort of weak, wiry, and he could probably get the better of me next time.

Both Henry and I are feeding him the line out. But it's too obvious for John, too clear. Too honest, for the son of a Baptist.

"Alright, man," he says finally. "I lost control of the car. I fucked up. We almost went over the side."

I know he doesn't actually believe it, understand what it means.

But it calms me down. I stand up, knock the gravel from my palms and my thinly denimed knees.

John says, "I'm sorry, man."

I say, "I'm sorry, too. I'm sorry I hit you with the beer." I don't mean it. If I was sorry, writing from this distance so many years later, it's for the loss of that beer. Beer was hard to come by back then.

"Me, too," he says, and we shake hands limply.

We get in the car, with Henry driving and John in the back seat, me in the front. We get on the dark highway back to Brownsville and after a while, I crack open a sweaty beer and then hand one to John. Before we drink, independent of one another we each put the cold can to our respective faces, him to his eye and me to my mouth, to knock down the swelling, but it's mostly because we'd seen it done in the movies.

Henry doesn't play anything on his CD player with the tape extension.

We're approaching Brownsville from the rear when John remembers somewhere we can go.

"Hey, man," he says. "My friend Val knows this dude, Karsten, who lives in the Holiday Inn. No shit. We can swing by and see if anything's up there. It's still early." It was just after ten o'clock.

The idea neutralizes the tension in the car. For a full thirty minutes no one says anything while Henry drives us along the dark salt land that separates Port Isabel from Brownsville, where the Mexicans and the US fought the first battle of the US-Mexican War, on Palo Alto. Teenage ghosts gliding on a salt highway.

"That sounds like a good idea," says Henry. "The Holiday Inn over by the expressway?" he asks.

"Is there another Holiday Inn in Brownsville?" I answer, genuinely curious.

In the Holiday Inn parking lot, John spots Val's car. I know this Val of whom he speaks. He is ordinary Brownsville fare, like *bistek* ranchero, popular on every menu. (A corruption of *beefsteak*, did you know? Fascinating.)

Valentín sits next to me in some classes because our surnames begin with an "M" and he is partial to saying, "Shit yeah, dude" to any question that requires a response in the affirmative. He wears a long black army trench coat in 100 degree heat, because he thinks it looks cool. He has a round pale moon face, dark hair, and flabby build. He eventually fell in love with the first girl that had sex with him at a graduation party, though he didn't graduate with his class. His mother took out a quarter page ad in the annual, saying, "Maybe next year, Val!" Ever the optimist, his mother.

John and I gingerly remove ourselves from Henry's car and bring what's left of the twelve-pack of Budweiser, neither of us looking at each other. We walk to the back of the Holiday Inn, by the big air conditioner, and find Room 124. There's music coming from inside, something radio pop and terrible, like Gloria Estefan. John bangs on the door loudly, disrespectfully. After a few seconds, it opens and reveals an odd little spectacle. Val, recognizable in his black trench coat, opens the door and leans in the doorframe, seemingly territorial.

Behind him is a curious scene. There's two twin beds unmade and rumpled, a bolted hotel television on a horribly littered dresser with Mario Bros. playing on it. It is the total catastrophe of a teenage boy's bedroom unveiled, except inside a regular Holiday Inn unit. The wet moldy cold of South Texas air-conditioning valiantly expending itself hits us in the face like a prop blast, and we all stand there for a brain-beat, taking each other in.

Thinking about it now, remembering that moment, I think I miss it, or moments like it. Because they get less frequent as you get older, don't they? The opportunity presenting itself so clearly. The escape unfolding itself before you. It just needs a bit of help to take form, needs someone to nudge it into focus. Because here, clearly, was God talking to me, this night we almost died.

Val, at the door, clearly thinks he is in charge.

Inside, there's a guy I do not recognize, a small tubby Mexican guy, sitting on one bed, and two fat Mexican girls sitting opposite him on the other with the bedside table between them. Both beds have their bedclothes bundled at either end, and the Mexican girls are drunk and leaning into their pile, laughing and whooping it up. Tubby Mexican guy thinks he's got a chance tonight. There's a stereo still playing something terrible near them, now discernable: Paula Abdul. The girls and the tubby guy are laughing, taking shots of cheap white rum and not registering us in the doorway. Playing a drinking game. Quarters, it looks like. I take all this in as I enter the room behind John, who immediately takes Val over to the bathroom to talk, probably about me.

At the foot of the bed closest to the bathroom sits a tall guy with a comforter wrapped over his head like a nun's habit, forcibly staring at the game on the TV. Val and John had to step over him to get to the bathroom, and he doesn't move, doesn't flinch. He's a white guy, looking a lot like David Schwimmer will look like in *Friends* some years from now, but thinner. He's playing Nintendo, which, at the time, is the hottest thing around. Mario Bros., a fairly high level, from the looks of it. He's ferociously ignoring what's going on around him, concentrating on the video game in full seethe. Resolved in keeping the people around him, who are obviously using him, foreign to him, away from him.

I love him, right then, somehow.

❖

Several years from this moment, I'll be visiting a zoo in Seattle because my mind is coming apart at the seams and my then-girlfriend Rebecca and I think that maybe a stroll around the zoo, around controlled nature, might help with the panic attacks I've been having. My anxieties have become unhinged, and I've been experiencing these periodic bouts of terror, especially when I'm trying to sleep.

It did not actually help, the zoo.

But it did remind me of something, when we got to the monkey house.

The chief orangutan sat square in the middle of the display, on a hammock, holding a potato sack over his head like a nun's habit, and he tried to keep the constant stream of fat families and crying children in strollers away, tried to get some peace, some privacy, by hiding under that potato sack, and I saw that he desperately needed to be rescued, and he looked me in the eye, and we both held the stare, and I totally remembered this moment, from before. Room 124.

It put me back to that night, when I met Karsten, playing his little video game and forcibly ignoring the terrible human beings around him, in his own monkey house, and I thought I could rescue him. I would rescue Karsten from these people. Though, thinking about it now, maybe it was the other way around. That I was looking in the universal mirror in the reverse.

He would rescue me from being on the roads, the predatory roads of Texas, by sharing his loneliness, his autonomy, and giving me access to Room 124, when he wasn't there, which was often. And I would introduce him to better people.

We would rescue each other.

❖

Karsten was the first person I ever met who was truly elitist, or maybe classist. I liked him right away. He saw himself as an intellectual, and apparently the drunken soul-searching conversations in which my small circle of friends would engage seemed to pass for intellect.

I introduced him to my friend Chris, another relic of the crowd that skipped with Tony and one of the stained myrmidons like myself who no longer held any credibility with teacher or administrator as to why we were not in school (too many dead grandmothers), and whose ethical slips could be marked by the resin stained fingertips and boozy ten in the morning hiccups.

Chris was literarily inclined, however, considered himself a poet and had adopted a middle name of "Hill." He insisted that it had been given him at birth, but I suspected otherwise, until I met his father, who was of hippie age, and then it made sense. (I've always had an innate distrust and irrational hatred of people who rename themselves. Seriously—if I dealt with "Domingo," then you can live with "Juan.")

Chris rarely spoke of this, but he had lost a younger brother, a toddler, who had been killed by a car, and the few times when he did mention it, I was too insensitive to realize what sort of hurt something like that could bring to a family, and wasn't it any wonder that his parents divorced—what marriage really survives the death of a child? I personally only know of one, and what a toxic marriage that was—and his friendship is one I regret never having attended to more, understanding him more than I did, being a better friend. But there would be many more of these regrets to follow in my life.

With him and Karsten, we'd talk about books and authors and music that wasn't popular (or popular in Brownsville, Texas) and foreign films that became less foreign as we became developing cineastes, limited as the availability of good art films were to us.

But all of this was bosch, remember; we were teenagers in rural Texas with no map, no compass, nothing: just an underdeveloped instinct to guide us.

We were drawn to art, but art was nowhere to be found in Brownsville. If there was, we did not possess the right kind of vision to see it. There was nothing beautiful in Brownsville, Texas, we felt. And we would talk about that often.

That's what forged our friendship.

✤

After one long, quiet sober Friday night spent driving around in Karsten's car, avoiding my house because Dad had come back from one of his trucking trips and had been lately unbearable, I finally relented and had Karsten drop me off at home late, because I was starving, though there was nothing to eat there anyway, except a large bag of Doritos. The house was dark, empty. Dad had already gone out, and Mom was still at work. Derek was probably over at Gramma's, miserably watching Mexican cartoons he couldn't understand.

As he left, Karsten leaned out the window and asked if I wanted to go down to Juarez with him the next day. Said he'd already invited Chris, who was in. I said, "Sure: I'm in." I always wanted to see what Mexico really looked like. Besides, it was what Mark Twain would have done.

The next day, Karsten picked me up around eleven o'clock. Mom had already gone off to work, Dad was *in absentia* and I think Derek was ... I can't say I remember. But I had about $2 on me and knew I needed a little more, even in Mexico. I had tapped Gramma as a resource and she was always very reluctant to let go of $5, and I tried to disperse those terrible humiliations to a monthly minimum, so she was out of the question. A last resort? Gramma's cousins, our buggering neighbors to the west, the Guadalúpe Ramirezes. Joe's mother and company. I sucked up what humility I had and posed a very earnest argument (I forget what it was, but I remember it was slick), and I got $5 from it, from Joe's retarded older sister, Lupíta Chiquita. (Hunh. That's Spanish for "little Lupíta." I just got that, typing it here. Meaning she was named "Guadalúpe" as well. So there were *three* people with a first name of "Guadalúpe" living there: her mother, father, and her. Mail call must have been very confusing.)

So when Karsten pulls up, I'm ready to go, dressed in my usual jeans, THE CURE concert T-shirt, a camouflage outer shirt in case it got cold (never did), and loud white British Knights (not my choice; sale at JC Penney).

Chris is there, and we pool our cash together, and we have about a sawbuck each. No overnight bag, no change of clothes, nothing. But, Mexico: Here we come.

Karsten's car is something that should be explored at this point. As mentioned, it was a retired police cruiser, white with the blue plastic interior, and Karsten could not care less about its maintenance. Often he'd slam it into park before even coming to a complete stop. Other times he'd have no consternation rounding another car by actually going up on the sidewalk and then coming back down hard on the road, bending a part of his bumper upward. He didn't intend on destroying it or putting himself or others in danger while driving, but he was a typical teenager, though he looked thirty already. He'd be distracted in the middle of making a turn, and then turn too far, then overcorrect, and enter a street on the wrong side. Or he'd become frustrated and drive on the shoulder at top speed to get around a traffic jam. He never sped or swerved for the sake of the thrill, but his ordinary driving skills were enough to keep

Darwin guessing: Someone was going to get eliminated. Either him or someone else.

If you remember, I had a thing about irresponsible drivers. Ever since I was an adolescent, I was convinced that I was going to die in a car wreck in Brownsville, before I could get to a city where I didn't have to depend on a vehicle and could finally breathe a sigh of relief. Every year in Brownsville there was a natural culling of teenagers at every high school, an average of about five to ten students dying from vehicular accidents. Drunk driving, irresponsible driving, the usual stuff. The highway connecting South Padre Island and Brownsville at the time turned into a two lane death trap about midway in the salt marsh during spring break, when easily 90 percent of all drivers were officially DUI. It was just understood. Friends, football associates, people you knew by sight, we all dropped like flies. I had grown so terrified that I would die in a traffic accident, I had taken to pulling over on the side of roads and counting to one hundred, even if I was late somewhere, so that I could cheat the fates, not be there for the moment of the impact for which I was destined.

Anyhow, the combination of Karsten's kamikaze driving and the notoriously lacking Mexican driving "system" doesn't occur to me until we're well away from Matamoros and driving dusty urethra-thin back highways headed south to Juarez, and I am catatonic with fear in the backseat. Karsten is gunning his engine around festively decorated pink and blue buses, sombreroed men on mules, and decrepit farm trucks with no operating lights or brakes (all looking far too familiar).

I gave up shouting out potential threats of impact, collisions coming from all sides. It was like a Blitzkrieg dogfight over London skies. Catholic buses full of peasants would veer out of roads that were not there a second ago; an oncoming Volkswagen Bug would suddenly appear in your lane, materializing right out of the choking dust cloud of the Nissan Maxima that was ahead of you not fifty feet away, pumping sickly black exhaust in poisonous concentrations from the unrefined Mexican gas.

I am so sick with fear, I actually crumple into a fetal position in the backseat and simply let my fate go into the hands of whoever is listening. I actually go limp and, if you remember your *Watership Down*, I go "tharn." I just curl up into a ball and let destiny take over, like a trapped rabbit.

Three hours later, when we round a hillside and look out into a valley below and see the lights of a city, I realize we might actually live through this.

❖

We get to the Mexican town after dusk and the town is blinking sulfur pink and white below us in erratic geometry, carved into a valley between slow rolling hills, and I have a fleeting sense of disappointment that they have electricity, somehow. Hadn't thought out my Mexican Huckleberry Finn fantasy all the way through, with this running away.

We descend into the valley and Karsten makes an abrupt right turn, suddenly parks his car against a pink stucco wall with broken beer bottles cemented into the top as a form of security, to prevent people from climbing over it.

"We're here," he says, and leaps from the driver's side door, leaving us alone and bewildered as he disappears through a metal and intimidating gate, leaving us to wait for half an hour in the car without even the keys.

Chris and I are eventually shown inside, and I'm further disappointed to find out that Karsten's father's Mexican mansion is an exact duplicate of every other newly built construction in Brownsville: poured, solid concrete for a floor with tile laid indecorously atop, ceiling fans propelling themselves in dangerously unbalanced elliptical rotations, central air ducts added as an afterthought, exposed throughout. I could be at Anthony's house, a mile from where I live.

The lord of the manor is no more welcoming than the ride in: We are banished to a single, sterile room with a JC Penney bed with scratchy sheets and a thin polyester comforter to comfort us from the stale, dreadfully cold, and mildewy air. It is like sucking air from the bottom of a well, breathing in that house.

Karsten and Chris take the bed, and I figure it will be best for all of us if I stretch out on the oval rug with a pillow and a similar comforter Karsten nicked from another, unmade room. I shiver the cold night away, feeling thankful that we made the drive there in one piece, at the very least.

That three teenage boys would sleep together in the same room didn't bother anyone, or make anyone draw any sort of conclusions. This was something I always thought strange about Mexicans and machismo: They don't immediately leap to a conclusion of homosexuality, or get hostile with true, honest homosexuals.

It's a holdover from preconquest times, before the Catholic Church began its native programming. Mexicans innately consider homosexuals to be a third sex, leave them to exist on their own: Go on, do your thing; have fun.

Where they get weird and violent is when there is a question of a straight man who might be gay; I think it's the self-deception that gets at them, because they're caught in the same conflict. Does that make sense, the clarification? If you're gay and you know it: Clap your hands. Enjoy it. If you're straight and are *acting* gay, with the potential to *be gay*, then the other men will take umbrage.

Meaning that, if you're gay and pretending to be straight in Texas, you're far more of a threat, because that's what macho men are struggling with, while the fantastically out gay men are not a threat, because, well, they're gay, right? They know who they are. And we're not gay. We're men. Sexy hetero men. Who like women. Until, you know, we like … men, in a moment of drunken sincerity. And we make up sub-groups: you're only gay if you get penetrated. If you do the penetrating, you're not gay. That's just pleasure, right?

I saw this happen many times, growing up in Brownsville. Totally out gay men were left entirely unharmed and unto themselves. Very prelapsarian bliss.

But svelte boys that didn't fit any particular macho prototype were subjected to horrible things, punishment, for not being a model of macho masculinity.

So, if you were nominally straight and wispy and had predilections for all things British, like me, then you'd have trouble from the dicks in football. Try listening to Morrissey and The Smiths while playing football in Brownsville, then. But, that's another story altogether.

The fact that Karsten, Chris, and I sleep in the same room provokes nothing from Karsten's dad or the help in the house, other than ignoring us to our discomfort.

The next morning, after an uncomfortable breakfast opposite a silent father, Karsten herds us into the bed of a Ford F-150: white, dirty, and raised vulgarly in 4 x 4 fashion. Chris and I sit in shorts and the veneer of a T-shirt on an unfastened spare tire and sing Smiths songs aloud and in joking unison, because neither of us can carry a tune, not even in a tune bucket. Also, I think we are both quite frightened.

We drive farther into what can only be assumed was south, and then eventually west for the better part of the morning, and soon we come to a queue of tractors, buses, and Volkswagens— all the usual characters on the Mexican roads back then.

Teenage gendarmes, not much older than Chris and me, dressed in dark blue military fatigues point Vietnam-surplus M16s at every car, and then at us, and the ancient Mexican driver who speaks for us somehow calms their minds and we are let through with no problem, but Chris and I are shaken. This also didn't figure into Huckleberry Finn.

In the shifting bed of the F-150, Chris and I pass the time further by singing tunelessly and talking about girls, or rather, the same girl (Mishell) in whom we are both stupidly interested because she's the only girl who likes music from Manchester in our school, and we are both trying to keep the other disinterested therein.

If things ever got uncomfortable, I don't remember, or I didn't realize it, because we just kept screeching outward into the dry Mexican air as it whipped up around us as the countryside sped past, unusually verdant, at least for me.

Eventually we turn down a dusty brown country road headed—I think now for a good reason—west. West just somehow feels "deeper" into the Mexican wild.

During this whole ride, a good two hours, Chris and I are taking turns swigging water from a green one-gallon thermos with the little white pour thing that had been in the bed of the truck when we had jumped in. The water, after drinking it, had somehow made us thirstier, tasted dusty. Still, we drink more. Pass it back and forth the way hobos would pass a bottle of hooch, and then eventually the truck is brought up short to a shallow ford of a largish creek, and the driver, whom we see now for the first time fully standing—a lean, tough and leathery old man in his sixties—throws the truck into park and comes around, looks at us sideways in an odd dismissal, wordlessly grabs the thermos out of Chris' hands and begins to refill it, right from the creek.

About ten minutes later after fording the creek in the Ford F-150 at high 4x4 speed, Chris is convinced he's picked up some sort of bacteria from the raw creek water we've been unwittingly drinking and is curled up in a fetal roll as the truck lumbers deeper into Mexican lumber.

I'm not so sure I haven't contracted something either, but I manage to keep from hysterical vomiting as Chris is doing, in a ball at the end of the truck bed.

Eventually, I notice the truck slowing—and it isn't my fanciful imagination this time—because the low, gnarled mesquite trees begin giving way and we slowly crest a small, shallow hill into what is essentially a long ranch road. A lone, ramshackle building made of cracking white stone with a low, flat roof appears out of nowhere at the end of the lane, and we stop. We're suddenly surrounded by horses, and the smell of horses.

It's a small ranch outpost, atop a minor hill, and more hills roll away to the horizon as far as I can see. It's still one of the most beautiful things I remember, in its uncomplicated, unassuming simplicity.

"This is one of my dad's ranches," Karsten says as he gets out of the passenger side and sees me staring off into the north. (It felt like the north. Felt like I was looking at the underside of Texas.) I can imagine Karsten, from this distance, probably talking in his monosyllabic Spanish to the old man for the first few minutes of the drive, and then saying nothing for the rest of the drive, which probably drove Karsten crazy, but was perfectly all right with the old guy. "We're supposed to help take down the fences," he says, absently pointing with an oblique nod to a long barbed-wire fence that trailed off into the distance. His attention is acutely fixed upon a .9mm pistol he suddenly pulls from under his seat, making a show of chambering a round, replacing the hammer, and then checking the safety and putting it in the small of his back. He wore no belt, so for the next few minutes, the gun kept tilting forward precariously, like it wanted to slip into the seat of his trousers and disappear down into his ass, and Karsten, unwilling to divorce his own fantasy, refused to remove it from there. Instead, he chases off after the horses, while Chris and I hop off the truck and attempt to ingratiate ourselves with the old man and the remaining horses, both of whom are visibly repulsed by our advances. We're unsure of what to do, and what's expected of us, Chris and me.

The old man disappears into his home, and then reappears soon after with a boy who looks very much his simile, except reduced to 30 percent. They both stand there, taking us in.

We stare back. Fidget awkwardly. The horses and their horse smell are swirling at a safe distance around us. Very, very un–Mark Twain, I'm thinking, when suddenly Karsten comes shooting past us riding a large, speckled horse that seems terribly upset at having a rider on its back, making the point very clear by running at full tilt down the length of the road and throwing its head violently around. Karsten, while Chris and I had stood there gaping and wondering what to do, had disappeared into a stable and managed to expertly festoon the fastest horse with saddle and bridle and then put the thing into gear. And then, off he went, like he was on a Ferrari, charging the length of the road, whipping the flanks of the poor beast with malicious glee, and the horse could do little but run faster, and then faster than that. Still, Chris and I stand there.

The old man says something to the boy and the boy slowly dissolves back into their shack, and then emerges holding a bag of tools.

Karsten shoots around behind us and I approach the old man, attempting to say something to him in our native tongue, and realize, all of a sudden, that I can no longer speak Spanish.

All these years of pretending, of cultural snobbery, of emphasizing English and feeling that Spanish was the language of the poor and conquered peasants had suddenly crystalized, and my one chance to engage in a wholly authentic moment, to talk to a human being who lived simply, who needed nothing other than what he had around him, woke with the sun and slept with the moon and the horses and the mesquite and the rattlesnakes, that my chance to talk to my father's people was lost, right there.

So I point. At the bag of tools.

And he points back. At the fence, the one to which Karsten had vaguely alluded, some distance down the dirt road.

And I get what he means. "Get to work, tourist."

Chris and I take the bag and wander down the road to where the fence has been under deconstruction.

It is barbed wire, three tiers of it, held up every ten or so feet by some wood stake driven into the earth about a foot or so down. One of those "u" shaped nails holds the line to. Remarkable that it has stayed up, in this cracked earth. Most of the stakes are just mesquite branches, given a minimum effort at whacking it into something resembling a vertical stake, then pounded into the earth, before the next one was done, and so on, until the perimeter was created, extending into either horizon and obscured by the shrubby trees.

I look in the bag that the old man had given me. It has two pairs of pliers and a flat-headed screw driver and a hammer, along with a hot plastic bottle of Coca-Cola that is filled with what now is clearly creek water, tinged with particles.

I think we get about four stakes done before we quit, Chris and me. That was our contribution to the great acquisition of Karsten's dad's ranch barony.

Come to think of it now, I think I was the only one who attempted to help. I think Chris was off writing his meandering, nonmetered poetry, and who knew what sort of malfeasance Karsten had gotten himself into, and then out of. Then into again.

My own sense of Gramma's peasant work ethic had driven me to help, but my sissy idleness and a small gash on my thumb had allowed me to give in after only a few minutes, which perfectly captured my psychological profile at the time.

It is getting into the late afternoon, and I decide that I wanted to ride a horse in order to have something to remember the experience with, before we leave. Maybe not the dangerous one Karsten is riding, but another, slower, maybe crippled one, like at a children's hospital.

After cooing and fumbling through a few old Americanized Spanish phrases and a lot of pointing, I'm able to ask the old man about the horse. His look is suspicious, uncertain.

Finally, he relents and enters the horse pen to catch a lazy, marelike creature and begin to harness it with saddle and bridle, which is an amazing amount of work. I hadn't realized what I had been asking of him. But he helps me climb aboard the sedate and pliable mare, who, out of nowhere, turns into a hell-borne, meth-crazed hot rod and sprints toward the low trees to knock me from her back.

I hear the old man and the kid shouting instructions to me from their perch at the stoop of the old man's house, but their shouts are drowned out by my hysterical and unending cries of "Whoah! Whoah! Whoah!" and the horse starts bucking, bucking me up and kicking out her back legs, trying *really* hard to catch me on a branch by darting for the trees, and then I have a clear idea of what she is attempting to do, that she has it in for me, and so I try to think of the best thing to do in this situation and I come to the conclusion that I will lie flat on her back, wrap the bridle and my arms around her dinosaur neck, and choke the animal to death, because I'm like that when someone threatens me.

So I do, or at least I try, and in doing so, I yank the bridle quite hard to the right and she rockets off in a steady, ridable pace back to the house.

It was more frightening than riding with Karsten, being on that horse's back and it charging out of control with the intention of knocking me off. I dream of that short ride still, when things are not going so well.

The mare, under the stern direction of the yank, gallops right up to the old man who catches her by the bridle, and by now, Chris and Karsten have come out to see what all the shouting has been about, and they laugh, hoot and point at me and my near-death experience at the hooves of an old mare.

I climb off the horse shaking, and she turns away and refuses to look at me, wanders off to join the rest of her people and do what horses do when they're not trying to kill the unhooved. The old man, quietly tickled, can tell I've had a considerable fright and is sympathetic. *"Estas asustádo,"* he says, which is a kind of low-frequency shock, and he takes me inside the house and sits me in the only chair available—an old, unsteady wooden thing—and pours me a drink of water from the jug. I drink it with my hands shaking, no longer concerned about the bacteria in the water.

His house, like him, is lean and simple. He has a cot along the wall with a rough cut window above it, with no glass, screen, or bars, just a hole into the outside. Tools and rope are hung on the walls, all of them obviously for use and not decoration. Every part of this house is put to use, intentional, functional. I think he is the richest and happiest person I've met until then. Even then, as an idiotic teenager, I could understand that.

✥

The drive back to Brownsville the next day was every bit as treacherous and aging as the drive to Juarez had been three days before. That morning, Karsten's dad had been no warmer over breakfast—fried egg soup and fried plantains: Remember, these were Cubans, not Mexicans—and so I preoccupied myself with the paper while Karsten tried to bridge the gap between friends and reluctant family, before we took up the gauntlet of the drive back to Texas.

Chris rode in the passenger seat up front and shouted out potential threats while Karsten gleefully gunned his engine on the dusty highways back north. I was exhausted by this point, incapable of sustaining that level of alarm, so I laid back down on the back seat and slept, the cries and shouts of the two idiots driving in the front of the retired police car seemingly far enough away so that they didn't pertain to me, could not possibly harm me, and so I slept. I slept.

❖

When I got home, two days later, the house was dark, and I ate a half a bag of Doritos for dinner, as I had gone unmissed, except by maybe Lupíta Chiquita, to whom I still owe those five bucks.

Karsten disappeared a few months after that, when his father "made a donation" to St. Mary's Catholic School and they allowed Karsten to graduate finally, though he had not been to school for close to two years. He called me about a year later from a naval academy somewhere on the east coast, asking me for the telephone number of some girl he had dated twice, said he'd call me right back, but never did.

That crazy Karsten.

Chapter 20

NEIGHBORHOOD HEROES

Joe's house had been unguarded by any male of consequence for some years after Lúpe had died, and Martín had scuttled off to the north to find work fit for a seventeen-year-old who was now earning the family bread. For some time now, the lime green house with the shit-brown trim was protected only by Joe, who was twelve now, cross-eyed and fat. It was otherwise full of women, full of a powdery allure, awaiting penetration of any sort, to hear my Dad tell it.

Across from their house on Oklahoma Avenue, there was a forgotten brick shanty that had at one point of usefulness been a kind of storehouse used to keep feed or bales of cotton, some sort of farming thing. It had fallen into disrepair and was quite uninhabitable, but that didn't stop a series of families from taking residency in it.

For most of the time I can remember living on Oklahoma Avenue, a small dirty family of white transients had taken squatters' rights on the spot, which was eventually reduced to a triangular mud hole, next to a stinking stilled drainage ditch that I believe was used as a septic system and garbage disposal. There were no other amenities to be seen, besides a perpetually smoldering fire pit by a gutted car shell.

They had a boy about three years older than me, named Stephen. Stephen was a skinny, dirty boy who had been the focus of periodic intimidation from Dan some mornings on the bus to school, I think to impress me. I never said much to Stephen, except once when he'd been recruited by the Army, and, excited to talk to anyone about it, he tried to read the recruiting literature to me while we waited for the bus on his last morning attending class. He'd had trouble sounding out the most basic of words in the propagandist promises of the brochure, and I felt awful for him.

I never saw him again. Then the rest of his family moved, overnight. They were just gone one morning, after five or six years of living there.

Eventually a large Mexican family moved into the spot. They never quite mingled in Grampa's barrio. I don't know if they ever really tried and were rebuffed, or if they were simply met with a cold reception and took their cue from that, but there were no formal introductions, no shared breakfasts or gossip, or work. They remained unto themselves. They were male, mostly: teenage boys and a few men, maybe a matriarch, if I remember correctly.

And it was one of these teenage boys who found himself a bit too tempted by the fruits of Joe's mother's house, the large looming green house with the brown trimming, with the three girls and the mother just living there, with the boy. Sure, the big one was retarded, *but,* as the comedian Dave Atell once horribly said, " . . . those titties weren't retarded. . . ." (And shame on me for repeating a terrible joke.)

One night, the eldest Lupíta, the mother who was at this point long widowed, woke up and decided to get a drink of water. She walked right by a shape in the dark, said she didn't realize it was a boy at first, but then the shape moved, broke, and ran—ran right for the door and ditched her purse in the living room, spilling its contents as he kicked out the screen door.

He had been interrupted in his burglary, and Lupíta had watched him run right straight to the squat across the street.

The next day, the barrio was abuzz. Gramma came in and told Mom and me over breakfast, and later I got the story from Lupíta herself, as she told and retold the story of her nocturnal visitor and his unsuccessful theft to anyone who'd listen.

She performed the story like Blanche Dubois, fanning herself at the memory and playing up the sympathies of her audience, but—like most everything else in the barrio—I got a sense of something vaguely sexual in her retelling, like she was really saying, "Why, I'm just not sure what he all wanted with little old me; I'm just a lonely old widow with an empty bed. . . ."

However, I'm sure the terror she felt at the moment of realization was severe: The few times I've discovered I've been robbed, the shock of it stupefies me for a minute; I can only imagine what it was like for her to catch the thief under her roof, and the fright she must have had.

For a full day, nothing happened. The incident seemed to pass and life went on as usual on Oklahoma Avenue, and I'm sure the kid across the street in the squat was finally breathing a sigh of relief when out of nowhere the night ignited like the Alamo over at the brick shanty.

Richard and the Rubio brothers, Grampa's nephews, all of them in their twenties and in varying involvement of cocaine smuggling at this point, the "trucking business" having adapted to the 1980s recession, and all of them with large shiny 4x4 pickups with chrome roll-bars and KC lights—they descended roaring into the property, coked up and locked down for war.

Four or five trucks broke through whatever flimsy fencing surrounded the place, and six to ten men with guns shouting in Spanish erupted from the cabins of the trucks, kicking down doors and setting fire to anything that would catch.

The young thief had unknowingly stirred up a cocaine-fueled hornet's nest. The group of squatters were beaten, rounded up, and terrorized, and though many guns bristled, none of them were fired, I remember, and I was impressed at their discipline, because they didn't want the sheriff called. Or maybe they just forgot their bullets, because mean-fighting, coked-up Mexicans aren't exactly known for their foresight.

Whatever the truth, no one was shot, no one injured critically, and no sheriffs were called. The transient family was run off in the one vehicle they owned, piled in and bloodied.

The day after, while the heroes were still off celebrating their victory in some port-side bar that was tolerant of their cocaine use, the morning sun rose on the smoldering ruins of what just the evening before had been a perfectly good brick shanty.

Joe and I heard the battle reports from his mother, Lupíta, who told us about this new development while Joe finished his breakfast, like we should learn a lesson from it, that if we make a life of stealing, a horde of coked-up Mexicans will kick down our doors and run us out of town, and that this was right and good, and how justice is meted out here. More border justice.

We listened to her solemnly, but were suddenly itching to get to the scene of the fight and see for ourselves what had happened.

When she finally finished, and Joe shoved what was left of his breakfast into his mouth, we bolted (well, I *bolted*: Joe waddled enthusiastically) through the same door the kid had kicked apart in his hurry to get back to his hovel, the same place we were now in a hurry to reach, before the fires died out, where it had all just happened, not a few hours before. The place was still smoking, the ashes of burned belongings still warm.

We picked through the rooms, and Joe looked for things to steal while I just felt a sense of shame at the abuse these people had just suffered—all of them, as a clan—because of what one of them had done, and at the smoldering piles of secondhand clothes, mismatched and moldy, and their mattresses made from cardboard boxes and unwearable denim, all of it half burnt. This was the undeniable ugliness of border justice, at our adolescent feet, and I was confused by feeling aligned to our men, and ashamed of what they'd done.

The rooms were uninsulated, open to the weather, and even through the disruption of the attack of the night before, it was evident to my eyes that this place was not habitable for people, that humans should not live like this, and even then, they had fought to defend it, and that then, even this—*this*—was taken from them.

I thought back to Stephen, who had attended the same school as me, walked the same hallways feeling the same teenage crushes on the same girls, likely, the same desires, and I remembered the first night I saw that kid in the barrio, his family's first night on Oklahoma Avenue. How he leaned his whole skinny body on a loose board on the wire fence and howled in imitation of a dog who barked relentlessly back at him—how wild and dirty this boy looked—and realizing that this is what he had to come home to, every night of high school.

And besides feeling so terribly sorry for him, for the people who had just been burned out of this hovel for breaking the peace of the Rubio Barrio, I felt odd, picking through there, an uneasy gratitude for everything that Dad and Mom and

Gramma had endured to keep us together, however uncertain, in that house on Oklahoma Avenue.

I found a burned up tin of ravioli, split at the top with a knife and two plastic forks still sticking out of it—an interrupted dinner—and I felt like I had to give a little prayer of thanks to Dad, Mom, Gramma, for being stronger than this whole fucking system of peasantry, and exclusion.

Rummaging through the dirt, Joe found and began eating a Li'l Debbie snack cake with the plastic only slightly melted, fairly recoverable. He pulled at the plastic and didn't seem to mind as he chewed his way through the ash.

Chapter 21

CHEERING UP PHILIPPE

It must have been New Year's Eve 1988, maybe 1989, and I was finishing high school, nearing graduation. All around Brownsville, preparations were being made to ring in the New Year joyfully, and I was stuck with Segis and his sidekick, Arnold, yet again. Segis had become my friend by default, because he lived out in the sticks near Oklahoma Avenue and had a car. He was also marginalized, strange in his conviction to reinventing the 1960s in his fashion and music. We had very little in common except that we both liked to drink beer and talk about "profound" topics that neither of us knew anything about. Arnold was Segis's neighbor, and knew even less, but you couldn't get one without the other, so I was stuck with both of them.

Somehow we managed to scrounge up enough money for a rack and a half of Busch beer, which is a dreadful fortified swill unfit for hobos, but perfectly appropriate for underage drinkers, with their livers of coal.

I forget how we got our hands on it. Buying the beer was never really much of an obstacle, but finding the cash for it always was. None of us worked, and our parents were close to indigent. But there we were: flush for the night. Segis and I were the juicers of the troop; the booze was for us. This overlap was fundamental to our friendship. Arnold was a sissy, but he was a faithful sissy, as all sidekicks should be, though his lackey personality annoyed me most of the time.

We started the evening out friendly enough, holed up in the parked single-wide trailer house Arnold's sister lived in with her brand-new family, behind Arnold's dad's house. There was no running water, no plumbing yet, so in order to relieve ourselves, we had to go outside and find a shrub. This was all right, civilized, for Brownsville.

Something was troubling me this night. I was seventeen, had made a mess of things with high school, and I had no plans for the future after graduation, which was coming up soon. There was a palpable sense of despair everywhere that no one seemed to feel or want to talk about. Segis was going on and on about how he was going to "start a rock band, man," and "make it really big, man" and "go on tours, man," and I just wasn't seeing a way out except through the military, through the Marines, like my brother Dan was doing, except in the Army. The despair was growing in me, but wasn't as yet conscious.

I was moody, morose this night. Not the best frame of mind for a teenage piss up.

About ten o'clock, Arnold's sister's husband returned from his shift managing the nearby Pizza Hut. He brought home his spoils: two large, cold, and incomplete supremes, which Arnold and Segis set upon hungrily, relishing this perk of management.

I demurred, a few beers up. Rather, I took a moment alone with the husband. I cornered him in an unused room, full of yet to be sorted boxes. I sat down with my beer in hand, and he stood, obviously uncomfortable, holding his latest baby and bouncing it on his hip.

"Can I ask you something?" I asked.

"Well . . ." [this is in Spanish].

"I don't mean to be . . . I mean . . . "

"*Mira*," he says. ("Listen.")

"No; wait . . . I mean . . . Is this all there is?"

I think he relaxed there. He didn't know what to make of me, and I'm sure he had no idea what I meant, because he certainly did not take offense. In fact, he seemed visibly relieved all I was up to was soul-searching and rhetoric. This, he could get out of easy, as there was none of it for him. For a minute there, he thought I might have been getting frisky, in front of his wife and child.

He didn't even take offense at the implied judgment, or insult. "Is this *really* all there is? Work at a Pizza Hut and come home to your wife and kids?" I think I started to weep.

"*Pos, es lo que pasa,*" he said, bouncing his newborn up and away from me. ("Well, that's just what happens.")

And that's what was bugging me, I remember. This was one of two possible outcomes in the Brownsville I knew—falling in with some local hussy and having your first kid before you turn twenty-one, and thanking your lucky stars when you can pilfer some extra product from a franchise restaurant after the other help has gone home, or, if you're luckier, enter the unexceptional redneck low-literacy state university system, like my sisters had managed, and work for the city or state of Texas later.

Now, this was my problem with that: For all my advanced wit, I genuinely had no idea what college was. My entire life, I had been told my responsibility and goal was to graduate from high school. Then it was over. I would get a job with Dad or something similar. When others talked about college, or I would see it on TV, I would pretend to know what they were talking about and that I was going along with the program, but I had no clue what the hell it all meant. I certainly didn't think it was more schooling. I sincerely couldn't conceptualize what it was. Labs, and people sitting on lawns, talking about Aristotle, smoking pot with professors who looked like Donald Sutherland, like in *Animal House*. I had no idea what it was for. Seriously. No one told me. I didn't think to ask.

This is the reason I was so blasé about just skimming through high school. I had no idea there was more beyond it. College was not spoken of in relation to me or Dan. Though I can't really speak for Dan, but I do know he joined the Army a year earlier than was allowed, because he couldn't wait to get away from Dad, and I can attest that when it *was* spoken of, college was—at least for me—something vague and reserved for privileged white people, in places like Connecticut.

Meaning that, besides blowing it academically, I was fairly guaranteed that I couldn't continue my education past public high school because I wouldn't have the grades, not to mention *any* sort of financing. I had blown my chance at escape, I was beginning to understand. I was getting scared that I might be stuck in Texas.

So my only other option was now in the room across from me that night, holding a sweaty, milk-caked infant, uncomfortable in the presence of the darkly introspective drunken teenager.

It was going to be this or the military, it was slowly dawning on me, and the military was looking really, really good. Maybe the Marines. No babies in the Marines.

I drank far many more of the Busch beers than was really necessary. At some point, Segis's father joined the party. He was a diminutive carpenter, slow to anger, quite loveable. He was low to the earth and dark skinned, humorously bitter. It was from him that Segis inherited a certain gentleness that made the high school girls buckle at the knee and belt. He picked up one of Segis's guitars and took the piss up outside, brought it out into the driveway, presumably to watch the fireworks way off in town, but Texas is flat: no curvature of the earth here, and as such, no fireworks to watch from a distance. Well, not in the sky.

Segis's father's guitar playing and joking around made our having beers in the cooler acceptable, in a way. When he wasn't playing, sidekick Arnold marshaled the boom box and cued up some Led Zeppelin or Motorhead, and we set to bring in the New Year, Texas-style.

A while later, something else started to bubble up, watching Segis's dad and his family enjoying themselves like that. The atmosphere was nevertheless tense, with Segis's mother bemoaning the fact that we'd bought beer. (Not so much that we were drinking it, but that we had spent money on it, though she was convinced we were doing every drug under the sun as well. Truth be told, had we access and the money, we probably would have been guilty of that, but alas: We were innocent of the charge. No, she was upset because we'd spent the $20 on the beer, when we could have bought a nice shirt, or a pair of shoes. Obviously she did her shopping outside the mall system.)

Actually, that's not altogether accurate. She blamed all of Segis's misdeeds—his drinking especially—on me. I was the bastard that made him drink. The year prior, or perhaps the year before that one, when Segis had been one of the regulars who skipped with Tony, he had been picked up in the parking lot of Sunrise Mall, pissing against a Buick. The mall cops caught him in mid-stream, while Tony and his other group were watching from the safety of a car, getting stoned. They laughed, and left, as the Brownsville Police Department came around to arrest Segis and book him in the city jail.

His mother had been called, and when she'd sprung him and started to read him the riot act, he did something he'd never before done, and raged right back to her in an adolescent fury, yelling and throwing things and otherwise acting out like a drunken teenaged kid would, against an oppressive mother. He said terrible things to her that she now liked to wear like jewelry, to keep him guiltily obligated to her. And she'd never forgiven me, though I wasn't involved.

So things might have been uncomfortable if I'd have paid her any mind, but I didn't: Segis's parents were more peasant-minded than even Gramma, and if I didn't have to answer to my own family, there was very little chance I'd answer to his. But this was, in fact, the problem.

This is what was bubbling up: The house on Oklahoma Avenue had been functionally vacant for months now, with Mom and me communicating exclusively by scribbled messages left on the kitchen counter, or on the answering machine, when I needed $5. When Derek was home from kindergarten, he'd have to suffer Gramma's daycare, which meant his watching her watch Spanish television and smoking menthol cigarettes while she blended sweatily into her easy chair. My sisters were off in school, and Dan was defending South Korea.

And Dad, well, Dad was doing long-distance hauling now, driving 18-wheelers from Brownsville to Detroit, moving GM parts from their cheaply manufactured origins on the Mexican border to the dying rust belt.

The isolation was finally settling into me, into my heart, after being left alone for so long, and I was becoming a real son of a bitch.

No other evidence was needed at this time than the afternoon that Dad called home from one of his road trips, and I happened to answer. His voice was desperate, frightened. He was calling from Detroit.

"June? Aye, Junior! *Aye mijo sánto!*" he said. ("My holy son!")

I was already bored, trying to get off the phone. "Yeah?"

He began to tell me this story, how he was just released from a hospital in Detroit, and he was finally able to call from the trucking office because he'd been in the hospital for three days, and he couldn't figure out where he was in this fucking Detroit.

He said he'd bought a box of chicken wings from a KFC near his drop point, and after he had eaten them, he had started to get really sick, and the next thing he knew, he was convulsing and vomiting, fell out of the cab of his truck to the ground—which is a pretty hard fall—and as he was lying there, wretching and convulsing, trying to call for help, the first person to come over to help was a stringy black guy (I won't use the word dad used, even in Spanish) who took his wallet while Dad lay there defenseless.

Dad, horribly poisoned, was prodded by the Detroit police, and he managed to explain in limited English who he was and what had happened by pointing at the cab of his truck. They understood, ambo'd him off to a hospital where he had his stomach pumped and was allowed to recover for two days in an alien, inner-urban American environment. Dad had been terrified.

And when he called, he was desperate for a bit of home, the warmth of something familiar, and it just wasn't me anymore; I was unrelenting, as alien now as the hospital had been.

I said Mom wasn't there, to try her at the JC Penney, where she spent most of her time now, working. I remember almost consciously making the decision to keep from being comforting, a sort of "Take *that*, you fucker," response.

Dad, however, did not sound hurt, or that he was in any way dissatisfied with my response. His voice was thankful, hopeful, when he blessed me over and over again in Spanish for simply answering the phone, and then he hung up and tried his disappearing wife at her job.

I hung up and went back to my usual moping, not thinking about that episode again until that night in Segis's driveway.

"Can you imagine how fuckin' scared he must have been?" I said to no one in particular.

"Who?" asked Arnold, who fit the bill perfectly, as no one in particular.

"My dad, man. Being sick like that, falling out of his truck."

"Your dad?" asked Segis, not tracking and not sober.

"Yeah, in Detroit. He got food poisoning and was so sick, he fell out of the truck," I explained, the gravity of the moment finally dawning on me, just how scared Dad must have been.

"While he was driving?!" asked Arnold, incredulous. And *he* was sober, hardly every drank.

"No, you idiot fuck, at the KFC. In the parking lot. He got food poisoning and ended up in a hospital. He could hardly speak English, and his wallet got stolen by some crack head. They thought he was drunk and were gonna arrest him first, and they treated him like he was a drunk illegal."

"Fuck," said Segis.

"Yeah," and here I started choking up. "And when he called home, man, I was a total prick and didn't . . . you know . . . I wasn't nice to him. I was a dick," I said, sobbing. "He was trying to tell someone at home what had happened to him, just trying to get some comfort, and I was a total dick."

"Man," said Segis. "You're a dick!" and he started laughing.

"Fuck this," I said, and walked off into the night, making my way home.

＊

Now, this might sound revisionist, or like absolute drivel, because it is, but a large part of my behavior that night came as a result of the fact that I was—in Texan terms—within walking distance from home. I was only about three or four miles from the house on Oklahoma Avenue.

Remember: In Texas everyone has a car and a car is necessary. In Texas you're consistently ten to thirty miles between everywhere you are and where you want or need to be—school, home, work, friends' houses, etc. I knew a family who had a Hyundai just to get to their bathroom. It's a big fucking place, covers more square miles than France. Look it up.

Segis's house was relatively close to our house, less than five miles. I could do that tonight, I thought, walking. I felt no obligation to anyone. I felt like I was in Manhattan.

More to the point, I felt I was no longer accountable to—or held hostage by—the people who held the keys. Which is, of course, terribly unfair to them, to Segis, who was always good to drive.

Segis was lonely, felt misunderstood by everyone, but especially his family. He believed himself to be an artist, a musician, an iconoclast of legendary scope. At some very fundamental level, he really believed himself to have the heart of a visionary, someone defiant and revolutionary, but he had very little chance to explore that, growing up how and where he did.

He felt he had large, universally important ideas, but he possessed very limited communication skills, and his ideas were painfully simple, but that did not keep him from attempting to write meaningful verse, and poetry. Lyrics to make you think, man. About the earth, man. And "society," man.

On top of it all, he had incredibly limited musical tastes, for a musician. He listened to very little else that was not mediated through the local classic rock stations. I felt bad for him; no one took him seriously, except maybe his girlfriend du jour. Still, he was my friend. What are you gonna do?

Anyhow, so I stomped off.

I remember I was actually excited to walk home, through the booze haze. Seriously. This was as metropolitan as I'd felt up to then. Thing was, between Segis's house and mine was El Jardin Elementary School.

Now, if you recall from back in chapter five, El Jardin was really quite the Garden of Eden for me, as a child. A garden of promise, of the best feelings I'd ever felt as a human being, from kindergarten to the fourth grade.

It was blissful there, nothing but fond memories. And to be this close to it now, as a tortured teenager with his options closing down around him, not to mention the sense of betrayal I had felt when I had been gerrymandered out of attending that place with the other English-speaking, upwardly mobile children of promise—well, there just wasn't going to be a civilized outcome.

And here it came: I scaled a ten-foot gate—the same one my older brother Dan had impaled himself on, by the beef of his bicep, which was sizeable, even as a kid, during football practice, the scar still evident even today—and I leaped down on the inside of the abandoned school like a very drunken Spiderman. Or Venom, his evil alter ego.

I made my way to the wing that I had remembered to be mine, when I attended school here, and instead of the dark, 1940s brick building that had been there—possibly the only thing in Brownsville that had any sort of antiquity—I instead found those cheap, awful squat one-room buildings that the government likes to hand out to overburdened schools. Change had come to my idyll, and this infuriated me further.

I picked up a dislodged concrete block and shoved it through the shatterproof fiberglass window of the nearest building, and it just sort of "spelunked" into the room, the fiberglass unsurprisingly adhered to the aluminum framing simply with glue. I could have foregone the ambition of hostility and just pushed it through.

Not to be deterred in my rage fantasy, I hoisted myself up and in, and—weak from the intoxication—tumbled inside, then I risked turning on the light.

It was a beautiful room, with Lilliputian desks, children's things left behind as if in an archaeological find, frozen in time, colorful, lovely, full of promise. Full of everything I was missing now.

So I set to destroy it, starting with the teacher's desk. I raged. I sullied. I shattered. I destroyed. I uglied.

But I did not defile, I felt. There was still love in what I was doing there. Because I was trying to get this school's attention again. Like I needed a parent's attention again.

Eventually I turned off the light and I sat down on the stoop, holding a tiny sweater from one of the kid's desks I had thrown at the chalkboard, which had shattered, the place in pieces behind me in the dark. I sat and I whimpered quietly to myself, thinking that I didn't have any more energy for the walk home. And then I heard sirens.

And then I booked it to the playing fields to the rear of the school, the alcohol thinning my blood so much that by the time I found a divot to hole up in from about one hundred yards away, in the dark of the football field, I was about to faint or throw up, panting horribly in the muggy night.

I slid into what was basically a ditch and kept down, using the kid's sweater to keep my face from getting wet, and I sat there watching for the cops.

No one came. The sirens died away, and still I lay there, unsure of what to do next.

Eventually, I grew colder and bolder and wetter and decided it was time to risk walking home again, and I got up, crossed the field, left the school by climbing back over another fence—this one far more unexposed—and started walking toward the main road, Boca Chica, which is when I saw it. A telephone booth. It was like the TARDIS, in Dr. Who.

It just appeared magically.

It had not been there six hours before.

It appeared sometime after dark, out of nowhere, at a crossroads between Segis's house and mine, a meeting place of two farm roads that went from nowhere to nowhere else. Our neighborhood was developing, apparently. Enough to warrant a full-standing, enclosable telephone booth, the sort that Superman would change in, in the middle of fucking nowhere.

Now, this made my mind tilt. I walked around it, the kid's dampened sweater still in my hand. I was like the neo-hominids in *2001,* walking around the monolith, circling, circling.

I could use this, I thought. But how?

Then I had an idea. I would blame someone else for what I did. Someone imaginary.

Fucking brilliant, I was. I dialed 911.

This is a rough but fairly accurate recreation of what followed:

911 Operator: "What's your emergency?" (The voice is young, fey.)

"Hi, uh, hello: I'd like to, uh, report a crime."

"Yes, sir. What kind of crime?"

"Um, a break in. At like, the school."

"What school, sir?"

"Un, the, uh, El Jardin Elementary School. Right by here, by this phone. It was kids. On skateboards. They were throwing rocks. They threw rocks at me. But they broke in."

"They threw rocks at you, sir?"

"Yeah, yeah. They threw rocks at me. And they broke into the school. I heard them talking about it. They were all like, 'Yeah, bro! We really trashed that school room!'"

"They damaged the school, sir?"

"Yeah! I saw them! And they were skating! And they were talking about it!"

"Where is the school, sir?"

"It's right here, on Boca Chica, man! It's El Jardin! You know El Jardin. Everyone knows El Jardin. It's a great place. If you get here quick, I bet you can catch them. They just left on Vermillion Road."

Now, this whole time, the voice on the other end sounds amused, playing at being thick, like he was playing a game. And he was: He was keeping me on the line until a sheriff's deputy rolled up next to the telephone booth and parked, turning on its lights.

"Oh, never mind!" I said. "There's a cop here now; I'll tell him. Good-bye!"

I hung up the phone and proceeded to tell my imagined story about the skateboarders (I always disliked skateboarders, quite possibly because I was jealous of their access to pavement) to the deputy, who, weighing nearly as much as a small moon, had by now managed to laboriously extract himself from the driver's side of the cruiser with tremendous difficulty.

He was wordless as he lightly touched my shoulder and moved me to the hood of his cruiser as I kept describing the imaginary skateboarders and pointing into the direction I had now convinced myself they'd run, and he slowly insisted I splay out my arms and legs and I do, totally unrecognizing what was actually happening as he patted down my waist and legs, my thin shirt, and that's all, as the purloined sweater had thankfully been left in the phone booth, on the phone. He grabbed at my right wrist and swung it back, and I think suddenly, *Whoah, this fat fucker's arresting me.*

"Whoah," I said, "Are you arresting me?"

When he spoke, it was slow and musical, full of the lilting pidgin elocution of the border. Sounded exactly like Pedro, from *Napoleon Dynamite*. (Hated that movie.)

"Please watch your head, sir," he said.

Still it didn't dawn on me that I was being arrested.

I was compliant and stepped happily into the back of the sheriff's cruiser. I was chatty, happy to have someone new to talk to, all the way to the Justice Center in downtown Brownsville.

"Hey, did you read about that boy last week in the detention center who was killed? The guards who sat on him? And they broke his neck because he was being loud? Did you read that? I wrote that story! I wrote it. I work for the *Brownsville Herald!*"

This was actually embellishment. I didn't actually "work" for the *Herald*; I was a stringer. I wrote stories through a program where high school students could contribute their raw material for about $5 an hour, and in return the publication got some local color and the kids got stuff for their portfolio. For me, I was pretty good, so I had been taken under the wing of one of their chief reporters, Basilio, one of the people who would help define my life. Basilio was a 1960s brown-proud radical from Colorado, very aware and in possession of an incredible command of language, had really impressive diction. And a nuclear reactor of hatred, both of self and in general, I would later see.

Anyhow, I was under Basilio's spell and this episode would unknowingly make him much more fond of me. (He bought me my first copy of *The Great Shark Hunt*.)

The deputy, however, was unimpressed. He was obviously someone's morbidly obese cousin who could be doing little else, if he wasn't "doing law enforcement." He drove us to the Justice Center, and I still didn't understand what was happening, where I was.

It was when the cruiser entered a garage and the door closed behind me that I finally understood I was in real trouble.

The fat deputy managed to extract himself much more quickly this time, probably because he was in front of his peers, and he opened my door. I was suddenly surrounded by uniformed boys and one or two men with clipboards, looking simple, methodical, and bored, with an older man in his sixties watching from a bench a few feet away and smoking a cigarette. I found myself wondering about him fleetingly when suddenly, from the only door leading into the building, this wispy, fey Mexican boy erupted in laughter, hung on the doorknob, and said, "Is that him?! The drunk guy? Ha, ha! I kept him on the phone for you guys! Ha! Good night!" and, laughing further, went back to his business of answering 911 calls on a slow New Year's Eve. All in a night's work. Personally, I was starting to panic, realizing I was at the mercy of these government-funded Aztecs.

I was stripped down to my underwear and processed by the two bored Mexican kids with the clipboards, and when it came time for the cavity search, I cried foul murder. In *no way* was I going to allow these people access to my most private of places. I was suddenly in spitting, fighting posture. *They will have to kill me,* I was thinking.

And then, the second I started resisting, the whole processing group wordlessly flipped closed their clipboards, grabbed their gear and filed out, as if this had been expected, leaving me alone with the old man on the bench.

He was weathered and grandfatherly, reminding me very much of the old man on Karsten's farm, the horse keeper. He had sat there through the operation, observing the intake ceremony quietly, smoking a cigarette, and when I started to make a fuss because they were expecting me to drop trou and "spread them," it was his turn to do his job. The other men shuffled off, leaving us alone in the dark garage.

"Domíngo, Domíngo," he said to me in a calming tone, in Spanish. "*Pónte tranquílo.*" ("Stay calm.") "*Necesítamos hacer esto.*" ("We need to do this. It has to be done.")

I understood what he was saying. This was my second chance at doing this calmly. It would get rougher if I refused again. His reassurance, which I don't think was feigned, was in fact rather calming. There was something in his manner that neutralized the invasion of the impending cavity search, much like he was a veterinarian and I was cattle. It felt almost impersonal at that point. Like he was a drunk teenage whisperer.

I was calmed into courage, and I told the man, in Spanish, to be looking because I was going to do it, but it was going to be quick. He said, "Great." So I said, "OK, here goes," and before I finished saying it, I was done: down, turn, spread, and yanked back up went the Y-fronts.

"You see?" he said. "Nothing to it."

I was allowed to dress and was led through the little fey boy's door by the troop of silent clipboarded Aztecs, who'd watched all this from the other side of the garage, smoking borrowed cigarettes. The old man chuckled to himself behind me, shaking his head slowly as I turned and waved.

I was ushered into a newer, office like area with two large women in their late thirties and a guy about twenty, to finish my paperwork. It was their job to process me further and account for my belongings, flimsy as they were.

My outfit that night was my usual wardrobe: a thin concert T-shirt, a pair of denim trousers or shorts, and my oversize, untied stinking British Knights. I was never much into jewelry, but I was wearing a Swatch I had stolen from one of my sisters and a cheap lead pendant that my Gramma had recently given me. It was on a cheap metal chain, and the pendant was large and round, fit the center of my palm perfectly, and it had an image of St. Francis on it, with a prayer inscribed on the back. It was worthless, like everything else I owned, but it was mine.

So when I was instructed to hand it over, I finally revolted. I started arguing. I was finally scared—remembering the story I had helped Basilio write about the illegal Mexican boy with the broken neck that the jailers were trying to cover up because he was sat upon by a large jailer when the kid started making a fuss—and I had already begun making a fuss. I didn't belong here.

I had interviewed the police spokesperson just a few days earlier to get a quote on the progress of the investigation, and even at seventeen, I could tell that the police were uninterested in pursuing the abuse of justice because the kid had been an illegal, and he had no family pushing for transparency. The only people who were keeping the story alive were the Yankee do-gooders—copy editors and reporters sent to Brownsville from the colder states to earn their stripes, like the BBC dispatches its reporters to the Congo, or the Democratic Republic of the Congo, right here on the Texas border.

Point being, I was suddenly aware of the vulnerability of my situation. And I was frightened by it. So I fought back in the only way I knew: being loud and fashionable, like the Mimis.

I took off the watch and threw it into the box I was supplied for my belongings. The twenty-year-old kid was taking inventory. One of the thirty-year-old mother-types sorted and packed. This part, I'd seen in the movies, so I played along.

"One wristwatch; brand: Swatch," I yelled and threw it in the box, already pulling off my British Knights. "One pair, used, British Knights, size ten and a half! One T-shirt, white, with Robert Smith of the Cure on the front! One pair of trousers, blue denim!" Each one of these instances was punctuated emphatically with my thrusting forward the described item into the awaiting box. I had the whole office watching at this point. They'd never seen anyone with a command of English before, obviously. Or such an obnoxious prick getting arrested.

The older woman holding the box was not playing along. She muttered something to the boy who was trying to keep up with my list, obviously struggling with either the pen or the language. When I was down to my underwear, again, I leaned forward and said, "You get all that?"

He didn't answer, finding it difficult to wend his way through my verbal karate.

"*La cadena*," the woman said, pointing at the chain and lead pendant Gramma had given me.

Somehow, and I'm not sure why, but this infuriated me. Maybe because it was the last thing that tied me to my family. "Take it!" I yelled suddenly, and yanked it from my neck forcefully, and threw it on the pile. This made anyone who wasn't watching by this point begin watching.

The woman muttered under her breath in Spanish, clearly unthreatened. She shoved my jailhouse issue orange jumpsuit into my small chest. I'd be spending the night in these, like bright orange pajamas.

Now, I'm afraid I'm going to have interrupt my narrative here, bring down the fourth wall. Remember: I'd been arrested only for being drunk and making that fantastically stupid call. At this time only I knew what my larger crime had been that night.

I was absolutely certain they were going to realize at any moment that the vile, impossible vandalism at El Jardin school was somehow related to the drunk, "Where am I going with my life?", lying teenager at the phone booth not one hundred feet from the school grounds. At any minute, they'd make the connection. Any minute now. Now. Now. Maybe now.

The suspense was torturing me. But I dutifully put on my jumpsuit and waited for the other, heavier and dirtier shoe to drop. I zipped up the suit and stood before the twenty-year-old kid, still scribbling away on his clipboard, the older woman who was probably his aunt, and the three-hundred pound jailer probably his father.

When he finished, the kid handed me the clipboard with my list of charges and personal belongings and asked me to sign it quickly, so we could get on with the internment. (My words, not his.)

He handed me a pen and I stopped cold: Drunk as I was, I was certainly *not* going to sign something so ripe with misspellings and egregious syntax.

"What—who?" I stammered, attempting to make sense of this Arabic.

"That's not how you spell 'jeans,' just try 'pants,' in the future, and it's a 'Swatch,' a brand of watch, not '*suatche*' with a 'u' and 'e.' It's not Spanish. And it's 'British Knights' with a 'K,' not as in 'nights.' And it's 'public intoxication,' not 'drunken in public'—and *really*—can you call that 'public?' Have you ever been out to Boca Chica? It's a desert out there. And it's a 'broken necklace' not a 'neckless—broke.' I'm not signing this until it's right." I pushed the clipboard back through the window.

At this point, no one was looking my way, in my earnest attempt at making friends, except for the guys in the overnight cell: They were enthralled, lined up against the bars and snickering.

I was their copy-editing Spartacus that night. It was either that, or they wanted to kill me, for making a fuss. One toothless old man in the isolation tank, looking through a porthole, started making catcalls as I scratched out and rewrote whole passages on my induction forms after they were handed to me, for validation.

"*¡Traímelo páca!*" he yelled. ("Bring him over here to me.")
He cackled with his face pressed against the porthole glass, his
mouth open and revealing his one last remaining tooth.

He was asking the jailer to throw me into confinement with
him. To have sex with him. As soon as I was done correcting the
grammar on the arrest report, and he cackled again, I launched
across the floor—the jailer reaching out and just missing me—and
I slapped the glass as hard as I could with an open palm and frightened the evil buggering pederast and threatened to relieve him of
his final tooth.

Now *this* guy, I was pretty sure I could take. He was like,
sixty, weighed about a buck-five. Besides, his wretched deprav-
ity—you just knew he hadn't developed the taste for children in
jail—brought out a lot of primitive fear in me. Fear and anger.

But, oh, real power transitions quickly, and the gargantuan
jailer took real pleasure in hoisting me solidly toward the overnight
cage, opening the door, and shoving me through, now that I had
signed the paperwork. Paperwork good. Drunk teenagers bad.

The incarcerated men, silent, shifting about noiselessly from
foot to foot, or craning to view images on the television in the
enclosed office, most of them in Texas illegally and awaiting tran-
sit back to Matamoros in the border town "catch and release"
policy—only to make it back within the next few days—these
indigent men all parted like the Red Sea before me, and I stood
there nearly catatonic as I heard the gate close behind me.

They parted not because I was formidable, or an alpha male,
by any stretch of the imagination. They parted and avoided looking at me because they thought I was crazy, and they wanted no
trouble, transparent as the holding cage was. Had it been otherwise, I'd have probably been much assaulted, much beaten.

Guys like that don't like loud mouths, fast metabolisms, in the same way a pit bull doesn't like a yapping Chihuahua.

Once the cage closed behind me and the snickers of delight from office workers and guards had died down, the crowd healed itself behind me, and so I moved over to a corner where I figured I could fend off an attack, and tried to blend in.

I stood, then crouched, then leaned, but nothing felt natural, with all the men meandering and wandering and mingling as if nothing was wrong. Some of them slept. Some laughed at the television they couldn't hear. A guy I knew from high school with a terrible dermatology problem and who really *was* crazy walked by in front of me, smoking the nub end of a joint, and you can let your mind wander as to how that got in there.

A few hours later, after I hadn't been eviscerated, hadn't lost a kidney to a shiv or been buggered like a rent boy in Picadilly, I began to relax. I made my way to a bench where a guy was sleeping and I pushed him wordlessly over to one side, in a manner aggressive and unaccustomed to me. It wasn't me doing this. It was my jailhouse self.

He wilted perfectly—didn't even look my way—and just did my bidding. Moved over and gave me room.

I'm thinking, "*Hunh. Maybe I'm not the jailhouse bitch tonight,*" and then I hear, "*Eh, Domingo! Como va la cósa?*" ("Hey, Domingo! How goes the thing?")

And I respond reflexively, with a smile in my voice like I'm walking down Oklahoma Avenue, "*Eh, pínche Juan! Náda, náda aquí. Que es tú honda?*" ("Hey, fuckin' Juan, man! Nothing going on here. How's things?")

It was Juan, my neighbor from across Oklahoma Avenue, about three years younger than me, himself doing a little overnight time, just saying hey as he wandered over to palaver with his ilk, and I gave absolutely no thought at the randomness of coincident involved in running into my neighbor here, at the Brownsville City Jail, on New Year's Eve.

It was just understood that sometimes, as a boy king, you end up in slam overnight.

It was here, about four in the morning, that I started to nod off, thinking about what was going to happen the next morning. Thinking about the cops making the connection to El Jardin, and my stomach started to knot, and not from the hangover.

I forgot to mention my phone call home.

I got the "one phone call" right after that episode with the corrections, before I was shoved into the cell. They handed me a receiver and asked if I had anyone to call. I gave them my mother's number: 831-4961, that first home number like a tattoo on my soul, as every child from the 1970s must have equally scratched into theirs.

She answered on the seventh ring, I remember, waking her up, Derek likely asleep next to her, at four years old. I think maybe this might be the night that our relationship matured, changed colors.

"Mom?" I said.

"Yeah? June?" she answered, sleepily.

"Mom, I got arrested. I was walking home and some fat cop arrested me." I said this in front of the jailer, who was standing next to me, and the other people listened from inside the office. The boy who had processed my belongings had been adequately ashamed for his poor, poor grammar and busied himself elsewhere for a while. I was mad, but not crying yet.

"June, calm down," she said, her voice clearly awakening. "Where are you?"

"I'm at the jail, Mom. These people don't speak English, Mom. I corrected their spelling."

"June, tell me where you are. Tell me what happened," she said, trying not to panic.

"OK, you get off now," said the fat jailer.

"I'm at the city jail, Mom. They say you can come get me at six tomorrow morning. Mom, this is the fat guy that killed that kid!" I said, looking right at him, not sure it was really him, but it could have been.

"June, just be quiet. Quiet now," she said.

The woman and the guard became insistent, shouting that my time on the phone was done, behind me. Mom could hear their hatred of me through the phone.

"Mom, come get me at six, please; these people hate me." Here the guard grabbed for the phone, and I pulled away. "They hate me because I corrected their English!" I was able to yell into the phone, and I heard mom say, "Oh God, oh my God," before the phone was hung up. And for emphasis, I decided to slam the back of my own head against the wall. I'm not sure why, but it made sense at the time.

I managed about two hours' sleep, sitting upright like John Merrick, holding the blanket they gave me at processing, but I had given the pillow to some other bloke. I was doing time.

Breakfast sounded at five o'clock, and the place went fucking bonkers, though silently, like a buffet at a POW camp.

I sat back, still terribly hungover and totally overcautious. But I stepped up finally when everyone else was done and was given a tray, like back in elementary school.

A single serving of milk in a container and a white-bread sandwich with a powdered egg and ham mixture, with a cookie for dessert was our breakfast, and these guys took to it like it was manna.

I held it in front of me for a beat and then turned and held it out in offering to the swarm. Hands reached from nowhere and plucked each item from the tray, and then I handed the emptied tray back to the jailer outside, without looking at him.

An hour later, my name was called. Or rather, I was called by *el necioso*. The . . . well, shit. This is a tough one to translate. The annoying one. The nag. The jerky-asshole guy. The guy who corrects your English, loudly, in front of others.

I was given back my clothes and threw off my jumpsuit, put my cheap Swatch and BKs back on, the necklace looking back at me sadly and in pieces, and I put that back into my pocket.

I was certain by this time at least, they'd seen the damage wrought at El Jardin, and I was just waiting for them to enjoy that bit of "justice," where they'd let me walk and then quickly yank me back in. But it didn't happen.

Instead, I was given more paperwork to sign—photocopies of the copy-edited originals, and newer, jurisprudential ones, with the adopted corrections, some part of me noticed—and I initialed here, signed there.

"What happens now?" I said to the auntie woman.

"Now you come before the *jutch!*" she cackled. "We send you a notice and you have to come to *cort!*"

She yells this loud enough for everyone in the cage to hear. She was back in charge. Even the old man in the solitary drunk tank managed to express a mildly cross look across his silent face that his favorite potential bride of the night before was being given his papers.

All these things were stuffed into an A-9 envelope and handed over to me with a sort of delighted satisfaction this woman rarely experienced, it seemed.

I was shown to a side door that coincidentally emerged into the same corridor and past a dismal cafe that I'd visited not a week before, triumphant as a junior reporter and flush from a journalistic mission, feeling terribly superior to all the people needing to be here, because of work, because of misdeeds, because they wanted nothing else, because they were in Brownsville fucking Texas.

And now, clutching my legal papers to myself, cold in my T-shirt and denim jeans and humbled horribly, I walked this hallway like a beaten kid. The cafe was in its opening groans, and as I left through the front doors, I saw the sweetest sight I think angels and soldiers see, when all gets lost and then gets found again, and it's Mom, in her beat-up silver Taurus, too many years too old but still her reliable car. And Derek, standing in the front seat in his pajamas, and looking through the windshield, pulled his pacifier out of his mouth and waved at me, and I waved back, and Mom gave me a sad smile, waving back, and I walked toward them, got in the back seat without saying a word, and Mom drove us to McDonalds, a huge cleft in my brain waiting for the crack detectives of the BPD to make the connection between my arrest and El Jardin.

❖

Mom was gentle, left me to myself. No longer the mother of a child, she felt, somehow. Derek was a great comfort to me in his innocence, and for the next two weeks or so, as I worried, worried and slowly began to recover from the horrible anticipation of my foul, foul deed, and the shoe that never dropped, well, it just never dropped.

The citations and orders to see a judge never visited our mailbox. My record, when revisited a few months later by the Marine Corps recruiting officer, had no mention of a P.I.

(Point of fact: I didn't go into the Marine Corps, though I had done all the processing, went through all the preparations. Mare led me through the maze of Pell Grant applications and enrolling into college at A&I, where she was attending after I graduated high school, and instead of getting on that bus headed out to San Diego, at the very last minute, I ended up going to college. For a while.)

"You didn't even have to go to court?" asked Segis some time later, when I was finally able to talk about that night. He was the only other person who knew I'd been picked up for P.I. I didn't tell him about the school.

"No," I said. "It just sorta disappeared."

"You lucky fucker," he said.

I'm assuming that either I was still considered a juvenile, and it didn't stick after I turned eighteen—however Segis was sixteen when he was picked up, and duly processed—it was either that, or the paperwork was too embarrassing to bring before a judge and was ditched in a trash can by someone unwilling to point out his illiteracy to the court system.

Either way, I never owned up to what I did at El Jardin. I never told anyone about it, either. I never told Mom that the reason why I looked so dark for weeks after was not from the shame she thought I was experiencing from the things she'd known I did, but from the secret things that grew much further down in a person, things that have no explanation when they blossom virulently in the dark. Things that are not for a mother to forgive.

I never told anyone that story, or what had happened inside that jail. I was too ashamed. But somehow, the night I saw my very French friend, Philippe, worrying over a bad day at work, I just blurted it out over dinner at a Seattle bistro, where he was disgusted by the food. I didn't see him very often, as he lives in Los Angeles, and did remote work for the publishing company where we both worked, him as a publisher and me as a designer.

Somehow, I thought the *Sturm und Drang* of the tale would take his mind off things, if only for a bit. When I finished, he seemed puzzled, bemused as to why I was telling him that story.

"I dunno," I said, shrugging it off. "It was both horrifying and quite funny, I thought."

Philippe thought about that for a moment.

"That's certainly a stone in your garden," he said, as he picked something distasteful off his plate.

Philippe said things like that, things translated literally from the French, phrases that make much more sense in the places they originate.

Chapter 22

CRYING UNCLE

It was Father's Day when Mom and Dad were invited to Kingsville to be with my three sisters and their respective boyfriends for the weekend, at their college, to legitimize further nuptials.

I wasn't invited along, but I preferred it that way, as I was accustomed to being alone and I'd have the place to myself without having to wonder when they'd be coming home, what they'd see if they did. Not that it mattered at this time, since I was producing a crap local political publication and making enough money so that I no longer depended on them for much. I was nineteen years old and had just dropped out of college, though not consciously. I just didn't go back, for now, until I figured out what the hell it meant.

Mom and Dad would be gone, and I thought I'd invite my friends over, have a small, respectable party. It made me feel quite the adult.

Gramma, as usual, was across the driveway in her brick hovel dissolving further into her sweat-soaked velour easy chair, probably fresh from a shower and wrapped in a terry cloth robe, and dutifully working on her cigarette-butt sculpture of a porcupine, which is what she did when she watched Spanish *telenovelas*. She'd stopped being so hysterical about work at this point, stopped pressing others into service, a combination of her old age and the absence of work in the barrio. Dad was working long-haul trucking now, and I was the only one press-gang age left at home.

The publication I was producing had an ulterior function that was superior to muckraking the dirty local politics, but only I knew it. Its primary purpose was to score the owner, Alfredo, free breakfasts at his favorite "coffee shops" around town, in exchange for running the business cards of the coffee shops throughout the twelve-page tabloid. There was hardly any advertising besides that. Alfredo was nearly seventy, a bail-bondsman who specialized in springing Mexican prostitutes. He'd throw their bail, get a little something in return, then drive them to the border and they'd disappear. More often than not, he'd never see them again. I don't know how he made his money.

He would, however, pay me $200 a week to compose his "newspaper," which is what I was doing in high school and college for free. I was happy to do it, at nineteen. We had crap in the way of equipment, crap in the way of editorial content, crap in the way of printing and design, but somehow, we managed to get a twelve-page publication out every week. I was a production department in a pair of trousers, and I was happy.

So I was feeling flush for the moment, not too disappointed at catastrophically failing so many classes at A&I the semester before.

Segis and company were invited over that Saturday night, as a result. I was even making dinner—a tremendous leap forward in sophistication.

All afternoon, I was fielding phone calls on Gramma's remote line, installed in our house long before, back when the trucking business was booming and we had to receive calls on both her line and ours, and Dad had been concerned because he thought we were missing too much business when her line would go unanswered. The remote line, in our kitchen, was to keep us from having to run back and forth between the two houses.

Eventually, it would become our single means of communication because Dan had adventurously discovered he could dial out to the 976 numbers we'd found in the back pages of the skin magazines under Richard's bed. We spent a lot of our free time under that bed, reading every part of the magazines and then ensuring that they were sorted in exactly the same way, when we left them, in case Richard had left them in a particular order.

Dan had taken things further by dialing up these numbers with no regard for consequences. In a complete absence of sense, he wanked off a $500 phone bill and then just hid the bills, when they were delivered in the mail, sort of how I managed my manufactured report cards in high school.

One afternoon, while looking for a fresh magazine in our customary exchanging ground under the spare bed's mattress, I found three portentous phone bills from Southwestern Bell, the last one threatening disconnection.

This was way too big for me to hide, under the code of brotherhood secrets. There was a lot that I kept secret, things that I won't even divulge here. (Like the time he . . . no; sorry. Too gross. Too humiliating. Even for Dan.) Thing was, I had just started high school, and I lived by the telephone and getting calls, and the thought of losing that one metric of social standing frightened me—how do you explain something like that away, at that age?—and more than anything else, we lived ten miles outside of town. The telephone was *necessary*.

This was far too much.

So I timidly gave the bill to Mom, who raged at me for not coming to her sooner, who then gave the bill to Dad, who raged at both of us, and then gave Dan a tremendous beating while Dan was working at the sand pit, loading trucks after school. (Is it any wonder then, the pathology of our sex?)

When Dan drove the tractor home from the sandpit that night, awaiting a further beating at home away from the prying eyes of the hired truck drivers, Dan gave me a murderously silent look that told me what I already knew, that he wasn't the only one who would be bloodied that day.

Our phone line was eventually cut, and we were left to sharing Gramma's line. Plan B always had a way of becoming plan A, back then. Still.

✢

That Saturday afternoon, in 1991, I drive to a mom and pop store to buy beer, and then over to the H.E.B. to buy the makings for spaghetti, and not from a can, which would be that evening's dinner. Quite sophisticated.

Segis calls around five, excited. So does Didi, a mutual friend, a bit later, both on Gramma's line. Gramma picks up her extension each time so I talk over her, and she realizes it's for me and then hangs up. This is the arrangement we've come to, in sharing the line.

I ask Didi if she can pick up Segis and Arnold, and she agrees. She's been the girl Smurf for a while now, having just turned twenty. She'd been knocked up by some bloke named Ricki, who'd gone off to Nebraska to work on some farm job and promised he'd send for her in a few months. In the meantime, she's developed a crush on both Segis and me, but mostly me. She has a lisp, which makes her endearing, but mostly I avoid her; the embryo growing in her freaks me out, especially if it's going to be anything like Ricki—farmer chav.

Gramma's phone rings again and I answer quickly, saying, "Hello?" because if it's anyone important, I want to make sure they don't hear Gramma asking, "*Bueno?*" The further away from speaking Spanish you are, the whiter you could be, and I wanted to be white. So white I was Jewish, actually, like Joel Fleischman, from *Northern Exposure*. It had been my only intellectual nourishment at this time. So I would leap on the phone when it rang, tried to beat out her old, tired woman reflexes.

This time, when I answer, I hear a kid's voice abruptly demand, "*Quien es?*" It's obviously not for me. The phrase, as a telephonic hailing, is a rude demand for the person who answered to identify himself, immediately. There's no protocol or good manners here. It's vulgar, rude. Farmhand rough. Makes me angry. So I respond curtly in English, thinking the caller wouldn't understand, and say, "No one who wants to talk to you," and hang up, get back to my spaghetti.

I'm feeling quite advanced, feeling like quite the urbanite. I'm making a crap salad and thin noodles with Ragu and serving it on paper plates, but I'm immensely proud of myself.

Half an hour later, Didi's car pulls into our driveway, the northern one facing onto Oklahoma Avenue. I look out the front window and see Didi, Segis, and his sidekick, Arnold.

Segis is dressed in his usual black concert T-shirt, a heat-pressed image of Jim Morrison leaning drunkenly on a microphone on the front; ripped and faded blue jeans with dirty white tennis shoes, the laces undone. At this age, we had each identified with a particular band, like a totemic emblem to grow around, and Segis's signifier of choice was The Doors. He ate, breathed, and drank Jim Morrison. Arnold was in the middle of deciding between two other unremarkable bands from the 1980s, I forget which.

Personally I regarded myself to be far more stylish, so my totemic band of choice was obviously the Cure. Maybe the Smiths. But definitely the Cure. But you couldn't get the Cure or the Smiths paraphernalia in Texas during this time, so I had to be content with dressing as much like Robert Smith as I could, which wasn't much, since he wore cardigans and lipstick and his hair like Elizabeth Taylor after a hard night with Richard Burton. Couldn't exactly get there, from here.

Anyhow, Arnold is lugging about his usual charge: a boom box with the duo cassette player/recorder. Segis and Arnold take it everywhere they go, and as sidekick, it's Arnold's responsibility to lug it about, like a radio operator in a Vietnam war movie. The boom box comes up to Arnold's knee, and he wobbles when he walks with it.

Didi is taller than all of them, and she's got her hair pulled back. It's permed, basically in the same style as Arnold's, in the traditional lesbian cut, except Didi has clawlike bangs. She's wearing acid-washed jeans tucked into knee-high black velvet boots and a frilly denim jacket. Think Bon Jovi here.

Lined up together, we are like a rolling trip across the FM dial that Saturday night. I am, of course, public radio, over in the low 80s, while Segis and Arnold are both classic rock stations, in the high 90s and 100s, while Didi is a pop or R&B station, in the high 100s, in her New Jersey–ness.

We have beers with dinner, the Coors I had bought at the store, and Segis had brought his own case of Budweiser.

Fantastic. Dinner is simplistically short, abrupt, because they, as guests, feel as awkward as I do as host, so we get through that part of the night hastily and get down to the drinking beer and talking, which is something we are all far more accustomed to doing.

Sometime during our fifth or so beer, we hear an engine roaring from the shared driveway, between Gramma's house and ours, tires spinning out violently and gravel showering and skittering over concrete. We all look up at once from our conversation and see my Uncle Richard's truck, the high beams blaring through the dust cloud, as the source of this disturbance. I have no fear or cause for alarm as I walk out the front door to see what the trouble is.

Though he had the reputation of a ruffian and brigand in the neighborhood, Richard had never shown any of that ugly, violent behavior to our family. He had always been respectful to Dad's family, to us. He was, after all, Dad's stepbrother, and he had been a sort of older brother to us all.

Richard, dislocated as a baby and made younger brother to my father, had somehow become everyone's older brother, in the barrio.

He kept order, as kids. He was always the largest, the toughest, the guy who organized the scrapping matches between us smaller kids and jumped in when things got heated. He defended us against any unruly or unjustly aggressive neighborhood non-relations. Around him, we felt protected. He was, like I said, our oldest brother.

That would all change tonight.

In return, Dad had always kept him working, kept him hired as his first *leftenant*, kept him well rewarded and flush, until the work dried out and Dad had to take on long distance hauling for a corporate company. Richard had to go his own way at this point; leaving Brownsville wasn't in Richard's comfort zone, and so he eventually did what came natural to everyone else in the barrio, and he became muscle for a drug smuggler, one of Dad's best friends, a cousin, from way back.

For a few years after making the career change, it wasn't unusual for me to find the trappings of the smuggling trade when I'd poke around in Richard's bedroom, still looking for that mythical, Brigadoon-like collection of pornography (now sold off in a pawn shop). Once, he caught me in his room while he was sleeping, and rather than scold me for it, he had grabbed a black trash bag that recently held twenty pounds of Mexican pot from under his bed, and then shook it so that it all fell into a single corner of the bag, and then he twisted it off and told me quick, get it out of there, go smoke it with my friends. It was about $100 worth of free shake. My friends Alex and Henry and I got tired of it after a while, and tried to find out what were the largest-sized joints we could roll, since we couldn't afford Zig-Zags. We tried all sorts of different types of paper—newspaper, toilet paper, paper bags—with horrible, throat-scorching results. We eventually ended up with an unintended and clinical fascination with Pink Floyd. Good times.

The thing was, I had no idea how bad Richard's cocaine habit had become, until one afternoon when we were having an impromptu cookout on our concrete veranda. I was cutting up, making Richard and Dad laugh, and Richard was on his way out for the evening in his dressy denim, when out of nowhere his left nostril hemorrhaged horribly and a torrent of blood cascaded over his mouth, just letting loose and pouring over. Even then he was so high that I had to point it out to him because he hadn't noticed. I felt very sad for him.

Of late, things had been going bad even in the distribution/ security business, and things were no longer as good as they had been in the mid-1980s, when Richard's career in the border trades had started.

He wasn't doing well, and he had been reduced to being proud, in the way that white supremacists are proud, because they have nothing else to be proud of, really, except for the good luck of being born white in America—and if they're *really* lucky, being born in Idaho.

Richard, however, had not been born white, and it didn't help that the week before—pressed for time and harried to be elsewhere—I had offered Richard $20 to mow Gramma's lawn for her, a responsibility that had been customarily mine since I was about eight years old. I hadn't meant it to be offensive, and I was utterly naive as to what an insult that had been, but he had laughed it off, sincerely, I had thought.

The resentment had been building for years in moments like these, it would seem, and tonight, it would hit a flashpoint.

The small black truck skids to a stop after roaring and spinning its way into the driveway, and no sooner has it ground to a halt than Richard throws open the driver-side door and springs out of the cab and is stomping his way toward me, as I leave the house.

"¡*JUNIOR!*" he yells at me, as soon as he catches sight of me, "¡¿*Que le dejíste a JP?!*" ("What did you say to JP?")

He's still walking toward me, short but firm and stout, like a coked-up Sherman tank in a leather vest and cowboy hat.

I stop dead in my own tracks, uncertain. I don't usually have reason to interact with any of the natives, and it takes me a moment to figure out that Richard's talking about one of his kids.

JP is the second oldest of Richard's many abandoned and neglected children, traded off like a commodity many years before. JP was at least legitimate, having been born of Richard's first wife, Patty. When they divorced, two of the three kids they had together were abandoned by both parents. Patty had kept the oldest girl, Jenny, but felt the subsequent two were too much for a freshly divorced mother to endure. So when Gramma's infertile sister-in-law Chá-Chá asked to adopt the second-youngest girl, Cindy, Richard and ex-wife bartered: It was to be a bundled package, or nothing. Both kids, or no kids.

JP would have to go, too. To sweeten the pot, so to speak. Hell, to cook in a pot, if you so desire. To feed the girl, Cindy. But they both go, together.

Chá-Chá and her husband Robé considered it. So far, all they had was René, an illiterate mule of a teenager from Robé's first marriage who would wander off for months at a time, and then come back to drive a truck for a while, get paid, then disappear again. Chá-Chá really wanted a daughter. So they took the deal. Fuck it, they decided. There was always work to be done around the yard.

If Richard felt any guilt about this, we'll never know. Remember: Children were bartered like livestock around there, and Richard himself had been handed off as a favor to please Grampa, back when Gramma was into pleasing Grampa, before she killed him.

That being said, my only interaction with JP had been at a barrio party about three or four years before, where I had accidentally wandered into some sort of fiesta on my way home. JP was off in a corner alone: stringy, diseased, pale, and unhealthy. He was also mute. He didn't speak, just sort of grunted enthusiastically and pointed when he was excited about something. This would also make his nose run uncontrollably, so he'd make a sound like, "*Errrrr*," SNORT "*Errrrrrr*," SNORT "*Errrrrrr*," SNORT when he was happy.

He was off to one side eating a plate of food with a tortilla when I tried talking to him, out of pity. He didn't know what to make of me, what to make of my attempt to befriend and joke with him, so after a while he started swinging at me, out of joy, punching at my hips and laughing.

He meant no real harm, I could see, but he took my kindness as weakness, as something to easily dominate, because that was the only language he spoke, and so he tried to beat the pity out of me, but with a smile.

That was the last time I'd ever spoken to JP, who would be about ten years old at this point. I had never interacted with him otherwise. To have Richard, bristling now before me, in fighting posture, accusing me of doing something to his kid, to JP, left me befuddled.

Then I remember the phone call.

"Was . . . was that *him* that called?" I ask, genuinely curious.

It was just like Richard to abandon a child and then feel compelled to protect his besmirched honor.

"Yeah, and you said, 'Someone who doesn't want to talk to you!' and then hung up on him!" he yells at me, getting uncomfortably close. This, he spoke to me in English, and it was curious to hear my own words yelled back at me, like a weapon being discharged. Richard's face is pale with rage.

I've never seen this before, not from Richard. Richard was always my friend, my brother, in a way. For him to be this mad, for him to be able to reach this level of hostility and potential violence—it just never figured.

"Listen, I didn't know it was JP, man. All I heard was someone being rude on the phone, and I said something in return. I didn't mean any disrespect to your kid, man," I say all this in the most nuanced, plaintive terms. Neutral, calming. I've done this before. And I mean it, with Richard. He stands there, fuming for a minute, in conflict.

He has green eyes behind clear, frameless glasses, and they're narrowed in a way that is all danger.

I say, "Richard, come on. It's me. You know I'd never do anything to hurt your feelings intentionally." This seems to be enough, seems to quell the savagery.

He grabs the beer out of my hand and upends it, drinks it dry in one gulp as a means of neutralizing the moment, granting me pardon. But meaning it as a threat: *I can take what I want from you.*

He does this in front of Segis and Didi, who have been standing in the doorway watching this happen from the beginning but have said or done nothing. We all seem to relax a bit.

"So we're cool?" I ask.

"Yeah, we're alright," he says. "Just don't ever be mean to my kids again, Junior."

"Like I said, if I knew it was JP, it wouldn't have happened; why don't you come in and have some beers with us?"

We go back into the house and resume our evening at the now-cleared dinner table, the atmosphere much relaxed. With Richard at the table with us, we feel an odd sense of gratitude, like we're being graced by barrio royalty. We all feel this, I can tell.

It's Richard, after all, who had taken me to my first bar for a drink, when I was fifteen. I don't really remember how it happened, but I had come home after skipping school all day with Tony and found Richard drinking beer in our driveway. So I sat out with him, sneaking the occasional beer, when around ten o'clock or so he suddenly wanted to look up a certain floozy who had caught his fancy some days before. He decided right there that she needed finding.

To this day—and I mean this sincerely—that has to have been the toughest, most dangerous bar I've ever visited. It made the bar scene in *Star Wars* look like a daycare for vegan children. It was constructed from plywood planks and erected illegally in an uncleared lot near the Port of Brownsville, snug in the still-unrecognized projects, and the beer was served in bottles from an Igloo cooler, on the ground, for a dollar apiece.

Because he had decided to visit on impulse, Richard was simply in shorts: no shirt or shoes, which was obviously no problem.

The place was hopping, with a jukebox in the sagging corner of the one room playing *corridos* loudly. We got a table and sat, with Richard ordering a round of Miller High Lifes with no hassle at me being at the table. He threw a $5 bill on the table, and the waitress didn't blink, just set the bottles down and wandered off with her $3 tip. Richard spent his time questioning the other bar girls about his particular interest, and I took in the scene around me, transfixed by the people there, the lowest of the working class, people with absolutely nothing, and totally enjoying themselves in a horrible penny opera. They fascinated me.

"Junior, quit staring," Richard hissed at me, bringing me out of my reverie.

I was riveted by this one little fella across the bar, wondering about his backstory, how he had gotten that scar on his arm, what he did for a living, and where he lived. Would he stab me? Where was his knife? Gramma used to tell me stories about Grampa and his cousins drinking in bars such as this, and one night in particular when his best friend Mariano had been stabbed in the belly, split open like a melon, and how he'd clutched both sides of his stomach to bring it together to keep the beer from spilling out, bemoaning how much he'd spent on beer that night, and how they all had laughed about it later. . . .

These were *those* people, I was understanding.

"Hey, he's gonna get pissed!" Richard had said and smacked my arm, and then I realized I had been staring, so I smiled and waved, and the guy just sorta waved back, in a way that wasn't friendly.

The girl Richard had been looking for had already fucked off back to Mexico, and so we ended the night by going swimming in a pool at an apartment "complex" where Richard knew someone, at two in the morning. It had been a really great night.

Another time, he came home drunk the night before Mother's Day with a Grammy-nominated accordionist, and they set up a party in the driveway. They had made quite a ruckus arriving, had awoken me and I'd wandered out like a cranky neighbor. Richard was the first one to notice me.

"Hey, June. Don't tell your mom. That's a famous guy, on the accordion. I don't know his name. You want a beer? Don't be an asshole."

It was Esteban Jordan, or Steve Jordan, who had been in a movie by David Byrne, *True Stories*. I recognized him right away because of the one-eye thing. Holy shit: This guy had been in a movie with John Goodman and David fricken Byrne! *No one would believe me,* I thought.

This was my first brush with someone famous, besides Freddy Fender, who had knocked up my Aunt Diana in 1969, who had apparently brushed up against Freddy more than once.

I said, "Hey, you're that guy in that movie with David Byrne! In that scene, at the Mexican bar, with the red lighting, with John Goodman!" Steve didn't acknowledge me. He looked away.

His flunkie answered, though: "He was in *three* movies, *mang!* But two of them didn't get released yet. He's a pro, *mang!*"

Steve was elusive, aloof, wouldn't really engage except to play the accordion that night.

I slipped back into my house and found my microcassette recorder, which I had because I was still working for the *Brownsville Herald* as a stringer at this time, and then I slipped back out to the party to record the rest of the evening. I needed proof that he'd been there; proof for whom, I'm not exactly sure.

Apparently Mr. Jordan was releasing a new album, and all these songs he was playing were "bootleg, *mang!*" When he found out I worked for the *Herald,* he was reluctant to continue, worried that I might write a bad review, and I didn't have the heart to tell him that, besides the fact that I didn't write record reviews, all Spanish songs sounded exactly alike to me, and no one would really care about his new album. But please: Play on.

And, as predicted, no one really cared about the chance meeting with Steve Jordan in my driveway, in the middle of the night, on Mother's Day, except for Basilio, my mentor at the *Herald.* "No shit?" he asked.

"Yeah, no shit. He even played a couple songs for my Gramma, at her window, for Mother's Day," I said.

"*No shit?*" He asked again, impressed.

"No shit. I think he was there for the coke."

"Hunh," he said. "Can I listen to it?"

'Sure," I said, and handed him the "bootleg, *mang!*" micro-cassette tape and then heard Basilio chuckling for the next two hours.

"You're a hoot, Domingo," he said, afterward.

Basilio had taken a liking to me the year before, when we originally started working together and I had shown myself to be very much a part of the Hunter Thompson school of journalism, when I came in half drunk from a night out on South Padre Island during spring break, while all the other high schoolers reeled in horror at my terrible state, dressed in a camouflage jacket and matted hair, then managed to write a six-hundred-word feature that made the front page, while their high school stuff had ended up as paragraphs in the H section, if used at all. Basilio had bought me a Dr Pepper, and copyedited my story himself, had been very much impressed. We became fast friends.

But this? Steve Jordan in my driveway, coked up and playing Mother's Day songs while I niggled and prodded him and his entourage? I was creating a legacy here. All thanks to Richard.

That had been our friendship, up until this night. I always felt safe with him, protected. Had no reason ever to fear that the mask he wore with other people could be turned to face me.

When I invite him inside that night, the danger is over. It will then be a good and happy night, drinking with Segis, like equals. I feel it.

We sit around the kitchen table, trading stories and laughing as usual, and the mood has changed since the unpleasantness of earlier.

But then the hour has grown later, and I have grown weary of the bad music, weary of the company, and I'm looking for bed, suddenly.

I say, "Hey, guys, I hate to do this, but I'm really kind of tired and I have stuff to do tomorrow; can we call it a night?"

This doesn't go over at all well with the boys drinking at the table.

Segis makes an attempt to keep me from retiring, as he's not done with the drinking, and I resist, saying that I'm done, and Richard pipes in, says, "They can stay. They're drinking with me."

I don't take this in the least as usurping; in fact, I feel better that he takes the responsibility of host. The house will be safe. "Great," I say. "Just please make sure the door is locked when you guys go."

"Don't worry about the fucking door," Richard barks, and the whole room sort of goes quiet, even though Ozzy is playing on the stereo.

I hadn't noticed, but he has been steadily fuming since joining us at the table. When I said I had something to do tomorrow, he had decided to take it badly. He had taken it as me posturing. Perhaps he had been right. I really can't be sure.

I say goodnight, empty my final beer, and then retire to my parents' room. This is the only room in the house with an air-conditioning window unit. They have a queen sized bed, a recliner, and a TV. It's like being in a hotel room, and I'm looking forward to sleeping in it that night. The door closed behind me; I undress down to my Y-fronts with the window unit turned to high.

The drone it makes cancels any noise coming from the kitchen. The room is dark, pitch black with the curtains drawn, and I very quickly drop off into a heavy sleep.

What happens next is a long time coming, but completely unexpected.

I'm dead asleep when I hear the door to Mom and Dad's room explode open and slam into the wall behind it, the doorknob burying itself into the wood paneling.

I sit up and twist in bed and can see the door frame illuminated by the hallway light behind it, and just barely make out a figure rushing into the room before I'm punched violently in the back of the head and then once in the clavicle, just under my throat, as I'm grabbed by my hair and yanked forward. I have enough sense to grab the hands that are grabbing at my hair. I'm pulled sprawling out of the bed, and I fall to the floor, in a crumple, at the base of the bed, where suddenly I'm being kicked in the neck and torso by something that feels and smells like a cowboy boot.

This is all in the dark, and I have not had time to consider or think about what might be happening, and I think I might have caught a voice—sounding like Richard's—when I feel the hard sharp thumps of pointed cowboy boots kicking me in the chest, the stomach, the chest. I roll up with my arms up around my head and figure out where the kicks are coming from, and so I roll into the kicks instinctively. The lights suddenly go on, and I jump up and see Richard standing in front of me at the end of the boots, and it doesn't make any sense to me what's happening.

His cowboy hat is off and his face is a mask of venom, his green eyes wide and dilated behind his glasses and his balding head covered in perspiration. He is breathing heavily from the beating he's just given me.

The light going on has shocked him into stopping for a heartbeat, and I'm standing there, my body stinging and red from all the shots I've just taken in my underwear, and I hear Segis shouting, "Richard! Richard! No! Stop it! Stop it! I didn't mean nothing!"

It had been Segis who had run in here, had snapped on the lights behind Richard, and who was now trying to get between Richard and me. The shock of the light now gone, Richard suddenly resumes his assault, this time on both me and Segis.

Segis tries to get in Richard's way, but is leveled quickly with a single hard kick to the balls, and he falls to the side while Richard charges at me. I lean back into a window and curtains and just sort of thrust my hands forward to try to stifle his punches before they come, and it seems to work, seems to keep him from summoning too much power, and I can take what blows he's mustering. Richard doesn't seem to be much of a fighter if you fight back, I'm understanding, even here. He's swinging fat, wide haymakers at my head and arms, and I'm able to keep the full force of the blows from hitting me by flaring my elbows and ducking my head, which is the only way I'm able to survive the second onslaught.

Still, I'm scared out of my mind at this point. A stout little fucker, Richard could generate a lot of gravity behind a punch, if he did it right.

I was a skinny boy, weighing about 140 pounds at this point. and aside from the few scraps a male gets into in high school and the ones Richard himself had arranged against Joe and the kids across the street, I'd never been in a real fight, never been hit like this. Richard, on the other hand, weighs about 250, and makes his living slapping people around. He throws his weight around, so to speak, and he has a lot of weight to throw.

Finally, I'm able to yell out, "Richard! Richard! What the *hell* are you *doing,* man? You're my fucking uncle! You're not supposed to be *doing* this!!"

I say this as the last wave of blows glances off my head, and I use my arms to entangle his and keep it from being too easy to hit my head again. Already I can feel that a few of them have gotten through and my left eye is starting to swell, starting to throb deeply in a way that I know far too well now. He then changes tactics and grabs me and swings me around and shoves me against the dresser.

"Shut up! Shut up!" he yells, pointing at me, "Stop your talking! You think you're so fucking smart, you and all your fucking family! You think you're so much better than us because you got psychology and school and you read all those books! I don't care, Junior! I don't fucking care! I'll fucking kill you and your fucking father, Junior! You can't just make us feel like we're nothing and then just leave! I don't give a shit! Your sisters are up there in that college just fucking around! They're just *putas!* You're not better than us because we're fucking Mexicans! You think you're fucking white people! You're not white! You're just like the rest of us! And don't you fucking think I won't kill your father, Junior; I'll kill him! I don't care! I'll go to fucking prison! I'll fucking do it! I'll fucking shoot him!"

I'm reeling backward at this hatred, this gestalt of the entire barrio gushing out of Richard's mouth, like a spigot of vitriol, a toxic explosion of gossip, envy, and anger convulsing out of this poor, stupid dumb beast who suddenly became a vehicle for the sentiments that the whole barrio had wanted to tell the Martinezes, that we didn't belong here, on Oklahoma Avenue, in their barrio, by using the only other outsider, who had nothing, and so much to prove.

"Jesus fucking Christ, Richard; listen to what you're saying. What the hell brought this on?" I'm legitimately confused, and

I make my way to the mirror in my mom's bedroom, moving past Segis, who's sitting on the floor, holding his testicles, and I see that my eye is red and white and swelling, will soon be deeply bruised, the blood vessels in the white totally burst. Lots of punches got through to that side. My lips are ripped open on the inside and I have to spit out a lot of blood, but not a single hit to the nose, I notice. Richard can't throw a straight punch.

The betrayal of it, the hostility coming from so close within the family, and then bared so openly at me, I just can't get my mind around it.

"What did you say about your Gramma?" Richard demands from me suddenly.

"What?"

"What did you say? Did you call her a bitch or not? Did you call your Gramma a bitch?"

I feel caught here; I'm not sure what I've said, what this means.

Here, Segis calls out from the floor, "No, Richard! He didn't! He said it a long time ago! He didn't mean it like that!"

"You shut up!" Richard spits at Segis, who complies readily. "Did you say it or not?"

"He . . . He . . . " stammers Segis, " . . . it wasn't like that."

"What the fuck are you two *talking* about?" I yell, my mouth filling with blood again. I spit it out, on the carpet. It makes a puddle.

"*Junior!* Did you call your Gramma a bitch or not?" he demands, furious again.

"I . . . I don't know! I say a lot of shit!" I yell, trying to tell the truth. "Maybe! Probably! I don't remember! Why do you people listen to me? I say a lot of shit!"

And then he charges at me again.

His first punch this time hits me clear on the mouth, and I feel something click, in the architecture of my skull. The next few punches, I see coming, and I block them mostly with my arms and elbows. I start to get the hang of it, at this point.

Richard's not a trained fighter, just an average brawler, only has two swings and a planted right kick in him, if he can get his leg up.

In fact, the one time Richard went up against a trained fighter—a black belt from a *tae kwon do* school near the airport—Richard didn't do so well. One morning I was lurking near his door, trying to determine if he was home or asleep, and thinking of possibly risking entering and pillaging a fresh skin magazine, when he called out: "*Quien esta alli?*" ("Who's there?")

I held back, then said, "Oh, it's just June."

"Help me out of bed, please," he said, almost inaudibly. I entered and saw that he was still in bed, having trouble putting his feet on the floor.

"What happened to you?"

"Oh, I went up against Benavidez last night, at a club."

"The guy from the tae kwon do school?" I asked, intrigued.

"Yeah, he kicked my ass. I said something about his girlfriend in the parking lot, and he kicked the shit out of me. I'd never been hit like that before. I ended up under my truck. I stayed under there until he went inside."

"Hunh," I thought. This was news indeed; it was like Jackie Chan fighting Godzilla, with Jackie winning. But this also created a perfect snapshot of the barrio boy kings: pretending to be tough guys, but having no discipline or training. They were just cock-strong field hands talking shit.

But this night, I've still never been in a real fight, not in the life or death way it seems, and Richard outweighs me by one hundred pounds and a ton of anger. My best way out of it is to talk my way out, I decide.

"Richard, you've got to stop this," I say, and something is wrong with my mouth. My jaw doesn't align, I realize. And something is wrong with my teeth. I run my tongue over my front teeth and can feel one of the incisors split in two, cracked down the middle. Richard is wearing a ring, just for this purpose.

I spit out a bit of tooth, and it hits the dresser with a click. Fuck. "Jesus, look at what you did, you fucking bastard," I say.

I stop to look in my mother's mirror, and Richard sits on the bed, behind me, winded. My eye is swelling shut, and my bottom lip is torn open. "Jesus," I say.

"Shut up!" he yells from the bed. "You called her a bitch last week because she only lent you five dollars!"

I stop. I look at Segis. "Is *that* what this is about?"

"No! No!" screams Segis. "That's not right! It was a long time ago! I said he wasn't just an asshole to you and your kids, that he was an asshole to everyone! Not just us! That's what I said, man!"

Still, I couldn't put together what was happening, what had happened after I left.

"So you were lying?" Richard says to Segis. Richard gets up, looms over Segis. "Hunh?" he challenges Segis. "You were lying? Is that it?" He tries to kick Segis again, who rolls on his side like a puppy and gets kicked in the ass.

"No!" yells Segis from the floor. "I just said he was an asshole to everyone, man, even his Gramma!"

"Jesus, Richard; is that what this is about? You've known me all your life; you know how I am. I just say shit about everything without meaning it, to make a joke. You used to laugh at it all the time; I did it to make you laugh. You were like a brother to me," I say.

"Shut up!" he says and lunges at me again, but this time, I'm out of reach, and his glasses fall off and he almost steps on them. We end up shuffling and in a weird shifting of position, I end up near them, and I pick them up, hand them back to him. He takes them and puts them on without thinking about it.

"Just shut up, Junior! You don't use your psychology and books on me! You're not smarter than me! I know who you are! I saw you grow up, you *pendéjo!* You and your family! I've seen everything about you! You think you're so much better than all of us because you try to speak good English and go to school! But you're from *here* like all of us! You're *poor*, your father is *Mexican!* Like all of us! Your sisters are just sluts who think their shit don't stink, like your mom! And your dad is just *weak!* He's *weak*, Junior! I could kill him, and your brother Dan, and your whole fucking family if I want! I'll go to prison, I don't care! You fucking disrespect your *grandmother?* What's wrong with you, Junior? You don't have no respect for *nobody!* For none of us! You disrespect all of us! You're not *better* than us, Junior! You're *not!* You hate us because you're just like us!"

Through this last tirade, Richard has broken down, weeping, in dangerous spurts, his hand to his eyes, and continues to cry, on his own, me and Stegis standing or sitting around him, unsure.

I almost want to hug him, hold him, like my older brother, crying, because up until the point he restructured my jaw, I still loved him. He had nothing more, nothing. All he could do to save his dignity was to threaten to kill my family and take the prison sentence, he thought, the poor pathetic bastard.

To be totally honest, everything he's said tonight is true.

As I stand there, beaten up, and watch him cry, the detached observer in me is taking notes, in my mind, so I can write the story down one day.

When he is finished crying, Richard picks up his hat, and I say, "Jesus, Richard; you were like one of the family . . . " and, with what is probably shame, he walks past Segis on the floor, past Didi who is standing by the door, watching all this happen, crying still, and he leaves.

We hear Richard's truck light up and tear out of the driveway, and I take that time to find my shirt and pantaloons and get redressed, with Didi's help. I say to Segis, "Jesus fucking Christ, what the hell did you say to him?"

He's immediately defensive. "*Nothingk, mang!* I didn't say nothing! Except that we were just sitting there after you left and he said, 'That guy's an asshole,' and I just said, 'Yeah, he's an asshole to everyone'!"

"And that's all you said?"

"Well, he was talking about your Gramma, that you said something disrespectful to her, and I just said you called her a bitch once, and then he got mad."

"Nice."

"I'm sorry, man. Really sorry."

"Nice fucking work."

I want to see what kind of shape the rest of the house is in, so he and Didi help me limp through the house, and it is mostly in place, nothing broken or shattered. When I look out the window, I see Arnold hiding outside, cowering by the rear left axle of Didi's car. Not exactly the sort of person you want around you in an emergency.

Didi gets a wet towel and some ice for my face, and I take it, put it heavily on my head. I've been pummeled, beaten horribly. Disfigured. This had been the thing I'd been threatened with my whole life, as the most terrible thing that could happen to you—losing your manhood in a fight—and a very small part of me is proud that I've been through it, come out the other side. Though my eye looks terrible, my jaw is out of alignment, and my tooth is cracked. But otherwise, I've gotten through without a scratch. Bring it on, world, I feel.

We hear Richard's truck peel out of the driveway in a terrific roar and when we feel safe enough to leave the safety of my parents' penetrated bedroom to lock the doors, we do so. The pain of the beating has started to settle in like a flu, and my arms and chest have started to bruise brilliantly, and I can't stop spitting blood, but still I can't stop myself from thinking, "This isn't so bad. This is what I've been frightened of my whole life, *and it isn't so bad. . . .*" I've been beaten so badly, it's as if I've been in a car wreck.

But I'm crying at this point, I realize, into the wet towel. Not from the pain, so much, but from the horror of what has just happened at the hands of someone I trusted thoroughly. Didi is holding the towel to my face as I'm weeping into it quietly, and I realize I'm thinking about this, about the pain, about the beating, as an inevitability, that it wasn't as painful as I thought it was going to be, like the beating had been understood, was a foregone conclusion, and I had passed the test.

I could leave Texas. I beat Texas.

I had a personal understanding that if I stayed here long enough, stayed in Brownsville, that I would get the beating of my life like this at some point. Never knew why, exactly, only that it was because I was different.

And it didn't hurt, really, except for the shame of being marked like that, and having to mingle in society with a beaten face. That is the real problem, I'm thinking: facing my employers and coworkers, people I've begun to respect, with the mark of my origins imprinted loudly upon my face.

I ask them to leave, Didi and Segis and Arnold. Didi is herself in tears at this point, and Arnold won't even come indoors for fear of not having the option of bolting like a rabbit for the nearest hole.

When they leave, I grab the towel, now saturated in tears and blood, and walk across the driveway to the closest comfort I can think of at the time: Gramma.

This is a mistake.

I let myself in and walk through the dark house to her bedroom and wake her up, in the dark, warn her in Spanish before I turn on the light that Richard has gone crazy and beaten me up.

When I snap on the light, she pauses for only a second, and then puts on her bathrobe and makes her way to the refrigerator in the hallway and proceeds to pull out ice trays and peanut butter, jars full of strange things, anything with cold, and places various things against my head and tells me to hold them there. All the while, she mumbles prayers in low, resolved despair that communicate to me clearly that she, too, has long expected this to happen.

She sits me in her bedroom, in front of the triangular corner altar she built before Grampa's death, which still has the Polaroid shots of Grampa's face, bloodied and pulped, from the night his own brothers had set upon him and had beaten him bloody.

Gramma had done this very thing, in this very spot, for him. Cold compresses to his face, blaming him for it happening under her breath.

This time, however, with me, Gramma isn't taking sides. Or rather, she is taking a side, and it's not mine.

Her manner feels more like she is a reluctant nurse in a POW camp and I am the POW responsible for fire-bombing her village, some weeks back. Maybe raping her unborn sister, to boot.

She isn't exactly sympathetic, is what I'm getting at, as I sit there whimpering, and when Richard unexpectedly returns.

We hear his truck roar back into the driveway, and Gramma immediately gets up and goes to the door to warn him that I am there, in her bedroom.

At this point, I think I just gave up, accepting that there are no—or never have been—any safe places in the barrio, not at the hands of these people. I am a giraffe in a community of mules.

If my heart was hard and dark before, it has become the impenetrable matter of a black hole now.

Richard stomps by her and looks in the bedroom, looks me full in the face in the bright light, at what he'd done, and Gramma holds onto his shoulder in the senile, beguiling way she usually reserved for pleading with men when she felt infantilism would better serve her cause.

"*Déjalo, déjalo,*" she says. "*Ya lloró. Bien a comer.*" ("Leave him be. He's already cried. Come and eat.")

"You got what you deserved!" Richard yells. "I mean it about your father, Junior! I'll fucking kill him, I don't care!"

"*Déjalo, lla,*" Gramma continues to coo, not acknowledging that the adopted cuckoo is threatening the life of her natural-born son. If she realizes what Richard is saying, she doesn't care.

"*¡Mira, lo que hiso!*" I yell at her in Spanish, as she begins to cook for him in the kitchen. ("Look at what he fucking did to me.")

In Spanish: "Listen to what he's fucking *saying!* He's saying he's going to *kill* your *only son,* and you don't *do anything!*"

"*Stop fighting, you two,*" she says in Spanish, pulling Richard through the door, and then lighting up her stove.

"I did it for you!" Richard says to her in Spanish, as her back is turned and he's sitting at the plastic covered table, his eyes streaming.

"Yes, yes," she responds, finding a pan from her sink. "Yes, yes, yes."

"He called you a bitch and who knows what else he's said. His whole family is like that. They think they're better than us," Richard pleads to her hunched back, while Gramma continues grunting her encouragement. Gramma, I could tell, in her twisted way, was deeply moved.

As Gramma continues to make Richard's breakfast, I walk out the front door, leave the bloodied towel behind on the chair I last saw my Grampa in.

It would be a long time before I would be able to stand near her again and not want to punch her teeth out after this. Gramma, I could take; we weighed about the same.

It is close to 3:00 a.m. when I call my sister Marge in Kingsville and leave a message for my parents, saying, "Mom, Dad; this is June (sniff). Richard beat me up, really awful. Please come home. I don't know what to do."

Segis calls me after I make that call, and the phone rings both in our house and at Gramma's, and I talk to him for over an hour before we realize Richard has been on the remote line, listening all along. I simply can't escape this nightmare. Can't wake up from it.

At the end of the call, I have Richard laughing and saying he's sorry before he hangs up, and I never talk to him again. Still haven't. Richard woke up early and disappeared the next day.

The sacrifice he made that night, killing his connection to the Martinez family, us kids who truly loved him, I think affected him more than it did me, in the end. Richard had been subconsciously chosen to tell us what everyone really felt about us, to put us in our place, since we were becoming too "uppity" for the barrio, while they were falling further into declension and disarray. And after this violent display, Richard was never again a part of our family, a part of our fold, or accepted back into theirs, the people who hated us in that barrio.

I took the beating, I took the venom, because I'd always been the most vulnerable, the boy with the mouth, Freudian as that image is. But I was leaving anyway.

Thing was, Richard was staying in the barrio. Richard's life could have been much better, much more, if he still had the love of my father's family. I would have loved Richard still. Today.

But he lost that, that night, by doing that. And we lost a very happy memory.

Chapter 23

AFTERWARD

Mom and Dad pulled into the driveway around noon.

Segis, feeling responsible, had shown up around ten o'clock and tried to apologize. In all honesty I never really blamed him for anything other than just being his trusting, innocent, simple self. You could no more blame a soccer-playing kid in the third-world for stepping on a landmine and losing his leg, and the legs of a friend. More to the point, Segis meant nothing by it. And later, he meant even less.

Mom and Dad listened to our story, and Dad grabbed my chin and forced my head this way, and that way, and then up, to see what was disfiguring, what would mark, what was permanent.

All the blood vessels in one eye had burst; my mouth was so swollen, I couldn't speak without first spitting.

While this was terrible to deal with, what hurt most was the look on my mother's face, as she studied me. She was half ashamed, half accusatory, like she, too, believed I somehow deserved it, probably for drinking at home, with Richard. But I was accustomed to this response, from Mom.

What was really terrible was the offers of pity I received from Gina, the girl I had fallen in love with, whom I had dated for like, three weeks, and really liked, but didn't realize I felt totally outclassed—at the time, I had just felt weird, strangely nervous, but couldn't figure out why—until eventually I realized it was because I couldn't meet standards, as a boyfriend. I had nothing to offer her. Which didn't stop me from falling further in love with her, as adolescent boys do. That's why the Cure had meant so much to me, at the time, because of Gina, with all its sweet bitterness, the soundtrack for the lovelorn. And when I finally got her on the phone to tell her what had happened, she paused, asked me to hold, and then came back and said her dad, the very reverend Judge Hinojosa, had offered me a place to stay, if I needed it, and I thanked her, and knew enough to feel totally humiliated, to be completely ashamed of where I came from. And always very grateful to him for the offer.

Dad had listened to me and Segis with obvious disgust, frustration. He was going out of his mind with rage by two o'clock. He was vengeful and horribly ashamed in that machismo way at the possibility of impotency, that he could not protect his family, yet again, even after Richard had threatened his life.

The sheriff's department was called, and another morbidly obese deputy had driven by around one in the afternoon, saying there was nothing he could do now, should have called when it was happening. Dad went inside the house and came back with a photo of Richard and the deputy's boss, the High Sheriff Alex Perez, arm in arm, with two other drug dealers, drinking beer.

"Oh," said the deputy. "That guy. *Riche*," recognizing Richard.

After he left, Dad turned on both Segis and me. "Why didn't you both gang up on him, at once? You two together? Kicked his ass!"

Segis answered, "Well, because of respect," he said, confused. "He's Domingo's uncle . . ."

Dad hissed at this, cursed. Spit and nearly punched Segis himself.

I had a better answer: fear. Richard would have killed us then, if we had fought back. This was a man without an Id in those ten minutes. He was unchecked, insane. Anything we would have brought against him, he would have turned on us, double. We were kids, dealing with a werewolf on cocaine. This isn't hyperbole: He would have killed one of us, or both. Dad's macho pride wasn't there to see it.

Dad called Dan, who was living in Seattle at the time with his friend Dennis, and made Dan feel like this was his fault. Dan felt horrible, and I got on the phone, told him it wasn't his fault: There was nothing anyone could do. Richard just spiraled out of control. Dan was relieved to hear me speak, I could tell.

Eventually, Dad got so wound up, he worked up his courage and drove off in the Taurus, infuriated, but quiet. Mom tried to stop him, knowing how something like this could turn out. She loved him still, at this point. She did not buy into this barrio drama machismo bullshit, with knives and guns. Mom was America.

But Dad didn't listen to her and he went looking for Richard, like he'd been expected to do all along, like it had been scripted.

Every ounce of courage was summoned and Dad drove off knowing he was now getting into a fight that had been building since Richard was brought home as a one-year-old in exchange for a pair of brake pads, a muffler, and a four-barrel carburetor.

Richard had shoved Dad into a remote corner of the nest, and Dad now had to prove himself against the neighborhood bully, his own stepbrother.

We all held our breath, and the guilt I felt was crushing, bringing this unconscious resentment in the barrio to a head once again.

Richard, in the meantime, had quickly converted to a fundamentalist hyper-Pentecostal church group that happened to be leaving for Michigan that morning, to work in a diner washing dishes and helping build more evangelical churches for the poor along the way.

Beating me, and having to own up to it, had been a mystical experience. He'd found Pentecostal Jesus, who spoke in tongues and snake venom. So he boarded the van and had been gone by three o'clock that next day.

And his cowardice, his hollow shallow crust of a fighter had crumbled that day, when Dad chased him from house to house, from hideout to hideout, and his biological family had lied to my Dad to keep Richard safe, hidden, and then put him on an Econoline headed north. And when Dad came home again, unbloodied, untainted, and safe, he was bigger to me and Mom, because nothing had happened. That was civilized.

After that, Dad never quite re-integrated with the barrio. He had already been feeling a sort of drift—nothing he'd ever mentioned, or quite been able to place, but after this, all his friendships went cold and he never really tried to pursue them. Richard, when he returned over a year later, caught Dad in a Christian logic riddle, and apologized to him in such a way that Dad, now also a good Christian, was forced to forgive him and had no choice in the matter, like they were competing players in Dungeons and Dragons. But Dad never forgot what Richard had done.

Richard continued to live a remarkably miserable life. He married an "elder sister" in the church he'd joined, who already had three kids, and he added two more.

Then he moved on, and married again, this time with two more kids added to the original assembly of the third wife. He became diminutive, shrunken, defeated. Absent of joy.

His one source of delight eventually became the love he rediscovered from his discarded boy, JP, the kid from his first wife who'd called that Father's Day and I'd hung up on.

JP had learned all the mechanics of every sort of truck, from the gasoline engines of the 1970s to the thirteen-geared diesel engines of the long-haul tractors. School was never a problem because he just never went: JP's life had always revolved around trucks, and by the time he was twenty years old, he was making a good living working as a long-haul driver. He could drive like a Minotaur, to hear everyone tell it, driving cross-country and making enough to keep his dad happy. He did this just to get the approval and attention of his father. With checks that big, he certainly got a lot of both.

JP had forgiven all and had spent his every waking hour hungry for the attention of his Pa; his *real* Pa, Richard.

And now, flush with cash and a shiny new pickup, JP managed to get back in Richard's orbit, and things were going well for them. Richard had found a renewed joy in his abandoned son.

They would go out on the town like pals, like equals, and one night after they were out drinking late, JP dropped Richard off at the trailer park where his third or fourth family was housed, and as he was driving home drunk, JP fell asleep at the wheel of his shiny new pickup and was killed on a bare South Texas highway, had the good luck to run into the only tree for miles around.

"It's sad," my own father called to tell me.

I waited a moment before I answered.

I wanted to say, "No, it isn't. Fuck him. I'm glad that Richard lived to see his abandoned son die."

But I didn't say it. At least, I hope I didn't say it. It suddenly dawned on me that the reason JP called that day was because he had been reaching out to the father who had abandoned him, on Father's Day. Richard's response had not been about Gramma at all, but about his guilt, his failure at being a father.

Anyhow, Gramma had had a life insurance policy taken out on JP, like she had on all the young men of the barrio, myself and Dan and Derek included, without any one of us or our parents knowing. JP's death was like winning the lottery. Again. She made $15,000 out of it, gave his family $1,000 to help bury him, and $2,000 to Richard, to help ease his suffering.

I tried to feel something after I ended the call with Dad. I tried to feel horror, pity, disgust. Satisfaction. Ran my tongue over the chip in my tooth.

I felt nothing.

Chapter 24

SLEEPING WITH MONSTERS

Dan had moved to Seattle because he had nothing going on in South Texas, after he'd been honorably discharged from the Army. He'd married and divorced some Georgian girl in a traditional Army romance for twenty-year-olds (over in three months), had defended South Korea from Kim Jong Il, and could order a beer and a blow job in flawless Korean. But he had nothing going on now and was feeling dislocated, wandering.

His best friend, Dennis, had also been in the Army, had been stationed in Fort Lewis, Washington, just south of Tacoma. As is usually the case, Dennis had met some provincial hussy, a woman named Mary, just like my sister who broke his heart, from a town an hour or so east of Seattle called Enumclaw, or perhaps White Horse . . . I don't remember. It was one of those isolated redneck mountain towns in Washington that makes San Antonio look like Paris, and as a result, Dennis wanted to move to Seattle to be closer to her and other girls he could sleep with as a career waiter. Dennis, even in the Army, was a career waiter.

He needed Dan, though, in order to do it, so he convinced Dan to make the move north. This was about a year before the incident with Richard.

I had been in school at Texas A&I, having a tough time of it and wondering what the hell I was still doing in South Texas.

I had imagined that Texas A&I—being a certified "college"—might have been a bit more liberal, would have been populated with forward-minded hipsters, like-minded kids into music, film, and fashion. This was not the case; the "A&I" stood for "agriculture and industry," and not "arts and industry," as I somehow managed to convince myself. It was a small metropolis of rednecks, full of the sort of people to whom I'd already endured enough exposure, in the numerical isolation of Brownsville. These people were farmers, or the children of farmers, and were going to college to find a better way to manage their farms, tend to their livestock, and otherwise evolve their trade. Still, I tried.

Late one night during this debacle, Dan and Dennis drove into the campus and looked me up in my dorm, and I came down to the parking lot to say good-bye, glumly. Dennis had convinced Dan that starting over in Texas was a wash and that he needed to be in Seattle, with him, paying half the rent. I'd heard the word *Seattle* before but wouldn't have been able to point to it on a map of the United States, so I had no idea what they were in for, how far they were driving, and therefore hadn't made a fuss about saying good-bye. I probably thought he was just going to another part of Texas.

Dan, though, he had an idea of the geographical separation. His eyes welled up with tears as he hugged me and said a long good-bye, for the second time.

Dennis was eager to get moving, to drive west out of Texas in his used 1983 Mustang LX. He was never much for style. Or, rather, he had the style of a fatherless, nappy-headed misogynist kid in the 4-H Club.

Dennis had been my sister Mare's high school boyfriend, and Dan's best friend. Sort of. There was just something about

Dennis that Dan never quite trusted. Dennis had, at one time, felt some very sincere feelings for Mare, but after a few years, she had decided to end it with him. She had her reasons, I'm sure. And something snapped in Dennis, after. He became icy, reptilian. Watched a lot of sports.

By this time, though, he had been brought into the Martinez fold and had been accepted thoroughly, being Dan's best friend and Mare's erstwhile boyfriend. Dennis knew all our secrets, many as there were. He had arranged for my ugliest.

During the time that Dan was stationed in Korea, my sisters were all in Kingsville, at Texas A&I themselves; Dad was doing long-haul trucking; and Mom was busy grooming her dreams of escape. Dennis, too, seemed to lose his navigation.

He wasn't going to school, was living at home with his single mom, Necie (soubriquet of Denise), who was quite partial to dating the few black men who lived in Brownsville. Rather than being socially stigmatized by this predilection, it actually gave her some sort of raw appeal with the Mexican men of the area, like my father. It sexualized her thoroughly, I think because the prejudicial logic was, "Well, if she'll sleep with black men, she'll have *no problem* sleeping with me. . . ." So no one had a problem with Necie's boyfriends, all four of them, who were the rhythm section of a local salsa band.

Anyhow, Dennis, at this time, was delivering pizza for Domino's and feeling pretty lost. He still came by the nearly vacant house, still needed the anchoring of the large swarm of family we had once provided for him, being a single kid to a single mom, but by this point, all that was left was me, and he and I weren't exactly simpatico. I didn't mind Dennis anymore, had by this point learned to cope with people who had suspicions of bound books, who wouldn't read anything larger than a sports page and felt that the atrocious music coming off the South Texas FM radio waves was for nothing more than getting girls to wobble their naughty bits. It was a survival mechanism, learning to coexist with people like him, because they outnumbered me greatly.

He had no more friends in Brownsville. I had no friends either. And so one Friday night, when he wanted some diversion, some chance at being out, Dennis had no one else to phone except for me.

He knew I'd be home at ten o'clock on a Friday night. He called on Gramma's line and I answered quickly so that it wouldn't wake her, over at her house, and he demanded, "Hey, get dressed. Come with me to Matamoros." He didn't want to go alone; I was good for that.

I said, "Sure. I'll be ready in fifteen minutes."

It wasn't the first time he'd called like that. Another time he called quite late, came by, and picked me up in his Domino's Pizza truck, said there was something he really wanted to show me. I was asleep, but I agreed. I was game. Let's go.

He drove us at top speed through the midnight streets into Brownsville proper, into the old downtown area, and then steered us into neighborhoods I'd never before had reason to visit. He brought the truck right up to a large, unkempt and crumbling concrete cemetery gate, right smack in the middle of old Brownsville town. I'd never seen it before. I'd read about it. It was the oldest cemetery in the city, dating back to the Fort Brown period, from the origins of the area, and the city had grown around it.

"Get out and open the gate," he told me.

"No fucking way."

"Come on, don't be a puss!" he said.

"It's one in the morning! I'm not opening the gate!" I said.

"Junior, don't be a puss all your life," he repeated, something he'd say to me when I'd have misgivings about doing as he asked. He said it often, and with real venom when he said the word, *Junior.* "Open the fucking gate."

With encouragement like that, at sixteen, I got out and opened the gate, then got back into the Domino's Pizza truck, and then Dennis turned off the headlights and crawled the truck slowly down the main path, which descended narrowly through a vast, open graveyard, glowing eerily in the moonlight.

In the low glowing light, the cemetery looked like something out of a George Romero wank fantasy. It was wide open and rolling, with unusual aboveground crypts among the forgotten tombstones, uncommon in the area. Very likely, all this is made up in my reconstructing the memory of that night, because I can see everything clearly in my mind, though it would probably be impossible, unless it was a full moon, which I'm not saying it wasn't.

Anyhow, I was expecting a scary scene, or Dennis getting very quiet, then shouting loudly, or maybe a fellow driver jumping out from behind a tree—asinine and unimaginative behavior, relevant to the limits of Dennis's creativity.

But what I certainly didn't expect was the impossible number of corpses climbing out of their graves, these huddled and dark shapes in the moonlight, groaning and yelping, hollering and moving unreasonably fast for dead people, all coming out of the fucking ground and chasing us down in the truck.

"Holy shit, Dennis, there's something moving out there," I said, starting to realize what I was seeing, and slowly going out of my mind with fear. "There's lots of things moving out there, Dennis. Holy fucking shit, Dennis, are you seeing this? There's fucking zombies! Fucking zombies! They're behind us, Dennis! Get us out of here! It's like a fucking movie! Get us out of here! What the fuck are you doing! Why aren't you driving! Get us out of here! Now! Now! Fucking *now!*"

Dennis, meanwhile, had a wide smile on his face and was letting the truck crawl slowly with his foot hovering lightly on the brake pedal like a good sport, letting the idling engine pull us through the cemetery while the hollering zombies started to catch us, the brake lights illuminating in red a horde of bodies stumbling behind us.

"Roll up your window, at least!" I yelled to Dennis, who surprisingly complied, and locked his door. I was leaning on my door and making certain that the window was up and tight and locked down, and I could see in the moonlight that there was definitely a horde of zombies behind us, and many more from the surrounding hills lurching and stumbling down slowly to join in the human-eating fun.

My mind reeled: It wasn't Halloween, it was way too large and coordinated to be a joke, it made no fucking sense whatsoever, no fucking sense at all, until I hear them yelling in Spanish, saying, "*Píssa! Píssa! Tráen pissa!*" and then I realize they were hobos, hanging out in the cemetery on a warm night, who had been trained to run after the Domino's Pizza truck for free pizza.

They were hobos. Not zombies.

Dennis had been laughing enjoyably at my fear. "Isn't that great?" he asked.

No, I thought. No, it wasn't. But, yeah, kinda.

This was why Brownsville had no homeless population, I suddenly realized, because they all had a general delivery address: the open-air historical cemetery. No one would fuck with them there, on the bones of Davy Crockett. And they'd get regular pizza deliveries, conditioned by generations of Domino's Pizza drivers who pulled this initiation trick on rookies, keeping the evening's leftovers in the bed of the truck.

The homeless horde, looking very much their role, and like they'd had help from the costume and makeup department, all made their way down to the truck's bed and helped themselves to the pizzas that Dennis had thrown back there before he had picked me up.

To this day, I've never had a more convincing trick played on me.

Anyhow, on the other Friday night that Dennis had called asking if I was up for a night in Mexico, I was up for it, but *en guarde*. He drove us to Matamoros and parked on the street, which was forebodingly empty. We visited the three clubs that the underage kids usually swarmed, and all of them were quiet this night. Mexico was empty, the party obviously elsewhere, and Dennis had not been invited.

Brownsville, back then, was like that. Every weekend night, there was only one place to be, one place that was happening. No two nightspots could coexist, let alone a third or fourth. There was only enough imagination and capital and mirth to sustain one address at a time. This was not a place that enjoyed unnecessary decision-making.

We ended up talking over beers in the quieter of the three bars that served minors, Los Sombrero's. It had always been my favorite, because it promoted conversation, in its own way. More accurately, I ended up talking; Dennis ended up looking around shiftily, distracted. Endured my conversation that was designed to casually annoy him into a discussion with mild irritation, like a UTI.

I'd had about three Mexican beers and was finally able to sort of breach the station of little brother, had started engaging Dennis as an adult, and I was slowly realizing there was actually very little to bring out of this priapic, sports-betting professional waiter, when we both noticed that this Mexican woman kept walking by, her blouse exaggeratedly undone.

She eyed Dennis en route to the ladies' room, and then eyed me on her return to her table, where sat, quite convincingly, a husband. We both watched her, uncertain from that amount of overt attention from a woman.

She sat down at the sidewalk table, overlooking the quiet street, and the man looked just like Tom Selleck as Magnum P.I., if he lived in Texas rather than Hawaii.

I couldn't figure out the alchemy, so I just continued my attempts at getting a depth-reading of Dennis' Neanderthal appetites, and he had finally admitted that Mare had broken his heart when the woman with the exposed tits sat down at our table, uninvited and unexpected.

She introduced herself. I forget her name. Tits Garcia, maybe. She asked Dennis how old he was.

"Twenty," responded Dennis, adding a year.

"And you?" She looked at me.

"Seventeen," I said, doing the same.

"Oh," she said to me, a smile growing knowingly on her face. "I could get in trouble with you."

She said, "You two guys want to come back to our hotel and party?"

Dennis says, "Absolutely."

Personally, I was wary, not sure why I was so repulsed by this invitation, but also totally caught in the inescapable gravity of sex here. So I didn't say anything. Besides, Dennis was driving.

She wrote her room number on the back of a receipt from her purse and handed it to Dennis.

"We're at the Motel 6," she purred with all the grace of a neck tattoo. "We'll be there in about an hour."

I started to say something, started to ask about Magnum P.I., when Dennis interrupted me and said to her, "We'll be there."

And there we were, in less than an hour. Sex was happening, Dennis could tell. Personally, I knew something was up but didn't know it was sex. I had an idea, but it didn't fit into any profile I could possibly imagine. And Dennis was driving, so there was really no chance of me not being there, either.

Both groups arrived at the same time, meeting awkwardly on the open-air gangway outside their room, as we were about to knock. They opened the door, and inside on a crude table was a full spread of Johnny Walker Red, wine coolers, and beer in a Styrofoam cooler. We had brought a six-pack of Budweiser, like gentlemen.

She sat us at the table, and faced the man, who introduced himself as, well, as her husband. He told us his name, but again, memory fails. Johnny Swinger. He sat on one of the two double beds and slowly sipped his Johnny Walker and chuckled lightly throughout the evening, as we began talking small, and then impossibly smaller still.

The atmosphere in that room was charged, scaring me to the point of shaking and I was talking ever smaller to her, talking in terms so minute, so atomic, so that they never could come close to describing the frothing, lubed-up sex-pounding elephant in the room, and I did this well, so well in fact that the man eventually left, making an excuse about getting more ice, maybe more beer, and left both Dennis and me alone with his wife, who lit up a Capri cigarette and took five milligrams of valium, giving another one to Dennis as her old man left the room at the Motel 6.

She was free and easy with her conversation now, telling us how she was reviled back in her native Houston, in her neighborhood, because all the women hated how she dressed, how she wore her shirts and walked around with her tits falling out, she laughed. She giggled at this and wiped at her mouth with her shoulder.

The man was gone a long time, and things did not progress sexually, mostly because I was still talking about nonsense, about sense, about anything except sex, and then she excused herself to the bathroom, and while she was in there, the man returned with a bag of ice and more wine coolers for her, and as he closed the door to the room, the door to the bathroom opened and she appeared, dressed in red lingerie that was not at all flattering and far too tight. She looked like the carotid artery of a hypertensive blue whale.

This was the break they were looking for, and my delaying tactics were locked out: The sex was on.

She sat back on the bed and Dennis leaned forward, laughing, and kissed her, like he was a swinger from the porn movies his mother kept readily accessible. They smiled while kissing like teenagers, and I felt graciously excluded from this. But then she pulled me to her from my chair by the belt and she thought she was sexy as she undid my pants. I was drawn by the horrible irresistible vulgarity of the availability of first sex. The stolen skin magazines under Richard's bed, the jokes and insinuation my father made at my expense, the stories of his fuckings and goings, the drainage-ditch muddlings I've grown up around shoved me into this scenario, made me defenseless, crushed down on me as I let myself go to her, even through my repulsion.

But I still had my standards: I would not engage with Dennis there. I made the decision to get to her first, if this is how it was going to happen: At the very least, I was going to be first to mount her, and I took off my shirt while she pealed with delight and her husband grunted satisfied encouragement from his position on the opposite bed, feeding another Lay's potato chip into his mouth, watching as his wife's hand went down to Dennis' clothes.

The next ten or fifteen minutes I hardly remember, would need tremendous shock therapy and LSD or lots of booze to have the courage to revisit those synaptic streams.

I mounted this stranger in bad lingerie, her stout body convulsing violently in forced pleasure under me as I awkwardly imitated the miasma of pornographic movies I'd seen since I was eight.

I thrust forward from the hip, skinnily, hard, and noiselessly, feeling, upon entering her, a sort of déjà vu, and then nothing else as I sweatily worked atop her, disgusted at what I was doing.

At some point, I became hyperconscious of the fact that Dennis had become bored, had pulled his knees to his chin while sitting by the bed, and was distractedly looking around the room. The husband was happily crunching away on the potato crisps, watching his wife play porno star under a stringy, frightened underage boy.

I had the good sense at this point to pretend to orgasm, to end this horrible theater macabre, and with a fairly . . . anticlimactic . . . thrust, I got up, moved away from her, and immediately went to the bathroom, into the shower. I stepped in there with the hot water turned to its fullest setting and stood beneath it, scalding myself, for punishment, like a good Catholic. It was like the shower scene in *Silkwood*, and I wished I had a way to remove my skin.

I had the vague sense that Dennis had moved into position, had mounted her freshly as I had closed the door behind me.

The bathroom steamed up around me and I scrubbed with the sort of fervor you would see after an incident at a nuclear reactor. I wanted to scrub down with napalm, with razor blades and fire and then bleach.

I stayed in there about a half an hour, could not bear to come out, with the awful feeling that everything had now changed for the terrible. Finally, Dennis knocked on the door, asked me to get out, because they needed to get in.

I did finally emerge, pink and raw like a piglet and frightened to death that I now had heptatitis, gonorrhea, and syphilis, and was due for an outburst of explosive AIDS within the month.

She entered the bathroom as I dressed, Dennis behind her, seemingly happy, like this hadn't been the most horrific moment of his life, too.

She was still in her crumbling, bad lingerie, her sagging breasts now utterly ignorable, and she just wanted to know that we all had had a good time, she said, coyly. She put her arms around me, and I caught a look at myself in the mirror, the look on my face, absent, but disgusted. No longer there, like I passed a test, and had moved on already, about a year ago.

On the way home, Dennis talked excitedly about what happened when I had been in the shower. He had been second, as I had seen, and after he had his turn, the husband had mounted her next, and after a few quick lunges, he had finished his own business, then gone to sleep as the wife showed us out. How peculiar, I thought, feeling even more disgusted.

I couldn't think of anything near the idea of sex for months after this. The girl I had a crush on in school was suddenly abhorrent to me, and I did something horrible to make her and all her friends angry, and so they all stopped talking to me.

For weeks I waited to see if the sores of various Venusian-type troubles would surface, but nothing ever did. When I had my physical for the Marine Corps a few months later, they gave me an STD test at MEPS processing in San Antonio, and I came up clean, totally clean.

Dennis never spoke to me about that night again, but he did tell Dad and Dan, which was further humiliating. Dan wasn't exactly encouraging, or insensitive about it. In fact, I don't think he ever mentioned it to me; knowing Dan, he saw it in purely developmental terms, like it was bound to happen, like it was going to happen anyhow—it certainly didn't happen under optimum circumstances—but it taught me something, so just get past it and move on; you had sex for the first time. Mazel tov. Now get over it.

I did get one round of ribbing some days later from Dad and Richard, after the fact, but I think the circumstances were horrific enough to be evident even to their deadened sense of right and wrong, and it was never brought up again.

This was the other secret that I kept to myself and told no one, no one ever.

And it took me about a year before I even told my therapist, Sally, in my mid-thirties, and I did it on a day when I did not want to talk about my catastrophic relationship with my then girlfriend. I suddenly realized that the story, to a strict Freudian, would be like hoisting a half pound of *foie gras* before the nose of a true, unapologetic Frenchman. (Sorry, Philippe.)

And I was right: She seized upon it and held on to it, right to the end of that and about two other sessions like a great white.

Later, if ever I became uncomfortable during our therapy, I'd just make a reference to that night, and she'd follow it there deliberately, away from where I didn't want her poking about. But maybe Sally was smarter than that, and I wasn't really putting her off the trail, because lot of things emanated from that night. Maybe I'm not as smart as I thought I was, and I didn't come out as clean as I had hoped, from that shower.

Chapter 25

DAD'S WARNING

When Dan moved to Seattle, he had done it in that sort of brazen, headlong sort of way you do things in your twenties, too stupid to know that you can't do something, so you just go ahead and do it. Dan fell in love with the place.

We have to give Dennis, and the Army, that: They found Seattle for us.

At the time, about two years before MTV and FM radio had found Nirvana and Pearl Jam and Soundgarden, Seattle was a hidden, mountain-cloaked rural metropolis unbeknownst to the rest of America, and a perfect starter city for me. I hadn't been invited, when Dennis asked Dan to come up, but that didn't stop Dan from asking me along, after living there a few months.

I wasn't ready, at the time, still reeling from the beating I got from Richard, still trying to disentangle myself from the mess I had made at school. Dan had been living in Seattle for nearly a year at that point and had become tremendously lonely, realized just how much my friendship and brotherhood had actually meant to him, after all those years as kids doing nothing but irritating and beating the hell out of each other. He would call me and tell me how clean and beautiful and cool and weird this place was; he absolutely drank in all the differences between this quiet Shangri-La and Texas, and all that we knew: the bitter heat, the entrenched racism, the limited possibilities, the large hair.

Seattle was subdued, a retreat for overeducated, liberal-minded people, a hideaway on the West Coast, with exceptional and fascinating drop-outs. It was a wet, quasi-British rain-soaked city full of promise and civility, where people judged you not by what you did or your race, but by your hobbies. It was the opposite of Texas. And beer. "Holy shit," he said, "the beer! Stuff you've never heard of!"

"What, like Heineken?" I'd heard of Heineken.

"No," he said, "microbrews. Beers that don't get out of the state."

"Micro-beers?" I repeated. "What, like, tiny bottles?"

"No, moron, just microbrewed—limited distribution."

"Oh," I said. I still didn't know what he meant, but saying "Oh," would get us to move on, give me more context. Maybe I could figure it out with more context.

Anyhow, it took me a week to find it on a map. Or rather, it took me a week just to find a map, and then find Seattle. It was up. Thing I always loved about living in Brownsville, Texas, was that the rest of the United States was always "up," same as how going south always felt like you were going downhill. Brownsville was always at your navel, or at the point you were in relation to the rest of the map. Everything emanated from that point. Seattle was up and to the left, the very far left. Near Canada.

"Hunh," I said to no one at all, in a library in Brownsville, looking at Seattle. "So that's where Canada is. Maybe I can go to Canada."

The incident with Richard was a few months behind me now, and my face had healed, but my tooth remained cracked, though it wasn't giving me any problems. Things had settled down around me. I had begun working very closely with the good Dr. Blum at a small and terrible political newspaper, *The Brownsville City Light*. He was an academic from Mexico City who had taken me under his wing at the developing publication. We were still struggling with bad technology, first-generation laser printers and the like, but we had a good relationship, talked extensively about many things. He was my first father substitute, which I tended to collect throughout my young adulthood. Dr. Blum was Jewish: spoke elegant Spanish and exquisite, if halting, English; carried himself with crisp manners; and was a very kind, very patient man, who looked like Inspector Poirot, but with a less manicured mustache. It was he who began my fascination with the Great Tribe, had created a passion for what he called "being a 'generalist,' knowing a lot about a lot of things. "'Specializing' in something is quite boring, don't you think?"

"Yes, I do," I said, though I only figured out what he meant some years later.

He'd republish many of his essays that he'd written for the *Economist* and other high-level publications that were far too complicated for the audience our publication was hitting. In the two years of printing the twelve-page tabloid weekly, the only response we'd gotten was a letter to the editor handwritten in a lengthy, sweaty, unpunctuated scrawl that went on and on about the horrors and consequences of drug use, which we had transcribed and printed, and then it turned out, in the end, to have been written by Segis's mother, because she was convinced still that I had been making Segis take drugs.

By this time, I'd dropped out of college, was working on the newspaper with Dr. Blum, and was feeling rather claustrophobic.

Dan's invitation to move to Seattle was looking better and better. Things at home had settled down—Richard had moved north with that Christian cult he'd joined in a hurry, and Mom and Dad had been well on their way toward separation, with Derek lost somewhere in the middle.

Gramma had gone on like nothing had happened, like she hadn't been a tremendous Judas goat the night of the beating, that she hadn't taken Richard's homicidal threats far too lightly. We avoided each other instinctively.

My only stimulation at this point had been *Northern Exposure,* I will admit with a degree of sheepishness. You might have called it a "boy crush" that I had on Rob Morrow, but I would call it all-out idolatry for Joel Fleischman. I wanted to be a nebbish Jewish doctor from Flushing, in the same way I had wanted to be Indiana Jones ten years earlier. The accoutrements would be different, sure, but I was certain I could carry it off. When I realized that *Northern Exposure* was filmed a couple hours outside of Seattle, the decision was clinched. I had been going a bit out of my mind, hanging around in a sort of illiterate limbo, knowing full well that there was a whole world of people with passions and interests just like mine right out there, and to get there, all I had to do was leave—just *leave*—and take that first fateful step out into the darkness. But it was frightening. Quite frightening. But I knew I had to do it; I was of age, but I had no money, nothing. I had saved about $500, that was about it.

I started to fester, in my own mind. Became very resentful of my situation, felt like the world outside of Texas was laughing, enjoying fantastic conversation about literature and art and coffee and . . . you know . . . things that mattered.

And I was stuck here, in Brownsville. Everyone I knew from high school had left, on their first leg of their eventual boomer-anging, now off spending their surplus grants and loans in the bars of Austin. Everyone from Brownsville who felt themselves adventurous had moved to Austin. I didn't want to go there; it seemed like high school in a different venue. Like pitching a tent in your parent's backyard and pretending to camp.

I was hitting a level of desperation that would soon force my hand, force me to do something important, like a howling teakettle.

One Saturday morning, Mom and Dad both happened to be in the kitchen, in a rare breach of mutual distancing.

"I'm going to live with Dan, in Seattle," I announced plainly. Loudly, too.

I was nineteen, expecting the same sort of response I'd had each time previous, which was normally utter denial, humilia-tion, or a command to stop talking nonsense.

Instead, they were quiet. Mom stood at the stove, Dad leaned his elbow on the counter separating the kitchen from the dining room, shirtless. He looked at me.

He nodded his head, faintly narrowed his eyes, and said, rather dramatically, "OK. But if I find out [heavy comma] that you are up there [heavy comma] selling your ass [heavy comma] I will come up there and shoot you in the head."

Mom, in the kitchen, didn't look our way.

I was surprised they let me go this easily.

Dad's response hadn't even registered. If it did, it was only that he'd had so little faith that I would have to resort to pros-titution to make ends meet. Well, fronts and ends. (Ha.) But I'd lived with the man for nineteen years now and knew not to take anything he said like it was coming from a human adult, more like a psychotic, tyrannical toddler, never to be taken seriously or trusted. His edict, saying he'd come up to shoot me in the head if he found I was down to rough trade, could be translated—as I did then—to something akin to, "Wow! Really? Good for you! Man, that's exciting stuff. I'm very pleased and happy for you! Good luck!"

To me, it was exactly the same thing. It was his way of blessing the enterprise.

A few days later, Mom asked me when I planned to make the trip. It was October when I made the declaration. I'd needed about another month or so of saving paychecks to get there comfortably. "Sometime in the coming year," I told her.

"Alright," she said. "Just as long as you plan for this."

"Sure thing."

But things weren't going well at that point. I was boiling over with a sense of abandonment, like something was happening, and it just wasn't happening *to me*. To make things worse, I'd stopped talking to everyone, all friends and acquaintances, after the beating from Richard, and the only contact I had with someone my age was the secretary at work, a cute girl a year older than me named Janie, from a neighborhood not a few miles from where I lived. Janie was a typical Brownsville girl, average, common, cute, and very Mexi-American. She was recently separated from the same boyfriend she'd had since kindergarten, was intending on marrying, the whole routine planned out for her by years of generational insulation and the unshakeable belief in the Virgin Mary. I had a crush on her, but she didn't know what to make of me. She had been really gentle with me, when she had first seen me at the office, after Richard had bruised me up. She'd even cried. We'd "had a moment" in the office some days after, but then she had reconsidered, pretended nothing had happened.

Then something triggered it, one night in mid-November. Boom. Dad and Mom had a big fight at the house, and somehow I got involved. I grabbed my stuff and went to the Holiday Inn, where Karsten used to live, and checked into a room. I bought a twelve-pack of beer and found a knife, sat in the room and made parallel cuts on my arm, leading across the forearms, about four or five of them from the wrist to the elbow. I did it slowly, cowardly, pushing down hard to feel the blade in the skin, watching the blood well up, then pulling down sharply. Then I did it again, and again. I still don't know why I did it. Dr. Blum and I had been discussing the various "sun dances" of the native tribes of the area, the evolved sensitivity toward anything that made one bleed, how the natives of the area had dramatic life-changing injuries happen to them every day, and they never reacted the way we would now, just sort of moved on, incorporated the new liability into their lives. How they would include this factor into their celebrations, draw hooks into their pectorals, under the armpits, string them out to a pole and run around the pole, stretching and bleeding and ripping their muscles out to ecstasy, is what they've written. I didn't agree, I told the good doctor.

I said, "Maybe they just liked the punishment."

Doctor Blum laughed. "That's very Catholic of you," he said. "No," he said. "They were just letting out the dragons."

"The dragons?" I asked.

"Yes," he said. "The dragons, all the demons that boil up in a person. The last of the dragons was let out in Durango, in

1967. Me and my two good friends, we had a ceremony, and we drank and smoked marijuana and shot off guns and let out all our dragons. That was the last of the dragons. We killed them, in ourselves."

And that night, I was surfacing my own dragons, with a serrated knife, making those cuts, needing that pain. I was watching those dragons come to the surface. I was going out of my mind. I stayed in that room, lonely. I'd placed a call to Janie, but she never showed. I didn't expect her to.

She wasn't really who she was, in my mind. I had been in love with another girl, Gina, and Janie reminded me of her now, but more approachable. Gina had since left, on her way to school, following her dad's career path, as a lawyer, likely a judge, eventually. She had a tremendous future ahead of her. Janie, Janie was here. Janie was staying here, not going anywhere.

The next day I showered, took care of the wounds, wore a long-sleeved shirt, and made my way to work.

At some point, I just left it all to hang and went home to pack. I drank a lot of beers while doing so, called and inquired as to when the next bus to Seattle was leaving.

"Where?"

"Seattle."

"¿A donde es esso?" (*"Where is that?"*)

"Washington."

"¿Donde?"

"Washington State. West Coast. *Norte.*"

"Oh. Hold on. Tonight, at 10:30."

"Thanks," I said. Click.

I got my things together, managed to sort and divide, cut ties to and shoved anything else I owned into two bags. I still hadn't told anyone I was leaving, right then. About seven or eight that night, I was overcome with a need to explain to Dr. Blum what I'd decided, get his blessing. I drove to his house, across Brownsville, and very timidly, in the dark, rang his doorbell. His wife answered, and I sheepishly asked for the good doctor.

When he came to the door, I think I wept. I tried to explain to him what was happening, but I couldn't. I was going crazy, I felt, like a top that was in the final stages of spinning, losing its center and wobbling out of control. And I couldn't exactly explain that to him. "My dragons," I said, and I pulled back my sleeves.

"Oh, Domingo," he said. "The last of the dragons . . . "

He was very kind to me.

I said good-bye to him.

I drove home, crying. It was still early, but I needed to get my car dropped off at the office—I had arranged for one of the owners of the newspaper to buy the car for $500 and send me the money later—and then figure out how to get to the bus station. When I got home, Derek was watching television, still unaware of what was happening. He was six years old and started following me around the house as I was gathering my things, preparing to go. He watched me finish packing.

"But why?" he asked.

"Because I'm going crazy, kiddo. It's hard to explain," I said.

"But why?"

"Because you're not my age. It's like, it's like you have all your friends, right?"

"Right?"

"And they like stupid music. And you don't like what they like."

"I don't like what they like. I like what you like."

"I know you don't, because you have good taste. You like the Beastie Boys. And the Butthole Surfers."

"I like the Beastie Boys. And the Butthole Surfers."

"Right, but your friends, they don't like the Beastie Boys, so they make you listen to other stuff. Stuff they hear on the radio."

"I don't like the radio. They play bad music there."

"Correct. And you want to listen to the Beastie Boys, with me, but they won't let you."

"Why don't they let me?"

"Because they're not as smart as me and you, Derek. We like things that are smart and funny."

"Like the Beastie Boys?"

"Well, yes; sure. See, the Beastie Boys are funny and do things that are different, and interesting, so they can't get on the radio down here. It's hard to explain. But they're smarter than the other stuff, because the Beastie Boys . . . that sort of music . . . that sort of art . . . they make you work for it. They make you think more. It's not given to you over the radio, not spoon fed . . . and you don't do it because everyone else is doing it. So yes; I mean, because the things you like are different from the things everyone else likes, that's why we're smarter. And you can either force yourself to like what they like or keep looking for the things you like, and keep finding them. But the thing is, if you stay around them too long, they start to win, Derek. And you start to like what they like, you start to be more like them, even though you didn't at first, and parts of you start going quiet, and the quiet parts start getting bigger, and then eventually, you're just quiet all over."

"But why?"

"I don't know, kiddo; but that's just how it is. And right now, I feel like I'm dying, inside, and if I stay here any more, Derek, I'm going to die. Little pieces of me at first. I'm going to start dying, and people will beat me up more and more, until I start to help them in killing myself. Like Richard."

"But why?"

"It's just how it is, Derek. There's no changing it."

"But why?"

"Because they don't like any one who is different from them. It's evolution, sorta, I think. Can't change the model too quickly. I'm a giraffe, born to a family of mules. Remember that, though, Derek. Remember that what you like, what makes you different, is that you are smarter than anyone here. If they were smarter, they wouldn't be here. So by that rule, you're smarter than everyone, get it? Don't ever let anyone tell you different."

"Because we like the Beastie Boys?"

"Well, yes. And no. Jesus, Derek, it's not just about music. It's about wanting more. Seeing more. There's more. There's so much more . . . and I . . . I just need it, Derek. Whatever it is, it just isn't here. It isn't in places like Brownsville."

I'm finished packing at this point, and I'm standing in the door to the front driveway, where my car is ready, too.

This is it.

I'm leaving the nest.

The only people present are Derek and Gramma. Gramma, this whole time, has been running around behind me, trying to pack food into my bags, which I then remove.

She hands me five packs of chicken-flavored Ramen, begins to tell me just how miraculous it is—even has a bowl of it, in her hands, the noodles just about swollen to perfection—and she goes on, "Just ten pennies a pack! And you get a soup! And noodles! Look! Look! You'll never have to worry about food!"

And it is in this moment that I finally see her clearly, like a figure standing in front of a lit-up doorway, outlined clearly, and because I'm about to leave, I'm breaking our definition, and I suddenly and forever understand my grandmother, her emotional and psychological development rusted shut at age ten, her one concern being food. I see her clearly at that moment as the young peasant Indian girl who had been farmed off because her family could not feed her.

Over a bowl of Ramen.

And it makes me cry for her, sort of. My eyes well up, seeing how poor this person really is, down in her soul, why she did the things she did. It hasn't been money or power she has been hoarding all this time. It's been food.

Gramma had brought all of us to America, but she could not enter. She was not allowed in. She had been our Moses, had made her covenant with America, for us, but it did not include her. This was as far as she could go. But here she was now, miraculously turning ten copper pennies into a bowl of noodle soup for me, showing me how I should never be hungry. Now, go.

Derek, on the other hand, cannot stop crying. He's six years old at the retelling, but in my memory, he's wearing diapers, and he sits down hard on the sidewalk leading to the car, and he cries, "June, please don't go."

I say, "Derek, I have to. I'm going to die here. I know it."

"Please don't leave. . . ."

"I'm sorry."

"Please. . . ."

"You'll understand when you're older."

He's inconsolable, and Gramma—nanny that she's been—sweeps him in, starts trying to feed him the Ramen, and my last image of my beautiful little brother is him on the ground, that night, crying, his face a mask of pain, of loss, as our hearts go pop, pop, pop with the disconnection of a time ended, of a change in circumstance, of one brother leaving another to fend for his little self.

And I never cried so much for Derek, not like that, not until the night fifteen years later when we thought he'd died. But that's another story.

In the car, my heart is collapsing at the idea of leaving him in the maw of a family falling apart, a family no longer capable of taking care of its innocents. I am leaving Derek behind, sitting down hard on the sidewalk, as I drive away, crying.

Just writing this now, it tears me up. It's one of my biggest regrets, in my life, how I hurt that beautiful little boy. In my wallet the only photo I carry is of him, one Easter, holding a rabbit with his pudgy little hands.

Before I leave Brownsville, I have to see my mother, who is working the late shift at the JC Penney, to pick up a bit of money we had previously agreed upon. The Penneys is near the bus station so I still have time. She takes an emergency break and follows me out to the parking lot, after I tell her my bus is leaving in forty-five minutes. I'm crying still, understanding what this means, and she isn't at all sympathetic to my decision to leave so soon.

"June, what are you doing! You said you weren't going for three months!" she says, when we get outside and are alone.

"I have to go *now*," I say. "I have to leave, Mom; I'm going fucking *crazy* here."

"June, just calm down; please, just calm down; what happened to your arms? Oh, Jesus, who did that to you?"

"Calm down; I did it yesterday, or the day before. You weren't supposed to see it. It's . . . it's nothing. I just wanted the scars."

"Aye, June; what is *that*? What are you doing? Just think about it. Just calm down. . . ."

"Mom, I can't anymore: I just can't. If I calm down, I'll just stay another day, and it'll happen again. And then maybe I won't go that time. I just have to go now. Now. I bought the bus ticket already. It was $197. I need the money you promised me."

"OK, I'll get it to you, OK. Now. You make me so worried to see you like this."

"It's Brownsville, Mom. It's this place. You don't get it, and I don't understand how you guys can just accept it, look at the same things I see and see something totally different. If I stay here, I know I'm going to kill myself soon. I know it. Really soon. Please let me go, Mom. Please, just help me this time. This last time. Please. I can't be here anymore."

There is a moment, and I see something in her eye, like a sadness, or an understanding. It may even be compassion, for the forgotten boy, at the end. "OK, June. OK. I'll get you your money, like I said," she says.

Motherhood, in the end, finally kicks in. And it's sweet, special, because between us it's rare.

"Yeah?" I say, unsure.

"Yeah. You need to be where you need to be," she says. "You need to chase down your monsters, like Max."

Here, I'm actually stunned into quiet, not even crying anymore. Some days before, I had pulled out *Where the Wild Things*

Are, and showed her an image of Max, doing his Rumpus dance, and I had said to her and Derek that it would actually make a really cool tattoo. Mom, of course, had balked. (This was before tattoos had become so fashionably rampant.) But we had sat and looked at the book—Mom, Derek, and me, in a rare triumvirate of family that night, and we had discussed what Maurice Sendak had meant with the book, about the rage of childhood, the deep betrayals and painful shifts, and she listened to me talk, and Derek liked how I was drawing so much meaning from one of his books. We had been happy.

"You go and do what you need to do, June," she says to me. "You go and find what you need. Your supper will be here, when you need it. Your supper will be warm. No matter where I am, that will be your home," she says.

And I can't believe it, watching her. That look on her face. It is all the love that I didn't have growing up, making a face.

Chapter 26

DAN'S SECOND TO LAST FIGHT

Dan is shouting.

Dan is pointing.

Dan is raging from the bottom step of a shanty bar in Kingsville, Texas, on the campus of a remote college specializing in agronomy. He's yelling through the door for some fucker to come out and fight him, square.

The night is thin and shallow, as murky as a recently disturbed mud puddle. It's the color of gruel, the low-hanging clouds reflecting back the dim sulfur lights that spot the campus and blot out the stars.

There are two fat Mexican bouncers at the door, looking very nervous and annoyed, trying to stare back at him. This isn't what they took the job as a bouncer to do, the look on their faces say.

Dan is shouting some more, challenging anyone he sees through the door to come out, to bring that fucker Larry out here. There are three steps leading up to the mouth of this low-shelf, black-neon college bar with cheap beer, and it's a Wednesday night, would have otherwise been slow and dull and uneventful, if there hadn't been that scuffle earlier.

I'm standing behind Dan, feeling remarkably unhappy about being there. I'm holding a nine iron, leaning on it, unsure of what I'm supposed to be doing. I want to pull Dan away from here, from the shoulder, tell him that this is madness and convince him that it is really OK to walk away from this, but he's blind with rage, intent on fighting this guy, Larry.

There's movement inside, blonde buzz cuts in cheap collared shirts holding spit cups. They can clearly hear him shouting, demanding satisfaction, are clearly unsettled by the pissed off guy at the bottom step calling out one of their "brothers."

From behind the two diabetic pillars blocking the door erupts a large white guy, blonde buzz cut, in shorts and a T-shirt, suddenly running out of the door and parallel to Dan, who locks him in, and they both begin running sideways, staring at one another, and sprint in this manner for roughly fifty yards to a field across the street, a grass parking lot for the football stadium.

The rest of the fraternity and anyone else who happened to be in that bar pour out of the doorway, and I have no choice but to run after them, run after Dan, who's pressed this way too far, and is now locked in a fight with a really big fucker and fifty of his fraternity brothers.

The crowd swarms around us, makes an impromptu boxing ring with Dan and Larry at the center, squared off. Up until this moment I'm clinging to the hope that this won't happen, that they won't fight, that we can get out of this and all he'll do is yell at me, take his frustration out on me—me, who feels responsible—and then Dan steps in and swings at Larry, connects, and all the life drains from my arms and legs. I go weak as one of the bartenders steps behind me and puts me in a full nelson, I think for my own protection.

✦

Seattle had been heavenly.

I spent a year there, taking in as much as I could, which wasn't very much: I wasn't prepared to see what I was seeing. It was an utter culture shock, and I just didn't know how to process it. Everything was far too different, and taking it in, absorbing it, was impossible with my simple understanding of the world. I would have had to develop the right sort of vision, the right sort of feelers to receive this bombardment of information, this new, wet wilderness of civility.

Because of the weather, what should have been a three-day bus trip took five. I traveled by Greyhound up the length of Texas, into Colorado, detoured to New Mexico, then Utah, somehow ended up in Idaho, and then I think we turned left. I met strange people, some of them recently released from institutions, who were horribly drunk and attempted to make sandwiches on my legs while I slept.

When I arrived in Seattle, Dan was terribly happy to see me. We lived with Dennis for a while, but in the end that wasn't a good fit, and Dan and I moved out, found roommates in a house in the "cool" neighborhood in Seattle. I was afraid to leave that ten-block area, and I found a job throwing pizza and hanging out with kids my age. And I had met a girl, Karis—the very idea of the slim-hipped gentile, the prize that validates every American immigrant's experience—and I had decided upon her, from the few times I had seen her.

At first the simple feat of getting out of where I was, in Texas, was enough for me. It took all the strength I had had just to do it. But scraping by eventually began to wear on me, since I had no plan beyond what I was doing then. But for that year, working on Seattle's most interesting stretch of commercial property, was brilliant; I basked in the delight of how utterly different everything was up here.

Most of all—and I know that this sounds surprisingly naïve—I was deeply moved by the sincere and institutional absence of racial prejudice in Seattle, which, back then, came naturally and easily to the area, which was, again, my experience there. People took interest in me, would ask questions sensitively. They would ask about my origins and experiences, and have genuine, unprejudiced delight in my answers. I had never experienced anything like it. In return, I began to develop that same instinct, that sensitivity of identification.

Seattle was a land of winter, an American Norway, a land of never-ending rainy days, as I had arrived in October, and I could lie in bed and read all day long with no one mowing the same patch of lawn directly underneath my window over and over again. Metaphorically speaking, of course.

It was different here, so very different. It was full of possibility, and the nights were deeper and wetter, and the moon was closer, made your eyes water when it was full. And the crows . . . slick, shiny, and dark and smarter than most people I had grown up with in Texas. My first week in Seattle, I saw a crow eating a watermelon lollipop. It was like the Mexican flag, with the image of the eagle eating the snake, but much funnier.

Eventually I began to understand that simply moving here was not going to be enough. I had to get back to school, back to the spring semester at the only school I knew I could get back into, in Kingsville, Texas, where my sisters were studying. Finishing school was the next step, I had decided, now that I knew what the outside world looked like. I'd get certified at something and come back and make a more comfortable living and seduce the girl, while I enjoyed the shit out of being away from Texas. That was my new plan. But in order to do that, I had to go back.

✠

There had always been many loud and terrible signals that Texas was not my home.

My relationship to Texas had always been disturbingly patriarchal: I don't know if Texas is capable of any other kind. I had the same emotional response to it as I had to my father: *I* can make fun of Texas, but if *you're* not from Texas, then you may not. And seriously: Don't push it.

Sure, ours was an abusive relationship, but it was an abuse that grew out of odd circumstances, like a plucky ragamuffin in a 1930s vaudeville sketch who is unexpectedly forced upon a bitter, racist, drunken war celebrity widely féted for the cannibalistic defeat of the ragamuffin's people. Sort of a:

— *Papá, more tabasco-infused tacos, pliss!*

— *Eat boot-heel instead, you lazy, no-good, diapered wetback worm!*

— *Aye, papa! Jou're so crasy!*

Texas has an image to keep up, goddammit. Didn't need a scrappy, artsy ragamuffin to complicate its drunken, colonial retirement. This was eminent domain, turned inward.

Texas, I still maintain, is a semiotic thunderbolt, can answer any cocktail party question about the superconscious power of symbols and signifiers across the widest cultural divides. Next to Bruce Lee, Texas is probably the most easily identifiable Western image that someone in deepest Kazakhstan or darkest Africa can recognize. Would you like to try that with, say, Nebraska? Or Maine? No, it wouldn't work. It wouldn't work in America, let alone Nepal.

Texas is in the shape of America's heart: As goes Texas, so goes America. It's the hoofprint of Jesus and would make a great tattoo.

The word *Texas* itself draws infinite responses from people the world around, mostly negative, and appropriately so. I won't pretend to defend it in the least—most everything reported about it that is negative is terribly accurate, but the thing is, if you haven't lived there, then you couldn't have met the Molly Ivinses, Anne Richardses, the Old 97ses, Audie Murphys, Kris Kristoffersons, Gibby Haneses, and Buddy Hollys.

At any rate, like anything complicated, the idea of Texas draws a tapestry of an emotional response, has many moving parts, eddies, and tide pools. Brownsville itself was just a conventional market on the banks of the Rio Grande, until it become a new phenomenon in the 1800s, as a "border town," when the delineation of a state—and moreover, two countries— was agreed upon by people who didn't live there.

Suddenly, a hinterland town that had been like any other— on a plain on the banks of wide dangerous river—was turned into a frontier, turned into dangerously complicated politically charged country. Turned into the end of one thing, and the start of another, though it was exactly as it had been just a week before.

It's no wonder it would create such perilous divisions in a person who grows up here. And the generations-old classism and racism insinuated itself like a prearranged agreement in which you were never personally invited to previously arrange.

Whatever the case, I gave it a second chance. I had to, like that plucky ragamuffin.

So coming back home to Texas, right back into the nook of the hoof, there was an immediate, inexplicable resistance to the culture, especially in the accepted patois of the area. To me, it had become palpable, this tap dance of language, a sort of psychic agreement in word choice, insinuating and dancing around the very pronounced idea that race was a factor in every uneasy discussion. It was tiring how much energy people put into concentrating emphasis to imply or divert attention away from certain racially charged phrases or words.

The word *Mexican* was especially leaden, dense, dark matter. Heavy with multiple meanings, with sharp edges, and none of the meanings really meant "originating in or from Mexico."

I had never felt the racial charge hang so heavy and so clearly as when I was reimmersed into the area after being gone for a year in bland, yogurt-covered Seattle.

It was now like a fog that only I could see, or couldn't see through, but everyone else pretended wasn't there. But I tried to reintegrate.

I moved back first; Dan would eventually move back later. He was reluctant to give up on Seattle just then. He took off a week from work and I paid for gas on the way back to Brownsville and he and I drove his Lincoln Continental all the way from Seattle to Brownsville in roughly two days, the sons of a truck driver with the bladders to prove it. (I whimpered all the way through Wyoming as Dan drove. Why is Wyoming *there?*)

But school was not to be.

✤

It was New Year's Eve again, I think 1993.

I had managed to enroll back into school and found a place to live, with the help of my sister, Mare. Dan had also moved back and was taking advantage of his GI status, had enrolled as well. I had no idea what I was doing at this school, wasn't really sure what college was about. Still, I tried. My sisters did it, and so would I.

I fell back in with some people I had known previously and had been invited to a party. Dan was spending the evening with Mare and her fiancé, Mark. We'd made plans to rendezvous later, and I went out with these people to some remote farmhouse and started mixing with the locals.

Things were uncomfortable from the start, but the evening started to turn when I began joking with my friend, Ernie, who was from Washington, D.C., and had somehow ended up in Ricardo, Texas, living with his grandmother, a retired journalist, and I said something funny and began getting some attention from a girl.

Her boyfriend didn't approve and said something like, "Give a Mexican some tequila, and he gets funny."

I took that as my cue to leave. I drank the rest of my beer and left through the side door. Ernie saw this happen and followed me out.

"What's wrong?" he asked, out in the street.

"It's just . . . I dunno; it doesn't feel right here. That was out of line, that comment," I said. My feelings were hurt; my eyes started watering. I wasn't able to endure that sort of language anymore.

"Dude, these guys are not like that; they're not racist. The guy throwing the party, Aaron, his girlfriend's Mexican." I liked

Ernie quite a bit. He was my favorite person in Kingsville, and it hurt me even more that he didn't get it.

"Just because you're fucking someone from that race doesn't make you racially tolerant. This isn't cool. This isn't right," I said.

I turned and walked away, walked a mile to a convenience store and called Mare's house, asked Dan to pick me up. No taxis, no public transportation in that part of the world. It's just too wide and flat.

Dan picked me up, and we went back to Mare's apartment and watched Dick Clark's New Year's Eve and had some more beers. A little after midnight, Mare and Mark showed up and asked what I was doing home, why wasn't I out with Ernie . . . ?

"He's upset because someone called him a Mexican," said Dan, burping up some Miller Lite.

"It's not exactly like that," I began, but Mare was suddenly livid.

"*What?* Who said that? Who hurt your feelings like that? No one's going to talk like that to my little brother! Get your keys, Mark. Let's go have a little talk with that person."

"It was just some guy, some guy named Larry, at a party. It's no big deal, really. Just kind of a misunderstanding, Mare. Please, let's just forget about it and stay here," I pleaded. I saw where this was going, and I knew the potential for harm, and I did not want to be responsible for this. It was boding ill, seriously ill.

Dan felt what I was feeling. He and I exchanged dark looks. He knew where this was heading, as well.

"Where is this guy?" asked Mare. "Is he at this party? What's the address?"

THE BOY KINGS OF TEXAS

"I don't remember where it was; I don't know the address," I said, thinking that I could put a stop to it there. But I had written it down on a scrap of paper earlier that evening, in case they had wanted to join us. Mare remembered this and found the paper.

"Here it is," she said, from the kitchen. "Mark, get your keys. We're going to this party. No one talks to my family like that."

Dan and I looked at each other again, caught in the tractor beam of family honor.

They were there because of me.

My sister leaped from the car intent on giving someone what-for. Her fiancé, Mark, standing at five feet ten inches and looking like he could bench press a truck, followed her, equally incensed. Dan and I followed gloomily behind, knowing what was going to happen.

Mare walked through the party looking for this guy, Larry. Larry had gone. That didn't matter to Mare, who was not shy about letting people know when she was displeased. "Who do you people think you are to make my little brother feel bad? Look at you! Look at how you dress, you rednecks. How dare you speak like that to my little brother?"

To the people at the party, it looked very much like I had become upset, gone home, and wrangled up my family posse to come back and start shit. How could it not? It was exactly what it looked like, from the outside.

How could they know what I was feeling, the low, razor-blade blood pumping through my heart, the shame and guilt at having my sister putting herself and her fiancé and Dan in harm's way, to defend my pathetic, skinny honor?

I begged her to leave, to get out of there, and panicked when Ernie came out and asked, "What the hell are you doing back here, with your family? *What are you doing?*"

And I just flipped out and put my fist through a window, as we left.

"Just go, Domingo," said Ernie's girlfriend, looking at me with shame, for even knowing me.

The next morning, things were quiet and dour at the apartment. I could tell Mare was embarrassed at her outburst. I looked through the phone book and found a window-repair person. I borrowed Mare's credit card number and had the guy go over to the farmhouse and replace the window for 35 bucks.

"Anyone else want to call June a Mexican?" Mare said, while we had hangover beers.

✢

We start school that next Monday.

Dan and I both know that the situation from the party is not over, that some sort of escalation is imminent, as a result. Kingsville is a small town. Texas is even smaller. We both move through our developing routine with some appropriate sense of dread, and after a few days things start to feel like perhaps they will quiet down.

Mare and Mark drive to Brownsville one evening and are not due back for a few days. Dan and I are left alone at their apartment while our own rental down the street is being readied for occupancy.

We stay up one night on a very limited budget, having forty-ouncers and watching *Ren and Stimpy*, when it's brand new and a novelty. Feeling a bit better, we decide perhaps we should go to a nearby bar and see if we can meet up with a local floozy. What the hell.

We dress up a bit better, scrape our collective cash together, and drive in Dan's Lincoln Town Car to a cheap, low lying college bar that serves $2 beers.

At twenty, I'm able to use Dan's military ID to gain entry to the bar, easily fooling the illiterate bouncer, and Dan comes in right behind me with his driver's license. The bouncer doesn't notice we have the same name and birth date.

Almost immediately, I'm accosted by Larry, who happens to be standing in the bar.

Unwittingly, we've walked into possibly the most hostile place we could have chosen: This is Larry's bar, as the head of Delta Tau Delta, in whose fraternity house we happen to be, during "rush week." This bar is their bar, and their . . . whatever the head of a frat is called . . . is Larry.

"Domingo, I heard you came looking for me," he says. He looks much bigger up close, outweighing me by about eighty pounds. Dan is standing behind me, and I turn to him and say, "Let me handle this."

"Listen, man, that was a mistake. It got completely out of control," I start to say.

Larry takes off his glasses and hands them to a slim, blonde-haired flunky, off to his left. I direct my attention to the little guy and say, "Give him back his glasses," dismissively. "He doesn't need to take them off. There isn't going to be a fight; we're going to leave right now."

But Larry hits me at the "Give him back his glasses" part, and I'm suddenly on the floor.

Well, not immediately. When he hits me, I rock back on my heels, stunned, unsure of what just happened because he hit me hard, but I didn't fall. I pop back up like one of those air-filled, bottom heavy clowns, to finish my sentence, " . . . there's not going to be a fight . . . " And technically, I'm correct, because he hits me again, with the same result, but this time he decides to tackle me as well. All this happens in seconds.

Dan, behind me, sees the first hit, moves forward, tries to stop the second hit, and is immediately rushed upon by the bouncers.

I am on the ground rolling with Larry, and I can't get out from under him. He is holding my arms down, and I'm drunk, bewildered, and coming to the realization, "Holy shit: I am in a fight, and I am losing." He sits on me and is saying something, but I can't understand him. I stop resisting, start listening:

" . . . so you and your family came looking for me, DO-MING-GO. What business you got with me? Cuz I called you an uppity MEX-I-CAN? That why you come back with all your family, to find me?"

It has all been a horrible misunderstanding, but it's too late to explain. I start to kick and push my way out from the spot, when a bouncer grabs Larry and pulls him off. I stand up, then the kid who is holding the glass rushes at me and swings wide and loose, and I block it and push him in the face—I don't know how to punch—and he falls down, stops. The bouncer looks at me and says, "Get out of here! You're causing trouble, I call the cops!"

I look around for Dan, and there are two bouncers holding him around the arms. He's incensed, saying, "Let go my brother, let go me!" And I can see he wants to fight everybody.

I just want to get out: I'm done.

We drive back to my sister's apartment. Dan's really pissed but doesn't say anything. The minute he gets to the apartment he changes into shorts and a T-shirt and his tennis shoes, and I know he wants to go back. He's not talking to me and is moving through the apartment quickly, with intention and palpable seething rage. This just . . . this just feels terrible. I want it to stop, but Dan is single-minded.

Glumly, heavily, I change into a pair of jeans, and I find the only thing I think is appropriate, and I quietly thank God I have them: a pair of combat boots, suddenly becoming more than a fashion statement. I look around, trying to find something that might work as a weapon. Anything.

I find Mark's golf clubs. I hardly remember looking through them, or what made me choose a 9 iron, instead of say, a putter, but I weighed it out, and it felt like it could be swung about like a weapon. I wasn't thinking straight.

By this time, Dan is stomping his way to the car, intent on finishing this fight, and I follow along, full of dread, a whole lot of Sturm and far too much Drang, nearly paralyzed with shame at getting my family into this, and knowing full well that there is nothing I can say to Dan to get him to steer off this course he is on.

Dan finally gets what he wants, after calling out Larry from the bottom step for twenty minutes.

Larry runs out after changing into street clothes, and we don't recognize him, but clearly this is the giant the frat has sent out to challenge Dan, so Dan and he sprint in that sideways crab-running motion to the field across the street, and we're surrounded by what seems to be a hundred people. It's rush week at Delta Tau Delta, remember, and everyone loves a fight, in Texas.

They're both pretty fucking big; I hadn't noticed how big Larry was before; Dan is out-classed in weight.

They square off, get in that foot stance, and I see Dan advance offensively, leading with a right jab cuz he's left handed. I see him swing once, and then that's it: We're engaged in this thing. There's no turning back; I feel my extremities drain with life, go leaden.

The bouncer comes up behind me and, almost with a gentle insistence gets me in that full nelson, while the other bouncer slowly steps up and takes my golf club, and I give it up without a fight, as it seems really idiotic and useless at this point anyway.

Then it seems like the whole fucking crowd decides instead to come up on me. They leave the two big fuckers to fight, and one hundred drunk, wound-up farm boys want a piece of the smaller guy who won't fight back, it seems.

Meanwhile, Dan gets in a boxing match with Larry. But Larry doesn't want to box; he wants to grapple. He brings Dan down, to the ground, and gets the better of Dan when they're on the ground. Larry, like I said, is a strong fucker. He gets on top of Dan, starts to choke him into submission. I see this because the bouncers have decided to start taking control of the situation by restraining me. I have a three-hundred-pound Mexican at each arm while I watch Larry pin Dan and put a forearm into Dan's throat, and the whole of the frat comes instead at me, taking shots at my Jesus Christ figure before the opportunity is lost. I kick at their thighs and knees and if I can reach, their hips. I am successful at keeping them all away: No one attacks me head on. I find myself wondering why this position is so popular in movies, when people are getting beaten up. This has to have been the easiest position to defend in, so far. No one is able to get within arm's reach, and I kick a tonnage of testicles from that position.

But Larry is choking Dan out. Dan submits to Larry. When we talk about it, years later, Dan says he admitted defeat to Larry, said, "Alright, alright; we're done. You win." Larry holds Dan in that position for a bit longer, then says, "It's done," and Dan replies, under the pin, "Yeah."

So Larry lets go, sits up, and Dan immediately jumps up and hits him with a round-house left hook, which knocks Larry flat on his back.

Larry turns over on all fours, about five yards in front of me. Dan immediately rushes forward and starts pushing and punching off all the guys who are trying to take a cheap shot at me. He runs up to guys and swings with big rights and lefts, and these guys run away. Larry is trying to shake off that left Dan gave him, still on all fours, and I lower my voice, speak in an unpanicking, unemotional tone, and I say to both bouncers holding me, "Let me go and this can all be over. If you just let me go, this can be over." I remind myself of the Bene Gesserit witch voice in *Dune*.

The bouncer, unbelievably responds by asking, "You promise?"

I say, under all the noise from the crowd, "I give you my word."

And they let me go. Then there's a small second when I think to myself, *Please, God, let me use all the strength I have in this leg to kick this motherfucker's nose in.* Then I step forward, and with my combat boot I swing with all that I'm capable and kick that fucker Larry square in the eye. He flops on his back like a fish and I am immediately attacked on all sides by all the guys who had been standing there watching, waiting their turn to take their swing at me, to prove their dedication to Delta Tau Delta during rush week.

And I fall forward onto my knees, my fingers interlaced on the back of my neck, elbows tucked in to protect my ribs, and I contract my whole body and wait for them to finish. Last I see Dan, he's just reached up on his toes and punched a seven-foot retarded farm boy who looks back at him in astonishment, doesn't drop his beer, and asks Dan, "*What'd you do that for?*" like his feelings have been hurt.

Suddenly, while I am still on the ground, this large Cadillac drives up, all four doors fling open, and six huge, fuck-off black guys from the black militant fraternity erupt from the car, shouting, "What's the problem here?" And the farm boys scatter.

The last glimpse we get of Larry, he's being helped up and carted off by two of his frat brothers, his hands covering his face. I hope I blinded the fucker.

Three of the black guys get between me and the mass of people trying to get in one last shot, and another guy helps me up. He's huge, nearly six and a half feet. He asks me if I'm OK. "My brother," I say. "Find my brother." I spit out a mouthful of blood and grass. The taste is familiar, from football practice.

"Your brother's right here," the guy says as he points me in Dan's direction. Dan has stopped fighting off the frat boys, started explaining our position to the new black frat. But they are not listening to him, they are establishing their dominance and perimeter around the Cadillac.

They put us into the car and ask what we're driving. "We can take you to your car, or home," they tell us, while we're inside, panting, looking over each other's wounds.

"Our car is right over there," says Dan, pointing just down the street. They drive us over, stick around for a second, watch us get in, and then peel away.

I never got to thank them, never knew who they were. They were like Batman, all of them, just appeared out of nowhere, then disappeared.

In the car, the radio is turned off and we drive quickly away, silently, feeling horrible, terrible things. Feeling shame. A stomach full of bile and humiliation at what we'd just done.

Dan endures his wounds from the fight alone, in a long cold shower, telling no one. Involving no one. He just takes it.

I can't do that. I'm made of softer stuff. I call Karis, after Dan has showered and I can soak in the tub. I'm able to get her on the phone, and we talk long into the night. I cry and tell her what happened, try to explain it, and Dan continues to bang on the door of the bathroom and yell at me, disgusted because I can't keep my mouth shut, am involving other people and talking about something that you can't do anything about.

Everybody hears about this fight. It goes down in Kingsville lore. If this had been fifty years prior, there would have been a *corrido* written about Dan and me that night, except the fight would have happened at three in the afternoon, instead of at eleven at night.

When she gets back the next day, Mare isn't finished with the Delts or the bar or the A&I campus police. She spends most of the day reading everyone the riot act for allowing this to happen, for standing by and watching as it did, and even comes home victorious with Mark's 9 iron, after the bouncers and campus security had been thoroughly shamed. This is why she's a teacher in some of the toughest schools in South Texas: Mare has never known fear, when she's feeling self-righteous. How I will always love and admire her for that.

Mare still has the power of the Mimis in her.

Chapter 27

THE HOUSE THAT
ROCK 'N' ROLL BUILT

Dan had stayed valiantly behind in Kingsville, continued with his schooling, but more to prove that the Martinez boys had not been beaten, had not buckled that night we fought Delta Tau Delta and their false champion and fifty-odd men.

I was more of the "Feets, don't fail me now!" philosophy and had split the next day, because I had never before in my life felt more helpless and weak and ineffective than I did that night, on that flat practice playing field, with swarms of rednecks trying to get their one punch in on the uppity Mexicans. My fight was over. Done.

The fantasy of college was shut solidly behind me, after the fight. I packed all my stuff and drove back home to Brownsville, trying to figure out what my next move would be. A&I was a small school, and I knew I would be seeing every one of those people who tried to take a shot at me every day, in every class I would take. There was no safety in this school, anymore. It was done.

I drove the two hours back to Brownsville in silence, in pain. I withdrew into myself and counted the minutes until I was back on my own again, and I don't remember even speaking to anyone during this time, after the fight. I was in a fugue and didn't trust any family with what was going on in my mind or heart. Couldn't trust these people anymore, I felt. Anyone.

The desperation of my circumstances thrummed loudly in my ears, my head hot with panic, and on my way home that evening, I decided to stop by a house I knew, where Georgina Haley lived. She was the daughter of Bill Haley, of the " . . . and the Comets" fame.

I had met her through one of Segis's friends, some idiot kid named Ronnie who thought of himself as a guitarist, the summer previous. Everyone in Brownsville thought they were a guitarist. Segis and Ronnie had put together an album of thrash music and had called it *The Abandon Church*.

"You mean, *The Abandoned Church*," I attempted to correct.

"It's a church for the abandon, man," Segis and Ronnie had both said, like I was the moron in the trio.

"Wait; so people go there to *get* abandoned, or does the church abandon *them?* Or would you go to the church in a sort of . . . reckless abandon?" We had been drinking, and I thought I was the one making sense. But instead, they just broke out in hysterics at how complicated they thought I was making it, so I dropped it. I think I still have a copy of it somewhere. It's just absolute crap.

Ronnie had somehow managed to hook onto Georgina Haley in some dramatic lapse of good taste on her part, and he had fallen hard.

Georgina was a spitfire of a red head, well schooled, well heeled, and quite attractive. Bill Haley had met Georgina's mother in Mexico, and when his career had begun to wind down, she had convinced him to move to Harlingen, in a sort of retirement where he faded quietly away, suffering through his final years with alcoholism and mental illness, outside the public eye. It was here that she decided to raise Georgina, at land's end, in South Texas.

Ronnie had already been talking marriage, while Georgina was enrolled in some arts college around Dallas and would be leaving eventually. I saw their situation already coming apart, so I moved in. Georgina was smart, sexy, pedigree notwithstanding.

One night she and I went for a beer run before the stores closed, and I leaned over and kissed her in my car.

"You know, I'm dating your friend," she said.

"He's not really my friend," I said, lustily reassembling logic. "He's more Segis's friend than my friend."

"He's my boyfriend, though," she said.

"Well, for now. You can break up with him when we get back home," I said, my eyes closed.

"It's a party, and he's staying over," she said.

"Alright, well, I'll give you a couple days," I said, suddenly realizing I was driving.

She looked at me in a way that didn't exactly mean no, and just kind of shook her head, smiling quietly. I would get that a lot in my life.

Still, I felt bad. I'd never done anything like that before, but Georgina was exceptional, had called for exceptional measures. Her dad had invented radio-friendly rock 'n' roll, for fuck's sake. He was Elvis's dad.

Though she hardly remembered her father, Georgina was really close to her mother, Martha, who was very religious, very Catholic, and a really good person.

Georgina's mother had endured the birth of rock 'n' roll—and all that this implied—and she was secluding herself in South Texas these last long years in her quiet isolation of raising Georgina, like a rock 'n' roll nun. Georgina's mother was wholesome. She was safe. And she had once liked me.

I think that's why I drove there, on my way back from Kingsville the day after the fight.

Georgina's mother, Martha, showed me in that night, showed me into her drawing room with the TV turned on but turned all the way down, where she had been meditating over her well-worn Bible and made us an awful herbal tea, this mongrel boy who knew her daughter, bruised and worried and incapable of trusting his own family.

The place was quiet now, with Georgina gone, and I was left with my demons in the house that rock 'n' roll built. I'll never forget the kindness she showed me, letting this monster of a boy into her house that dark night.

See, it was unusual for the time, this sort of kindness. People were never kind to one another, as I remember Texas then, so that when they were, when any sort of kindness was demonstrated, it was glaringly evident. Kindness slapped you in the face, kicked you in the kidneys, in Texas. Made you realize it was there. At least, that's how it was for me.

Very likely kindness was everywhere like a pollen, but I had not as yet developed the appropriate allergies to notice it.

Driving to Martha Haley's house that night, I hadn't expected to be welcomed in, nursed. But I was pulled there for a reason.

I'm sure I unsettled her, maybe even frightened her, but she would never know how her simple kindness for those few minutes had meant more to me than anything that would be waiting for me at home ever could. I should have told her so, but I couldn't really open my mouth to speak.

Chapter 28

BIOLUMINESCENCE

I spent close to two years recovering from that incident. I moved to South Padre Island, where I would end up writing and producing their weekly thirty-two-page tabloid newspaper and working as a bartender at a tiki club.

After a while, it was time to call on Karis, I felt.

Things were going well enough to call on the girl I had somehow managed to burden with the painful, twisted poison I mistook for love at the time, unregulated and torturous, the sort of suffocating peasant obsession that drives the tragic plots of early Russian novels.

Back then my heart was still capable of falling horribly in love with no intellectual administration, no real consideration for the other person. My love was selfish and existed entirely in my own body and head. It was an onerous munition fired without mercy from the impenetrable dark, and it asked its victim for help, as it killed her. Figuratively speaking, of course.

It was a hot, crude thing, destructive and jealous and petty, lucid out of hell and hell bent on being tragic, so all the songs that I loved could have more meaning, make them more real. Tragedy was the only song of love I knew. Couldn't sing in any other key. (By the time I was in my mid-thirties, I had assigned a girl to almost every one of the Old 97's's songs of heartbreak.)

I'd met Karis when she'd visited our apartment in Seattle in a mix of people who'd just gotten off shift from a dinner cruise on Puget Sound. I fell for her the minute I saw her in our doorway, as I let the group in, and she came in last, dressed in a man's shirt and tie, her hostess costume from the cruise.

One of Dan's friends, Ryan, worked on the ship and was dating Karis's best friend. I didn't know it, but Karis was just sixteen years old. When I found out, I thought that perhaps that was the reason she'd been so shy, quiet, but it didn't keep me from falling for her.

The group assembled in the living room, drinking and talking into the night, playing Trivial Pursuit and Karis became the target of my affection when she knew A.A. Milne as the author of *Winnie the Pooh,* especially in that tight sweater she was wearing when she got out of her work uniform.

She hung back in the kitchen on her own and was poking around quietly when I decided to make an excuse and look in after her. She decided to lean back into the stove and hold herself up with her feet pressed against the counter across, and she hung there for a split second, and then she fell sprawling onto the floor; I knew I was in love. It was too endearing, and today, I would identify it as the behavior of a child, but back then, I didn't know any better or any more than how she looked in that sweater and skirt and I wanted to have terrible, unfulfilling for the both of us sex right there, get all that other stuff out of the way.

What followed instead was a long and protracted wooing that lasted over the course of the next two years, and all the states between Washington and Texas, each coming day a crushing reminder of this girl I had felt was perfect for me—whose whole personality I had created out of the first few minutes of polite and awkward conversation.

It would turn out, obviously, that I knew nothing of this being, could never have drawn the person from those first impressions and had nothing in common with her except that I had the perfectly corresponding ability to ply her decision making with guilt like I knew her from birth. Every other assumption was wildly inaccurate, even the most basic ones.

Our first date established a theme for the rest of the relationship.

Dan and I had been in Seattle long enough to be a little hard to reach by people calling from Brownsville, which was kind of the point. We had a phone, obviously, but we disregarded all incoming calls from Dad and the rest of the family except for Mom. We talked to Mom, when we could. But Mom never spoke of herself, not usually, so when we found out that she was going in for emergency thyroid surgery, it threw us for a loop.

We were stuck in the U-District, in Seattle, while the rest of the family was rallying for her in the hospital waiting room. The reality of it caught me and Dan off guard.

I was horribly nervous about my first date with Karis, scheduled for later that evening, and Dan and I had started knocking back beers at noon. It had become an early and premature wake for mater noster, who survived the surgery with panache and is still with us at this writing; but for the first time in our lives, Dan and I had to face our parents' mortality. More than that, it was our mother's mortality—for whom we each shared an equally twisted, near-Freudian regard, sentimental and deadly.

Latins, I've come to diagnose, are capable of only one type of love, and all other forms of love are subvariants, or gradients of that one original imprinting, learned from the semi-erotic maternal handling of our children as babies, who are usually nursed and kept swaddled for far too long.

We don't *exactly* want to sleep with our mothers, but we can see why other men would want to. We don't *exactly* want to have sex with our same-gender friends, but hey, it's love, right? Love has no boundaries and all that. Like in the Marines. Every other type of love falls in between those two, from how we love our new iPhone (*way* sexy) to how much we love a television show (worth a wank.)

Love, as a means of communication, is eroticized too early, and it sort of fries our brain chemistry into a binary sort of "all or nothing" question, which, if it goes unanswered, and unquestioned and unexplored, then fosters the ground for the sort of relationship that's a bit too close to be healthy.

At any rate, this was the day Mom was going under the knife, and Dan and I got drunk at noon in order to cope with the grim possibilities. But then I had to get dressed for my first date with Karis. We were double-dating, with Ryan and her best friend, Julie. We were going to see *Naked Lunch* at a small theater nearby.

It didn't turn out well.

I wanted to talk to her all through the movie, resenting the fact that after two months of missed phone calls, communicating exclusively by voice mail and gossip, now that she was here, in front of me, I'd have to sit quietly and let the movie play. Plus, Mom was getting her thyroid removed.

So I whispered and annoyed her all through the movie, misbehaved and basically ruined the Cronenberg movie like a four-year-old, because that's how small I was feeling.

Meanwhile, during the whole playing of the woo, Karis had resisted heavily, her will a crumbling jetty to the inevitable persuasion of my tide, and again, if you forgive the further nautical metaphor, she was a lost ship caught in a typhoon that had centered itself directly over her.

I'd fallen in love with a sixteen-year-old girl with absolutely no idea who she was, her whole personality created in my own head, and the only overlap with reality was that she was cute, awkward, and a tomboy.

Mom came through the surgery just fine. Dad called Dan while I was on that date, and they had a long conversation that resulted in Dan freezing out Dad for a few years afterward.

"*Denny*, can I talk to you, *Denny*?" Dad started out the conversation, as Dan related to me later.

"Of course, Dad," he'd said. "You can talk to me. What is it?" I don't know what Dan was thinking this man was going to divulge.

"No, I mean like a man, *Denny*," Dad said. "Can I talk to you like a *man*?"

Dad had been talking to Dan like a man since Dan was six years old, but this, Dan suddenly knew, meant that Dad was about to divulge some ugly extramarital misdeeds, yet once more.

If Dad had a conscience, it was only this topic that gave him pause, made him want to relieve himself of it. Not the guilt, mind you, but the conscience itself. Dad wanted the relief of conscience, not the burden of guilt. To him, those were two very separate things.

"*Denny*, you know that I fuck a lot of women, *Denny*," Dad admitted to Dan. This wasn't news to anyone.

"¡Peró no póngo nada en la ríata!" he says. ("But I never cover my cock.")

"And your mother is going to get all those tests, *Denny. What if I have the AIDS, Denny?* What if I gave her something, Denny? What am I going to do?"

"You mean for mom?" Dan asked, not sure he was tracking what Dad was saying.

"¡N'ombre! For me! I don't want to know if I have the AIDS!" Dad replied, and then thinking about it a minute, added " . . . *Peró para ella, tambíen."* ("But, yeah; for her, too.")

Dan was disgusted and hung up on Dad after cursing him for his selfishness, and Dad later confessed to me that he was confused, unsure as to why Dan had a reaction like " . . . a little girl" about man things, after Dad had so clearly prefaced that the conversation they would be having would be between men about the things men do.

Personally, it was getting time for the long drive back home, and on my last night in Seattle (that first time), I put on my best jeans, shined my combat boots, borrowed a shirt from Dan, and wore a light jacket as I made my way down to Karis's work and waited for two hours until the dinner cruise docked down on the waterfront. When we finally had a moment alone, I gave her a bouquet of flowers I'd bought at a grocery store and a lengthy letter I'd written. We went to a diner and sat while she smoked and we talked. We said good-bye, and I promised her that she'd see me again. Then I ran off into the cold, clear night, the first time I'd been in that part of Seattle, just a twenty-minute bus ride from the neighborhood in which I lived and worked, but had been frightened to leave because I was scared I'd get lost.

A year spent on South Padre Island did little to offset the heartache I woke up with every day, and served mostly to make my fantasy of the girl more richly detailed, if utterly absent of reality. This isn't to say I didn't enjoy the spoils of vacationing young tourists who dotted the afternoons and evenings on the Island. Wounds fare better when licked with others, I found. But it wasn't the sort of "free-love" market one might imagine here; I think I mentioned that during spring break, visiting sorority girls are not interested in the local male population. They mate with their fraternal counterparts, and it was impressive to watch. Both sides of the female-to-male equation were fantastically identical, took an immense amount of care to dress in uniformity, wear their hair and their ball caps in exactly the same way. It was like watching penguins mate, from the sidelines. Hard to distinguish one from another. And penguins just aren't sexy. Cute, but not sexy.

But there would be the occasional cool chick who wandered down, amenable to a weekend fling, and that was good and right, in the logic of Jimmy Buffet.

At any rate, working both the bar and at the newspaper, I finally managed to save enough to buy Karis a round-trip ticket to South Padre Island, and after some tortured telephone exchanges, she agreed to fly out.

She said she'd had some flashbacks of her own, now that she was eighteen and had dropped out of high school. She had been thinking about all that she had left behind in Iowa. She wanted to go back and settle some scores about the way she had left things there when her family had left five years ago, she had been saying.

"Whatever," I said. "Are you coming to Texas?"

"Yes, I'll visit you in Texas," she said.

Even Dan moved to the Island, after a while. He finished his semester at A&I, had run into guys he'd fought that night every so often, but otherwise made it through those three months without further interference. He had proved his point, again. But he'd become bored. He had even begun listening to "tejano" music, and was very close to going "injun" in South Texas. Then he came down for a weekend visit and fell right into step with the lifestyle. I got him a job at the bar, and even had a best friend waiting for him, my boss and friend, Christian. They hit it off immediately (they could talk "sports," while I couldn't), and Dan was set to make the move.

It so happened there was a regular bloke at the bar who needed roommates; he had a huge place and wanted two guys to sublet, so Dan and I offered, and it came together in one afternoon. The new housemate, whose name I don't remember, was missing an eye. He lost it in an accident, where some chick he was walking behind was swinging her purse and he made as if to tickle her and she had swung it at him. He had paid for it with his eye. "A freak accident," he said. He got stoned at night when he watched TV, and his real eye would shrink and redden in the typical stoned fashion, and it would make for a weird moment, if you were stoned, too, and happened to look at him, with that one large, glaringly perfect and unmoving eye staring back at you, and the other one small and squinty red.

So the new apartment was set, and I was ready for Karis to visit. She had asked for the ticket, and I had sent it.

Her flight was due one Friday night, and I had her whole trip planned. Dan was gone somewhere, and I had his Town Car for the week, so I drove the hour to the Harlingen Airport in controlled delirium to pick her up and waited nervously at the airport bar. Against my better judgment, I started talking to the bartender, and the more questions he asked, the more I told him about what was happening, about this girl, about her visiting, about buying the ticket, about how excited I was that it had all come together after a year of planning. He seemed genuinely pleased for me. The bar at the time sat facing the two or three gates, so when her flight had emptied, and I stood there, right by the bar, and she didn't show, I slowly sank back onto my barstool. The guy, well, language wasn't his foremost strength, let's just say, and even if it had been, what do you say to a complete schmuck who just had his heart broken, except "This next one's on the house? I know you got a long drive ahead of you . . . "

Now, if I tell you here that Karis had cashed in that ticket I had sent her and booked another flight out to Iowa to see her old boyfriend and "settle things there," you might get the wrong impression of Karis.

In the end, her doing that—horribly deceitful as it was—brought us closer together, insists the revisionist schmegeggie in me, because she traveled that route, realized the dead-end, and then swung back around back to me. This is how I squared this all away, in my adolescent accounting, distorted by the twisted love I had for her. Well, for someone I had convinced myself was her. But see, because my emotional hold on her was mostly based on guilt, when she pulled this maneuver, I was—at some level—assured that our future was guaranteed. Horrible as it would be, but guaranteed nonetheless, because she would feel horribly guilty that she had done something so underhanded, and I would be there to press down on that lever as needed. It was how I knew how to love.

In the end, about a month later, she decided to move to Texas, and she bought her own ticket this time and moved in with me on South Padre Island.

Thankfully there was a different bartender this time, and I learned my lesson and kept my mouth shut while I waited for her at the gate. Bar. Bargate. Whatever.

She was on the plane this time. (Though, admittedly, when she walked through the gate, there was a thin bat squeak of a concealed good-bye to some khaki-trousered guy in his thirties to whom she'd been talking on the plane, and I wasn't supposed to see it, and I thought better than to point it out, though I had the sudden impulse to bash in his short, smug head right there.)

I'd borrowed a pickup truck to collect her, as she had packed large boxes for her three-month stay, and I didn't think the boxes would fit in my Oldsmobile, nor that it would have made the trip to Harlingen and back. It had become an island car: would run perfectly from one end of the island to the other, just about three or four miles in length, and about half a mile in width, but would begin to overheat if I tried to drive it any farther than that.

The minute I laid eyes on her again, this feeling of unease started glowing inside of me. It felt very much like the dog who had been chasing cars his whole life until the day he caught one and thought, "*OK, now what?*" I began to realize that above all else, I had no idea who this person was, and that the girl I'd fallen in love with did not exist anywhere outside of my own mind, and I had to do some *serious* readjustment to the "Madonna" fantasy that had been the drive of the last two years.

It was October already, in Texas. I'm not sure what month it was elsewhere. It was colder than usual, and the island was empty. I couldn't wait to show her this place, to see if she found the place as interesting as I did, in the off-season. I drove her to the end of the lengths of the roads, took her around and introduced her to my people there, and she was catatonic with fear, would hardly speak to anyone, entirely unsure of herself.

The second or third night, after dinner, I drove us to the southernmost end of the island, where the jetty system separated the island from the Brownsville Ship Channel, which headed all the way back to the Port of Brownsville, near my old house.

It was cold, and the night was deep at that end of the Island because of the absence of hotels, bars, and streetlights. This was Isla Blanca Park, and it was devoid of ambient light, so the night was raw out here, natural. It just so happened Karis had arrived during a red tide, when all the shellfish that have been saving up their toxins as a defense against larger predators suddenly purge it out all at once. The fish breathe it in and become too poisonous for human consumption, and the fishermen take their cue to just, you know, get drunk, instead of pretend to fish and get drunk.

I hadn't thought past the term *red tide* and hadn't really wondered where it had originated, until that night when I was out walking with Karis in the pitch dark and the waves on the beach lit up beautifully in a blue iridescence, while the water beneath it glowed a dingy but definite red. It was the biotoxins and algae in the water, glowing when the waves crashed on the beach. It was otherworldly, or this worldly, in my own backyard, and I had never seen anything like it. It would have been spooky if it hadn't been so lovely, and I couldn't believe there was no one around to witness what was perhaps the most beautiful thing on the island except for me and Karis.

She was equally captivated. In the crisp darkness of that night, the stars glowed like daylight above and around us, and the earth suddenly felt like a snow globe. We stood close to each other, but I couldn't make out her features. I could see the outline of her head, her hair, her shoulders against the starlight, but the detail within was gone, just not there.

She started telling me what she thought I needed to know, right there, as we were entering this relationship and the magic of the moment overtook her, too. Her biggest secret, she said, was that she grew up poor. And that. . . .

"Well, shit," I started to say, "so did. . . ."

"No, she interrupted, you don't get just how poor. Beyond poor. Hippie poor." Her mother, she gasped, was a lesbian. Going on for years now, all of Karis's life.

Her mother, Meg, had been molested by her father—Karis's grandfather—or maybe just abused. I forget which, in the retelling.

Meg married to escape the nest, like you do, and married a hippie carpenter in Iowa at the end of the 1960s and then moved around the Midwest in the 1970s until she realized she had been gay all that time and that was why she had never enjoyed or trusted men ever. Karis's absent father had come from a long generational line of hippies, so hippie they were like hobbits: Her father, she told me, never wore shoes. One time, they were walking home from the grocery store and they kept hearing a "tick, tick, tick," sound they couldn't quite pin down. When they got home, her dad realized he'd had a thumbtack stuck all the way into his heel, and he had not felt it, such was the derma on his underfoot.

Anyway, Meg had Karis and her two brothers, and they would have to come with her as she began her new life as an out-and-proud lesbian. She stole away with them one night and moved to a hippie lesbian commune, somewhere in Indiana, where Karis and her two brothers grew up on a perpetual camping trip where everyone was topless. They tried to assimilate into the public schools there, with very little luck.

Then they moved to Iowa, where Meg and her partner, Sue, had lodged themselves somehow as squatters in a house with no running water, no electricity. They lived there for at least a year, Karis said, now sort of crying.

They had moved to Seattle some years before because Meg had heard that the lesbian community and the social services were very good in Washington State, and then Meg and Sue broke up, which was hard on the kids. They had known Sue for most of their lives. On a couple of occasions, Meg had tried to commit suicide, and Karis had to wrestle a bottle of pills from her hand, dig a mouthful of pills out of her mouth with her fingers. And then Meg had begun speaking in tongues. Telling Karis that Karis was meant for bigger things, for great things, for . . . you know, big things. Stuff like that. In a sort of *Exorcist*-style voice, of course, which is great encouragement to do great things.

"Also," she said, after a while, when we were both sitting on a bench in the park, watching the waves break in blue, "there was a time when her and Sue were convinced that she had become pregnant."

"Your mom or Sue?" I asked, not tracking.

"Mom."

"Without, you know, help?" I asked, not sure if I understood correctly.

"No," said Karis, a spectral figure in the dark. "Just by the power of their love."

"This went on for about four months," she continued. "They even bought baby clothes and prepared a room in that house with no electricity or water."

Now this knocked me back a little. Why would two grown women believe that they could conceivably . . . well, conceive . . . outside the usual course of nature? I thought, *If a woman, who's had sex with a male believes she's been pregnant, it's usually because she's stopped menstruating. But if an older woman stops menstruating. . . .*

"How old was your mother?"

"When?"

"When she thought she was pregnant."

"She was about . . . forty-five, forty-six, maybe," said Karis.

"Early onset menopause, you think?" Leave it to someone prone to hysterics to leap to the conclusion of a spontaneous pregnancy at that age, when they stopped menstruating.

"Maybe," she said, bordering on defensive, and then fell quiet. The noise of the beach in the dark did wonders to dramatize this conversation, and I was on edge, waiting for the next development.

"Well, so what happened?" I asked after a while.

"She lost the baby."

"What, like misplaced it? After she had it?" I couldn't help myself.

"No, she lost the baby!"

"Her period came back?"

"Don't be a jerk!" she said. "You're not taking this seriously! I'm trying to tell you something that nobody knows, something that really . . . you know . . . changed our lives, and you're being a jerk!" she said.

I couldn't help it, at the time, but I managed to rein it in, my jerkiness. I had compassion for Karis, for being put through that, but I couldn't develop anything for her mother, couldn't understand why she'd put her kids through something so fictionalized as a virgin birth. Like the Catholic Church, except with a mullet and a pickup. And plaid flannel. And a tool belt. I could go on. . . .

The confessional download went on for about two days; I think she meant to give me full transparency, or else I was cheap therapy on that island. And it served to obfuscate our circumstances further, to doom an already futureless enterprise.

At that age, with my narrow, if precocious, understanding of the emotional mechanics of the world, of the interactions between people, I had the stubborn thought that we still had a fighting chance. Just by the power of our love, like that fictional fetus. We had as much chance as her mother's fictional fetus, I should say. We would prevail, I felt, because Kari was cute, and I was cute, and the world loves a cute couple. But our period, late though it would be, would certainly spot the lovely new trousers of our relationship.

Very early I began to realize that my ability to integrate emotionally and respectfully with other people wasn't what you would call at a healthy stage. Nothing magnifies your immaturity and inadequacies like that first relationship. How I related to people who were closest to me, after the initial charming, how I communicated was through humiliation and threat, through dominance and the threat of violence, and most of all, guilt. This was the Latin basis of my language. And I had no idea.

It was what I knew, growing up. It was how Dan and I talked to each other, more than in English or Spanish. It was the language that was booming out of our windows, and out of our neighbor's windows, and out of the towering speakers rattling out of Gramma's house, like the calls to prayer for the Muslims. It was our method of civilization, or colonialization, how we conquered one another.

Karis, Karis had no idea about this; her family spoke in some hippie lesbian gluten-free granola Chinese sign language, and I was yelling at her with a 1963 Chevy Impala and a sharpened taco.

All I could do, with Karis, was shout louder than her, in this language. All I could do was win at the shouting.

I'm reminded of something that happened much later on, around the time I was twenty-eight.

I'm in Seattle, playing with my dog, Stella, a horrible and rambunctious Shar-pei. It's actually Rebecca's dog, but you don't know her yet. Rebecca is in the kitchen, making martinis. (Bombay sapphire, like I'm having now . . . Oh, sweet heaven.)

So I'm messing with the dog, who's enjoying the interaction. We're playing tug-of-war with a rope toy, and—hailing back to my Moglai sort of ancestry—I have little compunction in taking this awful diseased toy fully into my mouth and chomping down hard on the thing, while Stella has a hold of the other end. (The martini will sanitize anything too diseased, I figure.)

In order to even the odds, I'm pitched forward, using only the strength in my jaws and shoulders, trying to keep it fair for the dog, but I still manage to pull it away from her, over and over again. Ha, ha! I think: Take *that*, silly thumbless animal!

Stella is getting frustrated, making that "*harrrooommmm*" noise she makes when she wants out in the morning, or when she gets really upset. I do it once more and Stella barks at me, having reached the outer limits of her frustration.

From the kitchen, I hear Rebecca say, "Domingo, would you let the damn dog win? Jesus fucking Christ already."

And it's here, in this moment, that the whole theory of nature versus nurture suddenly freezes on me, and my whole psychological profile sort of snaps in to focus. I am immediately transported back in an emotional wormhole to the day I came home from the first grade and announced proudly to my father, Dad, that I was the fastest boy in the first grade.

"And," I say to him in Spanish, "I even beat Nicholas Gonzalez, who's the fastest kid in the Special Ed classes."

Dad's not impressed.

"I bet I'm faster than you," he says, finishing his beer under the truck he's been working on.

I get hot for a moment, mad, while I consider this.

"No," I say. "You're not."

"OK, then," says Dad, standing up, covered in grease and perspiration. "I'll race you."

For this, he stops his business of trucking and mechanics, to establish his authority over his eight-year-old boy.

He points to the end of the driveway, which ends at Oklahoma Avenue, and says, "First one to get to the street wins. Ready? Go!"

And we charge down to the end of the street, the both of us, and I'm pumping my little eight-year-old legs as fast as I can— the race is in my heart, my legs, my face, and my arms—and Dad, who is about twenty-eight years old at this time, and has legs longer than the length of my body, is striding easily to the end of the road, standing over me as he's doing it and laughing, all the while laughing, saying, "Ha, ha! Ha, ha! I'm faster than you! I'm faster than you! Who's the fastest one now? Who's the baby? Who's the slow baby?" in Spanish, which, like German, makes everything sound far more humiliating than is absolutely necessary, and as we get to the end, I'm just fucking infuriated and exploding in tears and if I had had a gun I would have fucking shot him right in the fucking neck, right there. *Bam.* Who's too slow now, you fucker? Like that.

So I go back down on all fours and grab the rope toy in my mouth again, and Stella clamps down hard on her end, and so that she won't feel like the whole thing is rigged, I fight back for a few seconds and then let her have the rope toy.

I never learned to let Karis have the rope toy, not back then. I didn't learn that particular bit of social currency until I was much older, and sometimes still have trouble with it, if I'm not paying attention.

Doomed from the start.

Chapter 29

HOME

After three months of living on South Padre Island, Karis and I decided it was time to get back to Seattle. We packed all our stuff into the van I used for the distribution run of the newspaper I was writing and producing and moved it into Mom's house as we waited until we could meet the train in San Antonio. In the meantime, Karis would accompany me as I distributed the newspaper on a run from the top of the Rio Grande Valley to the South Padre Island office as part of my $300 a week negotiation. For the entire run, about four hours of driving, I would listen to the area's pathetic public radio, which would occasionally pipe in Terry Gross and some other network PRI stuff, which would give me a lifelong love for essays and storytelling mediated over the radio. The rest of the programming left me convinced that I needed to run as far away from the lower Rio Grande Valley as I possibly could, when the pitiful, pidgin English–speaking students of the local technical college who ran the one station that far down the left side of the dial would get on and try to kill the minutes in between the nationally produced stuff with banter. Oh, it was dreadful. It was painful listening to them, with their ambition to be on the radio far exceeding their abilities, and it would make me squirm for hours at a time, but still I couldn't turn it off.

Anyhow, Karis seemed to enjoy it also, as a sort of rude theater. We packed up our stuff and moved into my mother's house for a week, while we prepared to hike Amtrak to Seattle from San Antonio. Mom bought our tickets, out of unexpected benevolence.

One quiet morning, when it was raining outside and the house was quiet, with Derek at school and Mom at work and Dad elsewhere, Karis and I were alone, in my mother's room, with the air-conditioning droning, and the television turned all the way to quiet. We stayed in bed all morning long, and I made love to her in the way that I had hoped for from the moment I'd laid eyes on her, when her feet slipped off the stove and she had fallen, in that apartment in Seattle, and it was for me, the closest thing to perfect love as I'd ever come close to, in my mother's bed, in that room where Richard had assaulted me a few years before. It had been perfect, delicate heaven, for both of us. Just a moment of it, before it shifted away from us entirely.

On our last night in Texas, I drove us from Brownsville to San Antonio, in the dark, our car packed and a U-Haul trailer attached. Mom, Dad, and Derek slept in the backseat of my car, which had been overhauled at our mechanic's and was now in great condition. I was begrudgingly leaving it behind, as it drove as smoothly as it ever had. Somewhere in the middle of nowhere, on I-37, Karis tuned the radio to some midnight station and found old folk music, and she sang along with Joan Baez and Bob Dylan songs all the way to San Antonio, where we'd stay with Dan for the night. While she sang I fell completely in love with her, had capsized entirely, once again.

Karis's biggest problem in adapting to Texas life was food. She was accustomed to a much healthier diet, low fat and full of fruit and vegetables, and I hadn't realized just how limited your choices were out where we were if you didn't eat fast or fried or fast-fried food. She had lost a lot of weight, because we had taken to eating at home quite a bit, and then she had felt bad about cooking in my mother's kitchen. Gramma had tried to feed us a few times, and Karis had broken out in hives each time. When we got to San Antonio, Dan had a huge fantastic dinner planned at his neighborhood TGIFriday's, which Karis had never heard of, but was unable to order anything from the menu that wasn't fried or full of mayonnaise. I was embarrassed into not eating, either. But I had a few beers with Dan, to make him feel better.

Anyhow, we eventually boarded an Amtrak train headed west, and this was done in the dark, late that next night, and we climbed aboard with the lights off and were able to find a set of seats that were not occupied. When the sun rose the next day, we saw that the car was very nearly full and we were lucky to have found the seats, in the dark. The two day journey took a turn for the miserable as we both began to get horribly sick from the flu Derek had had in the car on the way up north, his last little gift to us.

We moved in with her mother, Meg, in south Seattle, near the heavily gentrified neighborhood of Beacon Hill. Seattle was an odd place back then, where the upscale neighborhood abutted the less-costly neighborhood, the status depending on the view, one would presume. All we could see were electrical towers and a busy road, right in front, but we were perfectly satisfied with that.

Meg didn't work, as she suffered from the Epstein-Barr virus and carpal tunnel syndrome and was in a new relationship, and living with her didn't last long, as it offset some sort of balance at home with her renter, a huge east coast lesbian named Ronata, who became quite displeased when I moved in for a couple months. Instead of renegotiating, Meg decided simply to move out on her own and abandon the home, and we all went our separate ways except for Meg, who suddenly found herself homeless.

Karis and I moved into an apartment near downtown Seattle, and Meg wanted to move in with us. It was a one-bedroom box, little more than a large studio, and we were already going to take in Ben, Karis's fourteen-year-old brother. Karis had to tell her mother no, for the first time in her life, and I think Karis blamed me for it.

We made the best of our situation, both of us having grown up poor and stressed, and we tried to carry on like two kids in love, in desperate and clinging circumstances.

One night Karis had insisted we go to the Indigo Girls concert, part of the Summer Nights at the Pier concert series in Seattle. It was July 1994. They had just performed Jesus Christ Superstar, and the one with the lighter hair played Jesus Christ, the other, Judas. Karis was electrified that night, walking in that long striding way she did when she was feeling really confident, really sure of herself.

Her hair was cut short and she was still very pretty, vaguely tomboyish. I hadn't figured out that she was gay yet; at this point, I thought she was just extremely codependent.

Dusk was falling when the concert was over, and the sidewalks were filled with more than the usual numbers of lesbians in Seattle.

We were moving with the crowd, closer to where we'd parked, and it took us past the aquarium. She was striding tall, smiling big, and I was happy for her; it was not often she was this sure of herself.

Up ahead there was a homeless man with a sign, asking for money. The crowd carved itself around him, giving him the space to market his gloom. They sidestepped his rank possessions laid out around him at his feet: a dirty bag, a tin can, a sleeping bag, some garbage.

Karis confidently marched up to him in an almost goose-stepping fashion, produced a crisp Washington State apple from her knapsack, and held it up in front of his face. "Here," she demanded of him. "Take the apple."

"An apple!" he cried out for all to hear. "What the hell do I want with an apple? I got no teeth!" he yelled, and we all could certainly see he had little need for a toothbrush.

Everyone within earshot burst out laughing, including me. This was the sort of thing that happened to Karis all the time.

Standing behind her I felt her confidence wilt, and I put my arm at her waist and ushered her away from there, and the homeless man began to cackle. "No teeth!" he yelled at us in a moment of rare triumph, as we walked away.

"You have to admit, that was kind of funny," I said a bit later. She burst out laughing through her tears a few yards away, as I opened her door.

Some months later, it was the building manager—an ex-girlfriend of Meg's—who decided that Karis and I should make friends with the couple that lived in the apartment directly above us. They were our age from Florida, and had moved out here to be "outrageous," as the girl, Janine, wanted to be a masseuse and felt that the holistic naturopathic school in Wallingford, Bastyr, was her best choice. And so she was a student, a tall Jewish girl with great hair, while her boyfriend, named Kip, who was bisexual and about a head shorter than her and was from Kansas, did nothing except sometimes imitate Alex P. Keaton from *Family Ties*.

"No, seriously," she told us, when we were high. "He used to dress like Alex Keaton and carried a briefcase, in Florida." Kip looked down and pretended he didn't hear her saying it, but he was fuming, I could see.

They were all right people, Kip and Janine. Well, Janine was; Kip was a five-foot asshole, into martial arts, and had been going to a "naturalistic, holistic" martial arts school in some warehouse he'd found advertised while waiting for Janine one afternoon at Bastyr. Kip worked for a moving company, in one of the Seattle suburbs, under the table.

Kip kept trying to get me to attend this secret dojo in a crappy industrial part of Seattle, and I'd never really thought about karate before, so I demurred, and just got more stoned, never fully realizing what was happening around me.

We started to see each other most every day, and I watched helpless as Karis developed a crush on Kip and he developed a crush on both Karis and me, and I wasn't certain about it all, never could prove anything for certain, and Janine and I started to develop a sort of charged friendship that was due mostly to the fact that we suspected our partners were either having an affair already or about to. The atmosphere was ionized and awkward, and besides his interest in my girlfriend, I couldn't understand the little guy's continued interest in massaging my "chi," rubbing my palm or inner ear lobe.

Then one day Kip suddenly came up with three pellets of mescaline. We took them one afternoon, me and him and Karis, in our apartment, and my mind was completely blown. I was flipping, freaking, with the anxiety of the situation, frightened by the very uncool atmosphere.

Things started to get really tense and things were feeling wrong, wrong, wrong, and so I went into our kitchen, and Karis had been standing there, staring into the cupboards in the dark.

When I flipped on the light, she was standing there and turned to me, except it's not her anymore but my mother, Velva, and she's looking really sad, smiling sadly at me. No shit.

And I flip.

It wasn't so much a hallucination as a revelation that I had started to re-create, in an urban environment, Mom and Dad's relationship, in all its disease and dominating behavior, just like all the literature had predicted, even though I'd fought so hard to prevent it. Except that Karis wasn't living the role Mom did.

Karis had been presented with an accelerated dose of the Martinez family love, telescopically formed in our one year together.

I'm not sure how my sisters were faring; they all seemed to have their hooks into men who were "upwardly mobile" for Texas, and Dan . . . well, Dan was full of the same sort of hot-headed Texan rage that I had, which gave him his own sort of emotional density. He had met a Canadian nurse on South Padre Island and was currently getting his accreditation as a nurse, in San Antonio, well on his path.

I felt I was suddenly alone, with my cheating mother in the kitchen of my apartment in Seattle, my mind a cocktail of Native American head cleaner.

It was in the middle of this disastrous scenario that Mom and Derek, as an eight-year-old, decided to visit. And here's where everything changed.

They flew up to visit Karis and me in March 1995, and I took Derek on a tour of the Holy Grunge City because I knew it would impress upon him the reverence in which he actually saw Dan and me, as the coolest people he knew. I took him past downtown bars where Mudhoney, Soundgarden, and Nirvana had played, told him tall tales about seeing each band here and there, with fantastic embellishments about knocking back pints with singers and roadies and such, and then I drove him to a house on Lake Washington and told Derek that that was where Kurt Cobain died, even though some old couple drove out of the gates as we stood there, and I explained that those were his lawyers, and Derek bought it all, of course, because he trusted me and was eight. (In fairness, I was only about a mile off of the Cobain house. And I did actually get the Bruce Lee gravesite correct, which is *always* surrounded by people, usually Polynesian families on a hajj.)

I had left Mom's visit and entertainment to Karis, who had warmed to her considerably, and decided to befriend Mom and take her downtown to Pike Place Market, which was within walking distance from where we lived, on lowest Queen Anne.

That evening, after we had eaten dinner and Mom and Derek were sleeping in the living room in an extendo-bed, Karis said, "Wow, your mom has seriously come from some bad situations."

"You mean with Dad, and all the kids?" I asked, not sure what she meant. It wasn't easy, that life. But Mom came from the same place as me, and so I didn't really think that it would have impacted her differently. It's like being a part of the 4th Marines, 1st Division: You just naturally assume that the other person has been through the same boot camp and same torturous training, so you assume that the other person can hack what you can hack. Anyone else is a nonhacker.

"Your mom was abducted as a young girl," Karis said to me.

"What?"

"She told me her life story, June," she said. Karis called me "June," like my family does. "You never heard this?"

"No," I said, sleepily, but getting interested, "Every time we talked about her family, my Dad would just say, 'Her mother was a whore!' and that kinda ended anything further."

"Well," Karis says, "Your mother's first memory as a kid is when she was separated from her twin Ricky, and given to her Aunt Hilly."

"Oh, I know that guy," I say. I remembered her brother, Ricky. I mean, I knew that Mom had a twin brother, but he would visit randomly and get belligerent when he drank. I remembered his favorite drink: Crown Royal and milk. Yuck.

"Then there's much more to the story than you know," she said, making the correct assumption.

Chapter 30

MOM'S STORY

Here's what we knew of Mom:

Her mother, who was, in some cosmic joke, actually named Dominga—a fact that I would keep desperately hidden all during elementary school, especially when I was accidently given her personalized pencils as school supplies, which had her name printed on them from back when she briefly sold real estate, and so I had to spend a panicked hour at the pencil sharpener grinding each pencil down to where they read Doming—lived in the city, Brownsville proper, behind the KFC. As my grandmother, she wasn't much of a presence in our lives. It was tradition that we would visit her house on Sundays, after church and lunch at Luby's Cafeteria, and Mamí, as we called her, would always be home because she was a degenerate gambling bingo-loving heathen and her third husband, Arturo, or Deddy, as we knew him, could be relied upon to be working on a car in his driveway, as a mechanic, with some or all or one of his recently bailed boys helping.

These were the guys who I had accidentally bought pot from way back when I was teenager, with Tony driving us to his new "secret biker hook-up." I'd been going there all my life; it wasn't too secret for me.

Mamí drank Tecate and would pour salt on the lip of the can, and she'd drink and smoke with the same hand. She was

actually pretty great, as a person, but not much as a grandmother, some might say. I never felt too close to her, felt like she
was more of a distant neighbor we'd visit, who had cable, and I
don't think any other of the kids felt differently.

She was also very light of complexion and hair, of European
origins, it was immediately apparent, though it looked like she
had fallen very far and very hard from grace. Her pale eye color
corresponded well with the way she dyed her hair in the strum-
pet shades of red and corn-husk yellow.

Mom had Ricky as a twin, and Diana, an older sister, who
were from Mami's first marriage, we thought.

At some later point her mother remarried, to the man who
was now her stepfather, Arturo, and bore him four fairly useless male children. Great, likeable guys when they were sober,
which wasn't often, but trouble when they'd been up to no
good, and they got up to no good regularly. Actually, this is
unfair; the youngest of the four, Eric, is about as successful as
you're going to get, in Brownsville. He's an optician, though I
think he still lives at home, with his mother, and he's just a year
older than I am, which is creepy. But Derek has some interesting stories about spending time with his Dear Uncle Eric.
Some very interesting stories involving a tremendous amount
of cocaine, and Satanism.

Anyhow, there was also this girl, Julie, who had been raised
in that last brood of children, and none of us ever really gave
much thought to Julie, because we took it as a matter of fact that
she was also Mom's sister, but Mom would go quiet when Julie
came up in conversation, and Dad would make crass veiled suggestions at Julie's source of origin, and then would make a point
of humiliating Mom's rather loose family moral code. It wasn't

until we were older that we found out that Julie was the illegitimate product of a quick and unseemly union between Mom's older sister, Diana, and—hold the applause—Freddy Fender, or Baldemar Huerta, as he was known in Los Fresnos, before he hit the big time.

Freddy had knocked up Mom's older sister, Aunt Diana, at a concert in the late 1960s.

"No shit; *the* Freddy Fender?" I asked Dan, when he told me, when we were kids.

"No, retard: *A* Freddy Fender. Of course, Freddy Fucking Fender. She was sixteen and was pretty hot, so they let her backstage after a concert, and he knocked her up," he said. Suddenly, Julie's Afro took on a greater significance.

"Does he . . . does he know about her?" I asked, trying to get my mind around it.

"Of course he does," Dan said. "Now, if he kicks anything her way, that's another story. That's between him and Diana and her current husband, I guess."

(He did, Freddy Fender. He did the nearly right thing and acknowledged Julie and would eventually help put her through nursing school, as an adult, to help her find her own way, when he got out of *la pinta*. If you remember your 1960s pop history, Freddy had served a stint in Louisiana for marijuana possession and theft after he had *Wasted Days and Wasted Nights* on the charts. Or maybe my chronology is off. Anyhow, he'd been caught stealing tires and had pot in the truck, was the story I was told by Dan, and it was a story I loved: Freddy had a record on the charts, and he couldn't help but steal a set of tires. I loved that about him. That's so barrio-credible. I still do things that . . . well, I better not mention here. Except that I was drunk, officer. One word: lawn mowers. Can't get enough of them.)

Anyhow, getting back to Mom: That was the extent of my understanding of my mother and her family. That was what we were allowed to know, by our father, who would proclaim Mamí a filthy *whore* whenever Mom's family would surface in conversation.

Instead of a curiosity with my mother's history, I had a vague association to those Sundays spent at Mamí's house, especially when I smell KFC gravy. But beyond that, I can't really say I explored any healthy interest in finding out more, of who we were. Of who Mom was. None of us did.

Dad and Gramma did a yeoman's job of beating that sense of curiosity right out of us. And Gramma had actually gotten drunk at a party once and squared off with Mamí and took a few swings at her. We still have pictures of that party. I was four, standing by a keg of beer.

Anyway, Mom, at the time, was too subdued to press more than that about her own family origins, and she—even she— didn't trust her own mother, it seemed like. Besides, what the fuck should we care? Dad said so, matter of fact. Her mother's a whore. Simple as that. Mom's family began and ended right there, behind the KFC, where Dad found her.

✤

So by the time Mom and Derek came to visit Karis and me in Seattle, Mom had already developed a strategy to divorce Dad, who had by this time fully embraced his new job as a long-haul driver, and all the freedoms it posed for him. I wasn't keeping track of Dad's movements, and I gathered then that neither was Mom.

Things had been on a steady downward trajectory since the first round of kids—ending with me—had moved out, and Mom felt her maternal duties at keeping the nest intact were mostly over, and Derek as the "Oops!" baby wasn't enough to singularly shoulder the burden of the dead marriage.

Mom had been getting faint tastes of freedom, first with her own job, and her own paycheck, and then with school, which she had started on the sly. And now with Dad gone for so much of the time, and even more so with a new group of friends who were well beyond the reach of Gramma and the Oklahoma Barrio, well, Mom's wings were spreading.

The trip to Seattle was a life-changing event for Mom, as if she had been waiting all this time to surface and tell her story to someone—*anyone* who would care, and Karis was as close to family as she felt comfortable at this time, and so she told Karis everything, from the beginning. They'd gone to Pike Place Market, on a very long walk, and Mom downloaded her story to Karis.

When she was just a toddler, Mom said, her mother had regifted her to an aunt, whom Mom called Tía Hila, who raised Mom as her own daughter until Mom was around six. This was the early 1950s, in Brownsville, Texas, when Dominga couldn't support the children she'd had. Another victim of childhood regifting.

Though the country had been at war in the 1940s, Mom's mother and her sisters had been living up a fantastic reinterpretation of the American Dream. Her sisters and she had moved to Southern California and gotten great jobs in the war effort and had more than enough gentlemen callers hanging about, by the looks of the photographs Mom eventually shared. They looked like movie stars, and dressed the part.

Their father, my great-grandfather, had been a French pharmacist, who had somehow ended up in Brownsville, Texas, after leaving France in a hurry with his family. He'd opened a pharmacy in Brownsville but still hated the United States with such French fervor that he tiled his floor in American silver dollars and was then told by the Treasury Department to cease and desist. They have an old portrait of him, with a bushy mustache, a stern look, and my mother's sad squinty eyes. This revelation explained a considerable amount about our origins and peculiarities, like my fondness for absinthe and pharmaceuticals, and *paté*.

But back to Mom. Or rather, her mother.

Mamí had come back from her time in California and was being courted by a well-to-do young man from Mexico with good prospects. His family owned a shoe factory in central Mexico, and he was very much in love with her, had asked for her hand and she'd accepted. She was quite the looker, and he had good reason to be jealously protective of her. He was forced away at some point, either militarily or for business, and asked his younger brother to look after his betrothed. Younger brother had agreed and off went her fiancé for an extended absence. Of course, in the stylized manner of these kind of stories, Dominga and the younger brother became involved during this time, and she came down with child.

When the older brother returned, there was a row, and the younger brother, scorned, wandered off ashamed and dishonored and jumped into the path of an oncoming train.

Dominga was vilified and blamed for the catastrophe, for destroying the family, and she was sent back to Brownsville, where she had her daughter in quiet illegitimacy, at her father's home. (This was Diane, my mother's older sister, who would, in turn, get knocked up by Freddy Fender in the mid-1960s.)

Dominga, at this point an unwed mother in the late 1950s, met up with a man who would marry her, named Frederico Garcia, who fathered a set of twins, which included my mother and her brother, Ricky, and was gone by the time Mom and Ricky turned three. Dominga just couldn't keep it together.

This is why my father would call her a whore and dismiss any further discussion of my mother's origins; he'd finally found someone he could feel superior to—since his own origin story wasn't exactly an uplifting or successful one with a happy ending—and he could intimidate and humiliate Mom whenever the topic came up. "She was a whore," he'd say of my mother's mother, and felt like he won.

But Dominga wasn't a whore, just a child who'd made some poor choices in what probably wasn't the most hospitable area for a good-looking single white mother. People can be far more punitive to the good-looking, if they have the opportunity, as a sort of punishment for being born with the luck of good looks. And an attractive unwed white woman would draw a lot of attention in a town like Brownsville, in 1958.

All that, I learned much later on; what Mom shared with Karis was this:

Dominga felt she couldn't take care of both Ricky and little Velva Jean and felt she had to give up one of the kids, as was acceptable practice in Brownsville at the time, as discussed previously. Dominga's sister Hila was the only one of the four sisters who remained childless, and unmanned, and so she gladly, willingly, appreciatively took on the responsibility of caring for one-year-old Velva Jean, as Dominga summoned all her womanly charm and ensnared yet another, and final, man to help her through those wretched Brownsville mornings.

Little Velva Jean was suddenly in heaven, cared for and mothered and encouraged in a healthy, matronly environment. The difference was dramatic; though Hila lived just a few blocks from Dominga and her new husband Arturo, it was a much more wholesome house, quiet and full of love.

Mom was eight years old when Dominga decided she needed more help around the house and figured it was time to call Velva Jean back to her house, where she belonged, so she could clean after her four new stepbrothers, who ran the place.

But her Tía Hila had other thoughts; Velva Jean was hers now. How could Dominga possibly think she'd just let her go like that? She had been her daughter for nearly eight years now, and she had nothing, no one else. Velva Jean was as much her daughter as Dominga's. More so, even; she'd raised her in her own home. Tía Hila fought back, tried to go the formal route to secure Velva's parentage. Started filing the paperwork.

Then one morning, in the middle of the conflict, while Tía Hila was still in the process of getting the slow-moving government to recognize her as the primary caregiver, she took little Velva Jean to the corner grocery store and was busy buying something, with her back turned. Dominga ran in and snatched little Velva Jean, put her in a car, and drove the few blocks to her house and locked her in. She wouldn't answer the door when Hila pounded on it, pleading, crying her spinster eyes out, begging for her little girl to come home with her, but Dominga was relentless.

She wanted her daughter back, now that the hard work in raising her was over and the hard work in raising the next brood was just starting.

I didn't know any of this. I'm not sure if any of my sisters knew this either. This is what Mom had told Karis that afternoon, while Karis listened, in the way that Mom didn't trust that her own sons and daughters were capable of.

And it wasn't over, the story.

Mom lived a Cinderella existence, at that house behind the KFC.

To say that she was beaten and treated terribly would be a terrible fiction; she wasn't mistreated or left to starve or anything too Brothers Grimm, but she did have to earn a considerable keep and look after four rambunctious and giddy, unfocused, and oddly loveable boys, who were headed toward a very dreary adulthood because of the sheer lack of discipline and formality at home. They were good and happy kids, and looked like they were pathologically stoned from birth, in the photos I've seen, this last brood from Dominga's overproductive womb. Her second husband, my stepgrandfather, was also a very easy going man who fixed cars for a living. He might even be called a mechanic; who knows. But Mom's stepbrothers made for a lot of colorful stories and bad moments. They were huffers, uncontrollable potheads, and thieves.

Once, when I was about fourteen years old, I'd run an errand for Mom and Dad some cold wet morning and had left some change in cash on our dining room table, which was right by our front door, and was then taking an *ahem* quiet moment to myself in the bathroom, enjoying the solitude, when I heard the door open and her stepbrother Johnny call out.

I called back, from the bathroom, "No, neither Mom nor Dad are home. Come back in about an hour, and they'll be back. You want me to tell them something?"

I heard him mumble something, and there was a tone in his voice that took me a moment to recognize as a sort of switch over to wile and subterfuge, and then I realized he could see the $35 I left on the table, and thought, *No; Johnny wouldn't steal that. . . .* I put my pants back on and hid the porn magazine I was reading under the towels, and by the time I opened the bathroom door, he was gone, and so was the money I'd left on the table.

His stoned friends, though, weren't so quick, and I caught Johnny trying to get back in the car, which didn't have a reverse gear, and I said, "Johnny! Hey, Johnny! Did you happen to see what happened to the money on the table?"

And he said, smiling, "What? No, man; no way," and then to the guy in the front seat, "Hey, get out of the way, man, come on, move!" By this time Gramma had noticed what was going on, and she saw the look on my face and had dropped what she was doing and ran back inside her house to get her .9 mm pistol, but by the time she came back out, chambering a round over her head very theatrically, they'd driven off through the U-shaped driveway.

For a second, I thought, *Fuck. I could have kept that money and just framed Johnny. I'll remember that for next time.*

But again, that wouldn't come until later. As I said, Mom's stepbrothers were just likeable dumb kids, even before they got into drugs, and they didn't really treat her so badly, and neither had Dominga or her new husband. But it was still against her will, and she had cried herself to sleep for years, wanting to be back with her Tía Hila, who lived just down the street, and she was slowly dwindling away from her broken heart.

Mom made a plan, at that point. When she turned eighteen years old, she would move back in with her Aunt Hila, and finish college, though she did want to get up to California and see what the fuss was all about with San Francisco. Meanwhile, Vietnam had begun to rage, and across America, the ghettos were being razed by draft cards.

Dad watched in terror as two of his cousins who were his own age had been called up and drafted, defenseless against the legality of the little white cards. He was graduating from high school this year and was lean and Mexican and 1A.

So Dad made a plan, at that point. He would get married and have ten kids at once. He would marry a woman with ten uteruses, and impregnate every one of them. He'd be 4F in a matter of six months, if he was lucky.

Out of nowhere, and without prior warning, Aunt Hila died when Mom was sixteen years old, from a broken heart, Mom was convinced. And I can see that. Mom was a sophomore in high school, and her aunt, the person she considered her real mother, was suddenly gone. All she had left was this life, behind the KFC.

Dad had known Mom from Brownsville High School. They hardly knew each other, had only really known each other from a social studies class. Dad proposed to Mom, without actually disclosing why he was asking her to marry him, and she didn't exactly disclose to him why she had agreed, but she did, and they moved forward into this *X-Factor* of a marriage.

Mom took the opportunity to leave her family behind, and Dad took the opportunity to crank out children to keep himself safe, while he was still at Gramma's feet.

Chapter 31

ORIGINS

They hardly knew one another, but they agreed to marry. There are few photos from their wedding, and I don't remember if Mom wore white.

From the few stories Dad and Mom ever shared with us, during those moments when they'd break their resolve and actually speak about the origins of their union, you got the sense that when Dad told you a story, that he was lying, or that Mom, if she spoke about it, was ashamed.

It was evident to anyone really listening that they'd had very little in common except that each of them was as desperate as the other for some sort of escape that they both—as teenagers—imagined marriage would offer.

Dad, as a newly minted American citizen at seventeen years old and recent high school graduate, was a huge blip on the radar of the local draft board. When his two cousins had been drafted, it was brown-trousers time for Dad.

So he pounced on Mom—you get the sense that hers wasn't the first proposal he'd offered, though he was a good-looking, stretchy bloke—and then had her producing children like a Pez dispenser.

Mom's life had stopped there, sublimated to this role in a primitive and desperate farm-based family of natives, which was run by Gramma, who had the biggest cock in the barrio after Grampa's death.

Mom did the only thing she could during this time and absented herself, locked herself away in the single-wide trailer in her heart, after Grampa died. (It was what she could afford.)

Grampa had been kindest to her, in the new situation, in the same way he had been kindest to me in mine, for those eight years I knew him. Maybe that's why she resented me more than any of the other kids, in her way. Maybe it had struck some sort of primitive jealousy that Grampa, boozer and womanizer that he was—but who wasn't, in that barrio?—had reminded Mom of the love she lost when her aunt died, and was now watching it unfold with Grampa and me; maybe that's why she disconnected so cleanly from me for those years, and left me to the bitter mercies of Gramma and Dad.

There had been that period when she'd befriended her daughters, during their high school years, but had then become sorely disappointed at their collective betrayal when, after they'd reached college age, Mom had decided that it was her turn, and she had started college and started to leave Dad, and they turned on her, to her surprise. Her daughters had not been happy with this. Were not encouraging of their mother's impending freedom. See, Mom picked up where she left off, at age sixteen, and began her life all over again.

She didn't come right out and ask for a divorce—it wasn't something anyone in our family would even consider as an option—but Mom got a very clear idea of the displeasure and disapproval she would endure for years to come from her daughters, who couldn't understand why she wouldn't stay with her husband of twenty years. The idea of divorce had settled in the house like a layer of asbestos, and she and Derek would mostly come home at this time simply to sleep and eat, and then spend their days away from it entirely, now that it had grown dark and was the only other thing Gramma watched, besides her Univision, from across the driveway. With Dad doing long-haul driving, he was home maybe five days a month, and he liked it that way, until he heard from his mother that Velva wasn't coming home so much anymore.

Mom flew back to Texas, and my relationship with Karis continued to get more and more textbook, more and more Freudian.

One night, with the ridiculous tension and anxiety in the air, I took a lot of LSD with Kip and Karis, but not Janine, who had to go to school the next morning. And while we sat in their apartment waiting for it to kick in, I was convinced that Kip and Karis were making freakishly animated "I love you" faces at each other when my back was turned. I started whipping my head around, trying to catch them at it, but I never did, or they were quicker than I was. Then the acid hit.

I'd always taken LSD in copious amounts in the simple hopes for a hallucination. That was it: I wasn't asking for much. I simply wanted to experience a hallucination like the hippies used to have and describe in their music and literature. It was what we were after, in high school, when Tony and Chris and Frank and I would spend all day taking whatever we could get our hands on.

Hell, I was willing to settle for a simple understanding of *Yellow Submarine,* with LSD, the unusual amounts of it that I would take. I couldn't get this stuff in Texas; the first time I ever took it was the first night I was in Seattle. I managed to put my fist through the hatchback of a Volkswagen Rabbit, but other than that, it had been a fantastic six or seven hours.

I'd forgotten I'd actually taken it, come to that, because I'd been so happy to see Dan after a five-day bus ride—through fricken *Idaho,* of all places—and we had started in on the Henry Weinhards right away.

"Look at this," he'd said, and showed me a sugar cube he'd plucked from the open freezer door. Unremarkable.

"It's a sugar cube, from the freezer," I said.

"It's a hit of liquid LSD," he said. "There's a guy who lives in the apartments next door to the store where I work, and he never has any money, so he comes in sometimes asking for like milk and eggs and bread, and all he has in trade are drugs. Usually acid, but sometimes pot. I've been saving them."

I looked in the freezer, and Dan had a bowl of sugar cubes in a covered plastic container, in the door. There are about fifteen of them, and some pot.

"Holy shit, man," I say, and take it from his hand and just pop it in my mouth.

"Holy shit, man," Dan said. "That's quite a bit of acid you just took." It would have been better had he quoted from Cheech and Chong: "You just took the most acid I've ever seen anyone take, man."

"Wish me luck," I said, and then drank some more beer.

Three hours later, I was in The Zoo tavern, having made it through the door with Dan's military ID, and the dolphins in the floor tile started jumping, like animation. I looked more closely, and they kept doing it: splish, splish, splash.

Hunh, I thought, and then remembered: the acid. I forgot about the acid, man.

There was a wake in there, that night. A regular customer who'd committed suicide, and I ended up talking to a girl who was really sad. It was her ex-boyfriend, whom she really cared for, and then the back room started to glow, behind her, over the pool tables. I began to have very inappropriate thoughts, responses, to this wake. I wanted to make fun of her grief, make fun of his suicide, like it was a weakness. I was completely out of my mind, unprepared for the effects.

Anyhow, by this time, I'd done LSD more than a few times, and knew what to expect, but I wasn't prepared to enter that state of mind with the atmosphere so electrically charged with what was going on between those two apartments. I swear, our twenties are the times of sheer lunacy: children making grown-up decisions, creating terrible beds for themselves, and others.

Karis sat at my feet, waiting for hers to kick in. Kip sat across from me, his feet touching my shins. It was like an early Bob Dylan song. We were listening to some organic college band, like Rusted Root or something. Janine was sitting on her sofa, looking over her schoolwork, when she said something, and Kip's five-foot energy turned twelve feet tall out of the corner of my eye and he growled at her, in response, and she immediately shut down, like a beaten child, told to hold her tongue. *Whoah,* I thought. *Did I just see that?*

I looked up and over, and Janine said something again, and he did it again: He grew large at her and growled violently, and she buckled underneath it, and it all happened in milliseconds.

My perception had sped up, or time had slowed, and I started to watch people as they really interact, in microflashes and microexpressions. Kip, as a little guy, was hyperaggressive to Janine, who was taller than he was, and could be easily subdued.

When he tried to talk to me and Karis, I saw him turn into a sort of mechanical doll, repeating things he'd learned—he was trying to be funny, trying to go into schtick—but it came off horribly, like a sick pantomime, like a coin-operated grotesque caught in the same repetitive five-word phrase repeated ad infinitum, and his eyes were glowing and sharklike, dead, and Karis, who had not moved, suddenly looked first like a child, and then an absent fetus, a dirty glow peeling off of her in cakes as she smoked a cigarette. Language suddenly became impossible, and broke down into simplified multimeaning sounds that meant a hundred other things, and I concentrated more on the origins of the meaning rather than what was being said, like I was looking for the root of intention because I could see the layers of distortion as the person tried to hide some things, emphasize others, and disguise meaning. I understood far more from the body language and facial expressions of the people in the room, much more than what they were actually saying, which made no sense, when out of nowhere the stereo started playing the Grateful Dead and began to glow red, menacing, and I stood up and said, "I have to go, you can't talk about anything in here, you're all unhealthy," and then ran for the door, Karis following me, and I swear that in the panic and danger of the next few seconds, of me making it down to the lower floor and into my own space, I gave off a psychic charge that could have powered a car in that walk from their apartment to ours, just downstairs.

For the next eight or so hours, my primary focus was not to lose my psychological ground. I was experiencing a collapse of logic and higher function, locked in a Hunter S. Thompson–worthy freak out of epic proportion. I was very close to complete psychosis, was very close to losing it, and probably did a few times, when I couldn't remember my name, when I curled up like a baby and tried to write my name, so I could remember who I was, when I played an episode of *The Simpsons* to try to calm down, and the whole episode was written about me, when I could feel the moisture in the air, and then suddenly my body would suck it all in and become dry, cracked, like a lakebed in Arizona.

It was the ninth gate; I was going through the ninth gate, and getting the awareness of crazy panicked jazz, baby, jazz: I was seeing the notes between the notes, and it was freaking me out considerably.

But I came down from that, around eleven the next morning, in bed and looking out the window, while talking to Karis about a very uncertain future, and about all the things I saw, telling her in code that I had been aware of the affair she was about to have, or was having already.

Chapter 32

CHEATING

In my defense, I was trying to do the opposite of what Dad had done with his wife. Actually, in all of his life, all of his choices. I was using him as a reverse compass.

I think in my distorted thinking, if I didn't "oppress" her by demanding that she didn't cheat, perhaps she wouldn't. Maybe, if I gave her the choice to make, and allowed it to happen, I wouldn't be the asshole my dad was. That she would choose correctly, that she would stay.

Karis had started having bad dreams, where she would be surrounded by her family and lying in a bed, and they had all gathered there to help her commit suicide, by taking a large black pill. Her mother fed it to her, and Karis would be crying, begging her to stop because she didn't want to die, and they would force her to swallow it, and waited with her as she died, holding her and thanking her.

One afternoon, when Karis was supposed to be visiting her mother and I was staying at home, because Meg and I didn't get along—Meg blamed me when Karis told her she couldn't move in with us in the one-bedroom apartment, and so she decided she'd remain homeless, couch surfing at the hospitality of the women from the Lesbian Resource Center in Seattle—and I was staying in on that off-deadline weekday, just getting mildly stoned and listening to *The Freewheelin' Bob Dylan* and scribbling in my notebook, Karis suddenly appeared at our door and closed the door behind her with a look of sheer panic and fear in her face and announced, "June, I lied to you. Instead of being with my mother, I was upstairs with Kip and then Janine came home, and I hid in the closet, and she caught me, in the closet." She says all this without taking off her coat or dropping her purse.

Being high, and being young and in love and unsettled by this abrupt forthcoming, I was knocked off-balance, and all I genuinely felt right then was a sincere sympathy for her state, not really taking in what she was telling me.

I said, "Oh, you poor thing; you must be totally freaked out. Come here," and I hugged her, asked her if she wanted some tea, clutching her to me. She was shaking, started crying into my shoulder, and I tried to calm her down, wondering if we had anymore chamomile.

It took me about an hour to realize what exactly was happening, to become angry, and I did fuck all, because I didn't want to react like my father would have, didn't want to be seen by others as a dominating, patriarchal machismo Mexican man. So I just took it.

⁜

Meanwhile, down in Texas, Dad had come back into town and was drunk.

His first stop was with *La Señora,* the *cúrandera,* his witch doctor. He waited for an hour in the waiting room while the line of superstitious pilgrims in front of him got their medical results mystically diagnosed (no need for X-rays here) or were given useless assurances that their financial health would be guaranteed.

Dad was here for a different reason this time. He wanted to know if his wife was fucking around behind his back.

It made no difference that he was carrying on behind hers—that was none of her business, and he had been feeling guilty enough about it already, didn't need anyone else telling him it was wrong—but if she was doing it, then there was hell to pay. But he needed to know for sure. Gramma had been on the phone with him and told him already that things were not normal over at his house. The other night, Velva had a woman over, and she spent the night there, of all things.

Gramma had taken revenge on the lesbian affair by turning off the water so those two *marimachas* couldn't shower in the morning. (It had been Mom's friend and coworker from JC Penney, who had been afraid to go home because her live-in boyfriend had been beating her, and also another textbook case of projection, on Gramma's part.)

But Dad didn't care about Mom being with another woman. It was another *man* that Dad was concerned about.

Dad had suspected Mom was carrying on behind his back since she had started working at the JC Penney's in Amigoland Mall, near the border across town, because she'd been acting all independent and paying her own bills and seriously crimping his manhood by doing what he was supposed to be doing, and well, things just weren't the same anymore. And he suspected there was a man involved. So here he was, at his "spirit-counselor's" and was asking her if his wife was cheating on him. And so she asked her spirits what they knew. Was Domingo Martinez's wife cheating on him? She looked in the ball, and so on. Rang the glass of water and all that.

Then she said, "Yes; your wife is seeing a man who's short, wears a uniform, and she sees him when she's supposed to be at work, when she's supposed to be somewhere else. They think they love each other, and it's a secret for him, too. She still loves you and the house, and she is conflicted, but she needs more. She wants more than what is at home. They make the love in secret." Yada yada yada.

Dad got his money's worth. The information was vague enough to be specific, and when I heard all this about a week later from Dan, I found it fantastically perfect that all the information "mystically" divulged could have been describing my situation with Karis, and I wondered if the spirits had tapped into the wrong "Domingo Martinez," sort of pulled up the wrong website when they Googled the name.

Dad didn't take the news well. To him, getting it from the *cúrandera* was the same as getting it from a police report, or an X-ray. He paid his fee and went to a bar and got more drunk, then drove across town to the Amigoland Mall when it was closing and caught Mom *in flagrante delicto,* as Dad sat in a borrowed car across from the employee's exit in the JC Penney parking lot, and watched as a Border Patrol Jeep slowly crawled up and turned its lights off, waited. So had Dad, in his borrowed Cadillac, from across the parking lot.

Mom eventually emerged from the door and walked around the Jeep, saying good-bye to her coworkers as she got in the passenger-side door, like it was something that happened regularly. The coworkers drove off and Dad took his moment, left the driver's side of the car and the door hanging open, and walked across the parking lot to the Border Patrol Jeep. He opened the passenger-side door and surprised both Velva and the border patrolman, later identified by Mom as her "friend," Felípe, and he pulled her from the back of her collar onto the parking lot.

They had not been enclenched in a passionate kiss, but had been staring longingly into each other's eyes, said Mom. "We were just talking!" she says.

Dad didn't say anything about this because he denied it could have happened, or didn't remember specifics, or doing it.

Mom was on the ground, outside the Jeep, and began yelling at Dad to stop, stop what he was doing. He then grabbed the Border Patrol agent—who was armed with a .9 mm sidearm, a shotgun, and an M4A1 carbine—and Dad started to pull him out through the passenger-side window as the door had swung back, when Mom fell to the ground.

"Sir, don't do that, sir!" he screamed, this "Felípe," under his tiny little Mexican moustache. "Sir, please! We were just talking! Sir, please let go!"

Dad pulled Felípe across the console and into the passenger side and had to step around Velva Jean to get him out. And when Dad let go to get a better grip on the man's collar, the border patrolman took his own moment to force the door closed and scramble back into the driver's side and drive away, leaving Velva on the ground with her enraged, drunk husband who had just caught her cheating.

Felípe didn't look back, or stop. The Border Patrol Jeep turned onto the main road and drove off, into the night.

Had he, Felípe, looked back, he would have seen Dad backslapping my mother into the ground and kicking her before he walked back to his borrowed car and drove off somewhere else, to drink all this away, and Velva Jean was left in the empty parking lot of the JC Penney, crying to herself, under the sulfur lights and the moths flitting in crazy deranged circles underneath them.

Chapter 33

CHEATING II

I hadn't fared so well either.

I got drunk at the bar across the street, what was then the Romper Room, and then I put on my combat boots. Karis drove up in her yellow Toyota pickup with the bed cover and the bad brakes and waited at the curb, where I had been sitting, smoking cigarettes, waiting for her to get home.

I'd finally gotten mad. Said some things over the phone when she was at work at the PCC deli, making something with tofu.

She pulled up to our assigned parking spot and didn't get out, just sat there and smoked a cigarette out her window.

And then I stood up and walked across the street and I kicked in the side of her truck, with my boots, my combat boots.

I kicked the shit out of the side of that truck and a guy from across the street said, "Miss, miss, are you OK? Do you need help?"

And I looked at him, and I stopped myself, because I was being the asshole, and Karis finished smoking her cigarette, and then drove off, with her truck now looking much the worse for wear, and I walked back upstairs to our empty apartment and listened to Kip and Janine thumping around upstairs, as she threw him out.

When she did leave me, when we finally broke up about a month later, after I'd moved into that horrible karate studio and started taking classes every morning and afternoon like Remo

Williams, when she would finally go, Karis left me for a woman who looked exactly like her mother, Meg.

I had to sit down, when she told me. I had met this woman, one morning when I dropped Karis off at her job at Puget Consumer Co-op, in Ravenna. I forget the woman's name, think it was something like Chris, but she was carrying vegetable crates from a delivery truck, and I made the comment to Karis that she looked like her mother's brother: same hairy bow-legged walk, same plaid, same tool-belt, and same moustache. Karis had not laughed.

Take that, Mr. Freud.

Chapter 34

KEEP ON TRUCKIN'

Dad is doing long-distance trucking for a company out of Brownsville now for some time, and he's in the middle of darkest Mississippi headed for a Ford factory in the south with his new partner, an old man named Jim who's been doing the route for fifteen years.

It's three in the morning when they're approaching Tennessee and a tire in the driver-side rearmost axle blows and shreds and catches fire from the friction. Dad is driving and watches it all happen in the side-view mirror. He panics, wakes up Jim, and tries to pull off the interstate.

"Keep on truckin'!" yells Jim from the bunk, pulling on his pleated denim jeans in a hurry. "Keep on truckin'!"

Dad, unsure of what to do, does instead as he's told and he downshifts, presses hard on the accelerator, and moves the rig back into "the hammer lane."

The tire is alight, glowing orange in the sideview mirror as Jim climbs into the passenger seat and soporifically readjusts his glasses. "Keep on truckin'," he mumbles, mostly to himself, patting his shirt pockets for his smokes.

Sure enough, the tire burns out in a matter of minutes, shreds itself over the course of a hundred miles, and billows for a couple hundred more but they make it into Memphis, all the way to Galilee.

This is what I think about the morning I awake with a pain in my lower back. It's very likely my kidney, maybe my liver, and I get upset at my deterioration, so I grab a beer at nine that Saturday morning.

Take that, kidney. Screw you, liver. Gonna keep on truckin'. Gonna make it into Galilee.

Chapter 35

TEN YEARS LATER

Hard times. I've been unemployed for ten months now, working a temp job at the Starbucks Resource Center, answering phones, having recently separated from my last relationship of three years. I have to move out of my apartment. I simply can't afford to live here anymore. It's not a great apartment by any means. There's no view, it's near basement quality and if there is another bad earthquake, I will certainly die in my sleep. But it's mine, and I'm thirty-two, and I want my own space. Thing is, I can't come up with the $700 anymore.

I have to move in with Dan, who had moved back to Seattle after six years of living apart, and now lives across the way with his mute girlfriend, Orlene. She's not really mute, but you have to be able to talk about the things she likes or else she'll sit quietly opposite you for hours without any impulse to speak to you. I've tried this before and have been impressed by her ability to say nothing, and to say it without a single word.

We're going to try this out, because both Dan and I feel a great compulsion to live together, like we did when we were kids. Dan's helping me get my stuff out of my apartment and into the one we're going to share.

We're trying to get my couch out over the balcony: That's how we got it in, after I had to move out of Rebecca's, my last girlfriend.

The couch, my couch, was one of the contingencies of moving in with Rebecca, previously: When we had moved in together, she had a terribly uncomfortable couch, and I demanded something far superior to the driftwood obstacle she had bought in a display of sympathy for a Pike Place Market "artist." I'd received my severance pay from the union I unwittingly and unintentionally joined while working at the *Seattle Times,* and it covered the cost of this lovely, oil-clothed couch, dog proof and deep. And about 250 pounds.

It's coming over the balcony, and Dan is holding it while standing on the roof of a UHaul, lowering it down for me, and in my terrible cross trainers, my ankle gives way while I'm supporting the couch, shifting it to a secure point of rest, and my knee pops out of socket: I feel more pain then than all the pain I've felt combined for the last ten years. I collapse, but save the couch, shifting its weight onto the face of the rockery nearby.

My knee pops back in again and I'm nearly delirious with pain and worry, lying in the parking lot. I've been out of work for ten months and have no health insurance. I'm scared, scared a lot. The couch is safe and Dan, his Honduran girlfriend Orlene, and their tiny El Salvadoran friend Alex are all standing over me, looking at me. Health professionals, all of them.

"Is he going to be OK?" asks Alex in Spanish.

Orlene leaves without saying a word.

Dan says, "He'll be OK. June, are you going to be OK? Can you stand on it?"

I stand on it. Dan decides I'll be all right. Everyone gets back to moving.

I try to walk it into place; it feels odd and loose, the knee, but I think I can get it back into place. I've never been delicate, and my body has an odd way of adapting to its borders, like Japanese goldfish growing to the limits of their ponds. It's as if my knee, knowing I don't have insurance, will compensate with whatever material it's got available. I'm walking inside ten minutes, but by no means normally.

I ask Dan, "Seriously, what do you think will happen? Is this bad? Will I need to see a doctor?"

"You probably need surgery," he tells me. "You probably need a CAT scan, or an MRI. You probably tore your ACL and need to have it surgically stitched back together."

I'm petrified now, but satisfied the couch is being moved.

Chapter 36

DAN'S LAST FIGHT

This is the letter I wrote to my sister, Marge, and her husband, Corwin, the night Dan was in the hospital having surgery on his broken leg, the result of a fight outside a bar. Dan had asked me to keep it secret, but I called Mom in hysterics, crying, and she called Marge and Corwin, who managed to fly her out the next day, paid for all her emergency expenses. This is where my relationship with them changed, and my relationship with Dan began to die. I left the letter mostly intact, except where it needed updating, which is noted with parenthetical marks. When I wrote it, I was slowly drinking a bottle of tequila, the only booze we had in the empty three-bedroom apartment into which we had just moved, that day.

Dear Marge,

This is exactly the sort of thing I ran away from when I left Texas. Dan has just had that sort of hotheaded response all his life, and he couldn't back away; in this case I didn't get to him in time to stop his knee-jerk macho reaction when these snickering fishermen called us "faggots" for wearing similar black leather jackets.

We turned around, I think I said something snickering back, left it at that and I told Dan to leave it; what did it matter? Forget it. Come on.

Personally, I had forgotten about it and entered the cab of his truck in the parking lot of that bar, less than a mile from (our new) home. Dan couldn't. He said, "You going to let them get away with that?"

(And this is where I feel culpable. Responsible. I allowed our shared *verhuenza* to speak, I remember. I said, "So, what, you want to do something about it?" He didn't respond. I said, "Fine. Come on." Shifted like I was about to open the door. You see, Dan was challenging *my verhuenza.* My sense of pride.

I wasn't strong enough to talk him out of this significant challenge in testosterone. In brotherly, familial honor. This is where I failed Dan. This is the choice I will take into my other lives. This is where the relationship with my older brother ended. I should have said something else. Because I wasn't big enough to say, "Yes. It is beneath us.")

He put the twelve pack in the truck and walked around the back and confronted the tallest guy in the group (the one who said the snide things), as I watched in the rearview mirror. I sincerely did not think Dan was going to swing. But then there was a swing, the first one connecting before I even opened my door to get to them.

My whole life, since I was a kid, Dad accused me of instigating fights so that my big, "bad" older brother could finish them. This has always been very far from the case. You couldn't understand the depth of responsibility and guilt I felt any time Dan stood up for me. He is my older brother and as such, my biggest idol, from when we were kids. I absolutely *do not* ever want this man-boy hurt, especially for something I did, or could control. Dad used to say to me, "You are like a Chihuahua, barking and starting fights so that your bigger brother can save you!"

This again was another very wide chasm in my relationship with Dad. How he could believe that I would put Dan in such a position? Every time Dan has ever been in an altercation that involved me in any way, I have always—*always*—tried to keep him from doing so.

That time in Kingsville? I wanted desperately to keep him from going back to that bar and challenging that bastard Larry. But Dan was determined, and I couldn't let him go alone. He was fresh from the military, full of that fake power. He was my older brother, and he was basically calling me out as well. (Where was my *verhuenza?*) I had to go. I hated that I did. Hated that he did.

I don't know if you get what I'm telling you.

I am *not* a bad person. Neither is Dan. But he's yet to develop that sense of responsibility and accountability that would keep him from throwing a blow for something as stupid as being called gay. Frankly, that night, I took that as an underhanded compliment, coming from those common fisher folk dressed in old Eddie Bauer flannels, blue jeans, and white tennis shoes. I mean: Really.

For most of six years I took those classes in karate and boxing so that I could have that skill set, that defense/offense available to me should I ever need them. Those skills are so rusty now that I am deeply surprised they surfaced last night in the defense of my older brother, who lay broken under some weak, stoned fisherguy who was brutalizing him because Dan's leg shattered when Dan misstepped. (Dan was knocked out, I have come to realize.)

They engaged at the end of the truck. I heard Dan yell at the guy, "What did you say to me, you mother-fucker? What did you say? Did you think I wouldn't do anything about it?" (Dan liked to do a Robert De Niro impersonation, when he was being tough.)

The guy was backpedaling. "Now, hey man; I didn't mean anything by it; we were just kidding. . . ."

And then Dan clocked the guy square.

I didn't want to get in this thing. I didn't think it just.

I jumped out of the truck as three other guys were running toward them. Immediately my whole body went leaden, heavy. Slow to respond. My whole body was feeling, "I really don't want to do this."

But quietly I felt the inhibitors in my mind click off, like a military guy opening his attaché case of weapons, taking in the disability of my left leg. I ran in front of one guy and blocked his approach to Dan and the other guy. Dan was ten times as tough, ten times the fighter as the guy who was swinging back at him, I could tell even in my peripheral vision.

It was like lead, my right leg, as I faced the first guy in front of me and realized he was in for a fight. I kicked him in his left hip and turned his lower torso suddenly. I had to force it, that kick. My left knee hummed disagreeably in yellow. I didn't want to do this. He threw his arms up at me to block the combination to his face as the kick connected.

Stop, it says. *I can hurt you.*

My knee disagreed with this, and I reconsidered my stance. I had to protect myself, and them, and Dan. It was stupid, but it was the responsibility of the veteran fighter. (It was what I learned, in karate. You take the responsibility to keep yourself and others in control. You hit just hard enough to make your point.)

I was trying my best to think my way through this. I attempted to prioritize my goals, now that I was reluctantly in this situation. I didn't want to hurt my knee, primarily. I didn't want to hurt these guys so that the altercation became actionable. I wanted to keep Dan from hurting anyone and himself. First and foremost, I wanted it over and I wanted to be home so I could yell at him.

I was still not convinced I wanted to do this. I felt pressed, forced. These guys were just stoned fishermen who said something stupid. They didn't want to fight. I didn't really want to hurt them. I'm not a bad person. I really felt Dan was overreacting, but he's my brother and I couldn't get to him to stop. I had to protect him. I stood between the first guy running up in white and Dan, behind me, and kicked him in the hip and punched him square in the face, then set up to do it again.

The guy I hit stopped, stunned. He looked at me and he was like . . . I don't know what. He didn't want to fight. He wanted to talk. I wanted to talk, too, but my brother was fighting the guy not six feet from me to my right, and I couldn't stop and reason. I pushed him away and threw another set of combinations. The guy was saying something to me but I couldn't listen. I told him things, I talked to him while I was hitting him, things I don't remember saying. "Go away. Keep away. Just stay away. I can and will hurt you. You just don't know. You just don't know."

The guy in white was still talking, trying to get me to stop, trying to reason with me, and mostly, at this point, I just wanted him to understand: This is a fight. You're in a fight. (You wear a different face here.) Fight me: I'll try my best not to mark you because even here I can tell you don't want to do this.

(And I am a just person.)

From here I don't remember anything, because when you're in a fight, you don't think your way through it, you don't make conscious decisions, you react and act. I think, to his credit, the guy in the white swung at me and almost connected, to the back of my left ear, but nothing's there this morning. Not even a lump.

Then, I remember the guy in the blue ran toward Dan with another guy and the big guy Dan was engaged with (I think they were trying to stop that fight), and I ran in front of them, too.

I think that's where I broke my pinky, when I hit him with a sound combination of hooks and straights to the head and body and I kicked the guy in the blue square in the stomach, and this is where I heard Dan's glasses skid on the pavement.

This might be where Dan broke his leg. A bad step. (This is where he was knocked out.) The weight of his body crushed the tibial plateau—shattered it—and he fell. Stupidly, and one of those weird things, I focused on finding his glasses to minimize the financial impact of this, to be able to get up and out of here as quickly as possible and so I scurried after the frames when I heard them go and ran after them, when I got the chance.

I didn't notice that Dan had fallen. I didn't see that the tall guy was now straddled over him and going left/right, left/right on Dan's face—Dan's arms were held out defensively and he was screaming, "Cut it out, cut it out." (I might be making that part up. I don't have a memory of this. I just remember the guy straddling Dan, vague images.)

I picked up the lens and the glasses and saw the guy on Dan (from a few yards away). I was stunned: It was just *wrong*. Dan was not supposed to be the guy on the ground. It didn't make sense. I screamed and charged, ran at the guy and behind him and grabbed him by the collar and slammed him backward into the ground, where he fell hard, hit his head, and rolled, and then I hit him, I don't know how many times, in the soft tissue of his face. I remember, here, at this moment, thinking about how surprised I was at how much human facial tissue gives, how soft it is, how unlike the punching bags and padded structures on which I'd spent so much time and so much knuckle. (So much so, that when you hit it, it is almost welcome, and you want to do it again because it doesn't feel real.) I'd lived here ten years on my own and never been in a fight. But this was different. We were in a fight.

The guy stood up, and he was much bigger than me. We stood there for a millisecond and looked at each other. (He was tall, about six feet, three inches, and lengthy, thin.) He outweighed me by about fifteen pounds, and we looked at each other, both of us giving away our poker faces at the idea of having to fight each other. I looked at him and I was scared, and though in my "tough guy" moments I would welcome the idea of fighting someone larger and with a better reach at any other time—I just didn't want to do this with a bad knee.

But it needed to be done. A look came over my face. I yelled "*Fuck!*" at what I had to do, made a face, and charged at him, bad knee and all. (It was the best thing to do, with an opponent with a better reach. Get inside and hurt him structurally, limit his reach. Tackle him. I remember thinking I was going to wrap him up, use his height against him, pull his legs out from under him and exaggerate his own falling velocity to slap his body on the ground, headfirst if I could, my weight on top of his. The reserve inhibitors in my head were unlocked. I intended to kill him. I don't know if that's actionable, admitting it here. Because I finally got scared. This guy bested Dan, who has always bested me. That was the look he saw, the banzai charge of death. This isn't bravado writing this, four or five years later: I intended to kill him, when I charged him. I think he saw that, in my face, and he ran. Thank fucking God that he did.)

The other guys I had just fought started running toward their Chevrolet Blazer and then, suddenly, remarkably, so did he. They were gone. They all just turned and ran. It was all over in twenty-five seconds, it felt.

If this had been Texas, if they had been fighters, we'd have been in real trouble.

Dan was calling to me, at my feet. His face was covered in blood. This didn't make sense to me. He was in total control of this thing. Personally, I did what I had to do in complete reluctance. My brother couldn't get up. He was in shock. He was white, under the blood. His eyes were huge, pupils dilated completely.

"Get up," I said. "Let's get the hell out of here, before the fucking cops show up."

"I can't," he screamed.

"What do you mean?"

"My leg's broken."

"No, you've just sprained something or another."

"It's broken—is the bone sticking out? Is there blood on the blue jeans?"

"No, come on, let's get out of here, your truck is open."

"June, I can't get up."

"Dan, get up; come on, put your arm around me. Let's get out of here."

"I can't stand on it; you're going to have to call 911."

"No way."

"Call the fucking ambulance."

"No fucking way, come on."

"Please call the ambulance."

I couldn't lift him. He weighed 260 pounds. He was in shock. He actually blacked out from the pain of the fracture while the guy sat on him and hit him. He didn't remember that.

I dragged him to a curb. *This is my brother.* I dragged him to the curb and had to run to the AM/PM and call an ambulance. This was my brother.

The ambulance and cops got there, and I tried to answer questions, tried to keep Dan calm. He told me I had to get Orlene, tell her what happened.

"No," I said.

I don't want to write about that.

That was the most awful thing I've ever had to do, was explain this to Orlene. That poor girl.

I was so terribly tired of this Latin macho bullshit. This was not me.

This was Dan's last fight. I hoped to God it was mine, too. I'd been crying all day. I hope those stupid fishermen fuckers know the sort of restraint I took from really hurting them, because they were soft. They were like afternoon butter. I simply don't have it in me when I don't feel the cause, and this wasn't the cause.

I have never put Dan in a situation where he had to fight my fights. I have taken my beatings growing up, and I spent all that time and money learning how to defend myself because I felt it was critical to my psychological architecture to have that sort of confidence. And now that I had, I felt so dirty.

Dan will tell you the same thing. I never asked him or did that "Chihuahua" thing Dad accused me of.

That was so totally unfair, so completely wrong, and so fucking Dad. Anybody who really knows me knows this. Also why I can't forgive Dad for who he is. What he thinks of me.

This is not the life I want to lead. This is why I left Texas. I think Dan has finally learned the whys behind that, the way he saw Orlene last night. How she's dealing with this today.

For my part, I am so totally sorry. I didn't do this. I did my best to help him out of a really stupid decision. And he's apologized to me, so you know. Dan's acknowledged how incredibly stupid he was not to have walked away. He needs his mother. I need my mother. Thank you for getting her to me. To us. I'm sorry for all this. This isn't who I am. This isn't what I'm building here.

Your little brother,

June

Chapter 37

SETTLING ACCOUNTS

Dan and I had made the mistake of taking an apartment together after he moved back to Seattle with his girlfriend, Orlene. He'd met Orlene in Brownsville, where she'd been a certified nursing assistant at one of the many long-term care/nursing homes he'd finally decided were better suited for a man of his particular demeanor. Dan had a habit of becoming emotionally attached to his patients, couldn't see them just coming and going, like in hospital care, or clinics. He wanted to help, make sure they were comfortable, safe. This required him to have more control over their destiny, and them to be either disabled or old.

His patients responded, as did their families. Dan is a very good and conscientious nurse. As such, he has a treasure chest of things given to him by the families of his patients who have died after he'd watched over them for years at a time. When it came a patient's time to expire, he was there for them, and for the family, and the family would leave him with a memento of the patient: a favorite baseball cap, a Mickey Mouse watch, something.

That grown men who aren't fucking should not live together is something neither he nor I had learned at this point, when we decided to rent the largest apartment I'd ever seen in Seattle.

Dan and Orlene and I had moved into the topmost "suite," on the fifth floor, for an exorbitant $1,500 a month, which was a considerable sum, since I was out of work and responsible for half the rent. That the even 50/50 split on the rent was fundamentally an unfair determination since there were two of them and one of me didn't even occur to Dan: He would take care of the cable and the groceries, so it would even out, he explained.

We had a tremendous view looking east over Seattle, over the north end of Queen Anne Hill and the boat channel and the three or four bridges that crossed it, and of flight paths and the Cascade Mountains—a sight that was heavenly to us, having grown up on the salted flats of Texas, where you could only see to the end of a street, or a dusty horizon, and the world felt flat, fell flat, ended flatly right over there.

There was a strong, clear pull to throw ourselves into this housing situation that neither of us would identify for months to come. Dan and I were subconsciously re-creating our "Saturday morning cartoons" hour, the few times as children we were allowed to wake up and sit in front of a television and watch cartoons from six to ten o'clock with a bowl of cereal, and the rest of the house sleeping in. More often than not, even this little gem of childhood was interrupted by Gramma or Dad's hangover and we were forbidden to watch television. Something needed doing. Get dressed and get outside. There's a tire needing changing, a truck needing a jump-start, a radiator needing radiating.

So, with each of us silently raging and wishing hellfire to take either Dad or Gramma or both and not sharing these thoughts with the other, we'd slink into our shared bedroom, get dressed for dirty, sweaty work, and sometimes, because he couldn't take it out on anyone else, Dan would shove me in to the closet or to the floor to make himself feel better. I would get back up and then add him to my list of people I wanted God to kill that day, and we'd get on with our Saturday morning.

Now, more or less as adults, as men in our thirties, Dan and I were re-creating a scenario where we could sit in front of the television as much as we wanted, and if Gramma or Dad would try to tell us different, well, there would be hell to pay. We were big fuckers now, Dan and me, and beholden to no one.

Since I was out of work and living on a small stipend of about $275 a week, and Dan had broken his knee in that fight on the *very first night* we had moved in together, well, we had a considerable amount of downtime, time to reflect on what an awful and emotionally wrenching experience that had been, when I had to come home alone from the brief visit to the pub down the end of our new street, enter the apartment without Dan, covered in his blood, and find Orlene sitting in their new bedroom folding and organizing clothes while watching QVC. Then had to tell her that Dan was in the hospital with a broken leg. And her response, so appropriate and deserved, was to throw her dolphin figurines at me and curse me, curse him, for being stupid boys, for hurting ourselves in fights, hurting the people who loved us. And all I could do was just stand there, staring at the floor, staring at my brother's blood on my hands from wiping it off of his face, his nose, his eyes while we waited for the ambulance to get him. She cried. God, how she cried.

I drove her to the hospital where they had taken Dan. And, well, it had been more than a few weeks after that, with his leg in a cast and him on crutches, that we eventually settled into something resembling normality, routine. Orlene would wake up in the morning and get to work around ten or eleven. Dan, even on crutches, would drive her. Orlene did not, does not drive. I would sleep in and listen to all this from my end of the very large apartment.

They would leave, and I would maybe drift off or wake up and cruise the want-ads online and send out more meaningless résumés. Dan would return about forty-five minutes later with a twelve-pack or two and that evening's dinner. I would get out of bed, wash up, and we'd greet each other as we sat down to watch cable and drink beers, tinged with whatever painkillers Dan had available that day: Vicodin, Percocet, some opiates, whatever was around. Remember: Dan was a nurse fresh out of knee surgery; he had a fantastic medicinal tool kit.

We lived together like that for a year, plumbing the shared depth of a missing childhood and hoping to chart the bathymetry so we could start the swim back up to the surface, as human adults.

I could watch between four and six movies a day. Dan liked to intermingle his fantasy movie watching with ESPN, which was my cue to head back to my room and watch something a bit more BBC on my own, until he'd begin to make dinner, which he still loves doing, and then my job was to sit on a stool and entertain him with stories and conversation until dinner was on low heat. Then we would have a few more beers and wait for Orlene.

When Orlene came home, she was usually in a snit—Why is there a mess in the hall? Who didn't take out the trash? But when Orlene was upset she'd mostly yell in Spanish so we usually ignored her, or giggled, just ducked our heads. Then we'd have dinner, and she'd retreat into their bedroom and watch QVC or the Home Shopping Channel and talk for hours with her sister, back in Brownsville. Dan and I would serve up the final entertainment for the evening, drop a couple Vicodins or Percocets each to enhance the last three or so beers and off we'd go, reliving those stolen Saturday mornings with pharmaceutical encouragement.

Dan's favorite movies at the time were the first two *Lord of the Rings* installations, and in order to set the mood, we'd build huge conflagrations in the small fireplace, and because the undersize fireplace was incapable of housing so large a holocaust so often, we ended up melting the metal grate by the time we moved out. We watched the *LOTR* series endlessly, blending formlessly into the couch with narcotics, and we would discuss the movies, the books, and Peter Jackson's impossibly perfect special effects so often and repetitively that we became like Jews in a Talmudic exercise, so much so that Orlene started referring to our movie watching as "Bible study."

It wouldn't last, of course. No shared psychodramatic constructions ever do, and especially not one that began with Dan starting a fight with stoned fishermen who had snickered at our expensive leather coats and Doc Martens, ending with Dan getting knocked out and beaten severely and falling in such a way that crushed the tibial plane on his right leg.

This is when we really had the chance to talk about growing up, about our horribly complicated feelings about Dad, Gramma, and Mom, and our sisters, who were thriving and lovely and were having lovely children. Dan and I never used the word *sacrificed*, but it was the picture that we reluctantly painted as adults, inherently adverse to the idea of victimhood. We turned our noses up at people who claimed to be "victims." It was unmacho. And yet as we continued talking about what had happened to us, how we had been raised in the typical barrio mentality, that, as boys, as the indentured children of Mexican peasants, it was evident that Dan and I had been sacrificed so our sisters could marry upward. And it had worked: Our sisters were doing well, thriving with good husbands, and we struggled with being happy for them, excited for them. Our hearts were twisted with resentment, as he and I dug in and embraced fully the addiction and alcoholism and crap machismo that would be the only thing we would ever inherit from our father. Mazel tov.

We had successfully constructed a situation where we could, Dan and I, talk for hours and days without end about what we'd seen, felt, experienced, in a way that an extended weekend of me visiting him in San Antonio or Brownsville, or him visiting me and a girlfriend in Seattle for a week simply could not afford us. Dan and I wanted to talk, talk freely about what we had endured as kids and did not want anyone else to restrict that. And we wanted our cartoons and Fruity Pebbles, godammit.

As such, some evenings would get downright maudlin. There was one night when Dan was cooking something seafood in the halogeneous kitchen and things had been happy enough that day that I was comfortable enough entertaining him, chatting idly and telling stories while drinking beer and rolling an occasional joint. There had already been some days when the emotional rot had started squelching through, and we'd become terrifically hostile to one another, Dan and me. He'd clamber upright onto his cast, grab his crutches and make like he wanted to hit me. I would look at him, bewildered, bemused, backpedaling and taken aback: Dan and I had never—would never—get violent with one another. It was code. It just wouldn't happen. But neither Dan nor I could ever back down from a fight. And yet, there he was, scrambling to punch me. He never did. And I never would.

Those days, the apartment would glow with resentment and tension, ready to burst in conflagration at the first available oxygen.

But this evening, things were great. I had done my due diligence earlier that day: sent out résumés, jogged my five miles, filled out the requisite unemployment forms, belayed the banking. Orlene got home and she was OK, we were not too blasted drunk, and Dan had made her favorite dinner, so after she went off to bed and we were watching HBO, there was something on the TV that reminded us of the time I broke my arm when I was fifteen, in high school.

"Oh, yeah," Dan said, "It was a Sunday." I snapped right into the memory: It was indeed a Sunday. Street ball, with all the boys from Hannah High School varsity and junior varsity. and I was the only freshman allowed to play, because Dan was my older brother. It was a stupid, unstructured game on the front lawn of the high school. Just some boys playing ball.

But the star blonde quarterback named Shawn was taking it too seriously, and at the end of some dumb tumbling and fumbling about, he dropped the ball and I jumped on it, from the opposing team, and recovered the fumble. This didn't sit well with Shawn. (His parents couldn't spell "Sean.") My arm was broken quickly, at the end of his knee. I heard it crack loudly, right in front of my face.

Dan said: "Get up, come on; it's our ball."

I said, "Shit. My arm is broken."

Dan said, "No, it's not. Let's go."

I said, "I can't move it. *Look.*"

Dan saw it was in the shape of a Z.

I stood up and said, *"Fuck!* Thanks a lot, Shawn!" to the guy who did it.

Shawn said, "No problem," and walked away, and there was murder in Dan's eyes.

Dan's best friend, Victor, has an older brother, Carlos, who happened to be there. He drove us home, my left hand closed in a fist over the sharp angles of my right forearm. Carlos drove a black mid-1980s Thunderbird, just a couple years old. *I'm in shock,* I thought. Dan was panicked, in the back seat. I heard Dan talking to Carlos, directing him to our house that was very, very much outside the city limits and into farmland. Carlos drove his sleek car over the muddy roads and into our driveway. Dad was waiting in the doorway at the end of the concrete sidewalk leading from the parking spot, because Dan had called ahead.

I got out of the car; I think someone opened the door for me . . . I stepped out and my left hand was still on the Z of my right arm—both bones, radius and ulna, in a straight break, forced down where they shouldn't have been. I walked the length of the sidewalk to my father, who hadn't left the house in three weeks, unemployed, out of options, stinking of a cheap, recent drunk, fuming inaudibly but very noticeably—his dark black hair flaring this mask of hatred. He was unwashed, dressed in a T-shirt under a thin, red-lined flannel shirt, screaming curses and profanities at me in Spanish, his runted son who *had* to get hurt, *had* to break something, putting him in a position where he couldn't pay anything, *pay nothing.* And then, right there, as I walked to the top of the stairs, drawn magnetically to the open door to my house, where everything was going to be safe, my father punched me on the side of the head, yelling horrible things, and he was about to hit me again, and I fell into the doorway, onto my broken arm, and my brother, Dan, who is only two years older than I am, Dan rushed my father and slammed him against the wall, pinned both of Dad's shoulders to the weak plaster board and said, *"What the fuck are you doing?"* and Dad stopped, scared, speechless, his eyes wide and white.

Dan kept him pinned, panting. Gramma rushed forward, studying my adolescent arm, goosenecked. Dan let *pater noster* go, paced behind him like an animal, ready to protect his broken little brother again.

Dad, Gramma, and some other cousin looked, whispering in their pidgin ghetto Spanish: "Felípe. Felípe can fix it. Felípe has birthed breached calves. He knows what he's doing, medically."

So I remembered this just then, a little while ago, watching Dan as he was back in the kitchen, his kitchen, on his crutch, adding spices to whatever it was he was making, with his right eye changed a little—nerve damage from that last fight we just had a few months ago. I kind of started to cry, but of course I didn't tell Dan, who was sitting in the dark room across from me, but couldn't see me in the flickering gloom of the television.

In my memory, my mother rushed forward at this point. It might not be true. She was screaming and yelling that none of her children will be disfigured, if she has to work to the end of her days. I think that part is true. I woke up in the hospital a few hours later, when the pain had died down. The three middle fingers of my right hand were locked in a sort of Chinese finger prison, dangling from a metallic bedside stem. I was in a hospital. I finally felt safe. I was an American again, not livestock on a Mexican farm. That's how close a line I walked that day, where my brother and mother kept me.

An oddly attractive nurse with a two-pack-a-day voice told me, "Honey, it's gonna feel a little hot in your ass for a while, but then you're gonna feel real good after that, is that OK? Do you understand me?" and I wasn't sure if she was talking to me like that because she wasn't sure if I was conscious or capable of understanding her English, and then the Demoral sears this lightning path from my right ass cheek to my soul—and for the very first and only time in my life I hallucinated. It was fantastic. There were these figures fighting with swords and words and lines, in the sky, right outside the window. Geometric shapes, all of it. Language. Absolute communication. Undiluted violence. Purest redemption. Kindness in its most poisonous form. It all made so much sense to me. Right outside the window. Right out there.

The doctor snapping my arm into place with a sort of yoke in the crook of my elbow brought my attention back suddenly, and the pain was sharp, unbearable; I passed out.

Some minutes later, I woke up, and the doctor was wrapping a wet cast on my wrist.

I turned away and said, "Gramma."

The nurse asked, "Are you seeing things, honey? Are you hallucinating?"

And I said, "Is there a squat woman clutching her purse to her stomach in the doorway?"

The nurse said, "Yes."

I said, "Then, no."

I was totally disappointed. Gramma was the Devil. I thought maybe I was seeing the Devil.

Dad was gone by the time Mom drove me and Dan back home from the hospital that night. He was gone for two weeks, and one morning I woke up to find him sitting on my bed, dressed in the same red plaid shirt but looking like he was going off to work, and he scuffed the top of my head and laughed, tried to make a joke out of the cast I was wearing and his behavior that other day. I didn't look at him, couldn't meet his eye. I was throughly disgusted with him.

Dan and me, we were working through our own trouble. But Dan, in all his oafishness, I understood he was still just trying to save his little brother. Every fight he's been in, gotten me into, he was just trying to save our honor. Save something. Save anything.

In his own clumsy way, he was doing the best he could. He was like Stella, the unruly Shar-pei I used to have, defending his family.

But tonight, when I remembered what my father and grandmother could have done to me—the way they could have disfigured me, and it took Dan to throw Dad against the wall when Dad hit me, my arm broken the way his leg now was. . . .I think me and Dan are even. Getting closer to even, if we were keeping accounts.

And I said to him that night, "Thank you for protecting me from our father that day."

Dan started crying, over on his couch, in the dark.

If it has to be like this for now, I thought to myself, *I think we're on our way to being even.*

Some months later, I begin to get blue. Dan doesn't notice it because it's summer, and it's hard to be blue when it's summer in Seattle, especially with the view that we have from that deck. We're sitting outside one Sunday evening, lounging like real gentiles and looking east over the aft end of Queen Anne Hill, onto the Ballard Bridge, watching the boats sailing from Lake Washington into Puget Sound, or vice versa. Some evenings as the sun went down, we would sit outside and watch the planes directly above us on their final approach to SeaTac Airport, and we would plane spot, counting all the planes stacked up in the skies around Seattle as they lined up in tandem to land. It's still the best view I've seen in my twenty years in Seattle.

We're drinking light beers that night—or at least I am—and he's having a Shiner Bock, from Texas. Dan's got an assortment of Texan hits on rotation on his CD player. The Old 97's, Dwight Yoakum, Kris Kristofferson, Steve Earle. Drinking music. He's telling me about his sciatic nerve, how painful it is, now that his cast is off. And I tell him how much I jogged yesterday at the Seattle Pacific University track, then walked around with a friend of mine and her dog, and how I talked and talked and probably said far too much. And he tells me how he called in yesterday and is having a three-day weekend, about the ribs he's about to cook, boiling on the stove now, and we're having a great night, on the deck.

He gets on the phone with Alex, his Lilliputian friend from work, who is evangelical about his simple beliefs in a Latin American Jesus and sings Celine Dion songs at top volume, utterly without shame or irony as he wanders the halls of the nursing home. Dan is calling him and rattling off the opening bars of the *Mexican Hat Dance* when Alex answers because there's a patient at the home with Alzheimer's who belts it out in earnest every time she sees Alex, who is not Mexican, but Salvadoran. This makes Dan crack up, because Alex is a proud El Salvadoran who hates to be misdiagnosed as Mexican.

They've got another patient who's been circling the drain now for two days, circling like one of the planes we're watching that night, and Dan wants to make sure she was still alive when Alex saw her last. The patient, Mary Ellen, was eighty-five years old, but as Dan liked to tell her, she didn't look a day over seventy. She was a delusional alcoholic who thought she was in a bar and Dan was the bartender. Mary Ellen had drunk so much she was incapable of speaking most days and had been mostly reduced to autonomic function. She was the most difficult patient Dan and his group ever had. The rare moments she was lucid, she would claim to be Native American, though she was really Scots-Irish. Dan and Llambi, his Croatian nursing partner, call her "Dances with Whiskey."

Dan asks Alex if Mary Ellen has gone to the "Big Pow-Wow in the Sky" yet. You have to have a real sense of gallows humor when you deal with people dying on a weekly basis, Dan tells me when he's on hold.

"For some patients," he corrects himself. "Not for all of them." His eyes drift off at this point.

Alex begins to yell at him for being callous, hysterically invoking the name of Jesus, so Dan breaks drunkenly into the opening bars of the *Mexican Hat Dance* and Alex, fuming, hangs up on him.

We both sit there and laugh at Alex. Stupid Christians. Alex loves Dan.

I'm feeling a big shift that night, can sense it, whether it's happened already or if it's in the mail or happening now, I don't know. I feel like I am waking up after a year of the steadiest, most narcoleptic administration of morphines, opiates, and painkillers augmenting the regular booze outs. I'm headed for trouble, I can feel. I had made the decision to stop this lifestyle when I moved out in a couple months, since I had just started working at a trade publication, would soon be back on my feet. I am thirty-two at this point and need to steady myself, pull back from the edge, where my toes have felt the updraft of the plunge into an actual habit—my inheritance as an addictive personality.

I had taken to spilling out the contents of the medicine cabinet and playing Hunter Thompson: "What Would Dr. Thompson Take?" was my motto. I wanted to make it into a bumper sticker. But that lifestyle didn't have legs. Didn't feel right, no matter how I tried to rationalize it, justify my associates. Fold it all into something acceptable. Denying loudly the predisposition to addiction.

Then Kris Kristofferson comes on. Dan's playing all the big Texan hits that night.

There was one time some weeks previously when Dan and I had overdone it with the meds and beer, and we were having a loud, two in the morning debate about "Me and Bobby McGee" and whether it was homoerotic.

"It was the 1960s," Dan says. "Even Bob Dylan admitted to having sex with men and shit."

"He's singing about a girl," I yell back, from my impression in the couch. "Bobby's a chick, a fuckin' hippie chick he picked up in Montana."

"No, it's a dude," says Dan. "A dude that fuckin' dies."

"No, it's not, man," I say. "What fuckin' version are you listening to? You're confused because Janis Joplin sang it, too. Bobby McGee's a hippie chick he's traveling with to California to be with all the other hippies. It's the goddamn 1960s, man; they're all out there. They're all fuckin' hippies. Anyhow, she doesn't die, she just wanders off with another 'old man,' like. She trades her first old man for another old man, in like, Tucson or Arizona. Listen to the damn lyrics."

"*No!*" Dan insists. "It's a guy, and he *dies!*"

The next morning, Dan is incredibly sick, calls in to work. He lies on his bed, with a trashcan positioned readily nearby. The very memory of "Me and Bobby McGee" is making him nauseous, he tells me later. He's kept from puking all night and all morning long, but then he sings the opening lines of the song, in his mind, as he's lying there.

Busted flat in Baton Rouge, waiting for a train . . . he thinks to himself. Then he erupts in vomit.

Hunh, he thinks to himself, afterward. *Let me try that again.*

Busted flat in Baton Rouge, waiting for a train . . . Then he vomits again.

"OK," he decides. "That song goes off the playlist."

But this isn't what is bugging Dan tonight. Someone at work had asked him if he considered himself "Tejano."

"We're not 'Tejano!'" Dan yells at me in his usual oversize animation. He had been offended.

I say, "We're Texican," because I had just seen John Wayne in *The Searchers* and there had been a mention of that word, by the German or Norwegian couple who was carving out their livelihood in the middle of fucking nowhere. I'd been watching a lot of John Wayne lately.

I sing the opening bars to the *Mexican Hat Dance* to make him laugh.

Dan says, "No, no, no; we're fucking Americans; Texans next, godammit. We like our barbecues and beers and the cowboys and boxing." Hear, hear. And our drugs. I think Dan's overdoing the Vicodin as well, but I'm not in charge of his life. And I don't know it right now, but he's also made the decision to change this around, but we haven't talked about it yet. I'm on the verge of weeping because Kris Kristofferson is now singing about his "Sunday Morning Coming Down," and because it's been lonely out here, in between our own lives, slipping in between the streams of other people's lives, where I thought I really wanted to be.

Later on, I find a bottle of something that looked suspiciously like liquor in the fridge, with a label written in a foreign form of Spanish. It was a gift from Alex, from his travels in El Salvador, something called *aguardiente*. It's odorless, almost tasteless if it wasn't for the flavor of your own soft palate dissolving while it strips away your tongue. Dan pours out a couple of shots and down the hatch they go: We drink a toast to *Dances with Whiskey* and another to Luther, Alex's fictional black boyfriend.

Maybe it's a sort of withdrawal I'm feeling. It's too beautiful an evening to feel this weepy. I can see north all the way to Crown Hill, see Mount Baker in the distance looking like a musky ice cube in the reddening dusk at ten o'clock that night. It took us a long time to adjust to the summers here, the eighteen-hour daylight around the solstice. Dan decides he wants to play the Guns and Roses album, *Appetite for Destruction.* I am nothing if not a sucker for nostalgia, so I say, "Sure," and I giggle all the way through the first couple tracks, remembering the meteoric impact this album had when it hit Brownsville. Dan had enlisted in the army that next year, ended up in Korea, and he'd played this album nonstop while on duty guarding the demilitarized zone, he tells me. The idea of Dan in that position, of Dan listening to "Mr. Brownstone" with a loaded M16, staving off the yella horde, the idea scares me, frankly. Saving Texas from Tojo.

The sun is finally going down, at nearly eleven o'clock. We're going to watch *Raiders of the Lost Ark* and yell out Harrison Ford's lines before he says them, like we do.

As we're watching Indiana Jones, I begin to tell Dan how I had made our neighbor, Joe, play the role of Sapito when I was a kid, me pretending to be Indiana when I was twelve. I say, "Fuck. It must be a terrible thing to not be able to play the hero in your own imagination. Do you think it's my fault he's never left home and is managing the neighborhood Jack in the Box?" I feel really awful all of a sudden.

The CD player is unexpectedly playing the *O Brother Where Art Thou?* soundtrack, and Dan starts singing, "*You are my sunshine, my only sunshine . . .* " in the kitchen while he's preparing the barbecue sauce. I can't help it in the dark living room, and I start crying again, feeling hopelessly lost. Contaminated.

Something's over. Something's changed again.

By the time we moved out, after a full calendar year, Dan and I couldn't stand to be in the same room alone with each other. We had exhausted our supplies of stories, thinned ourselves to translucence, robbed each other of any sort of mystery or truth.

Any recollection or cleverness that got started out of one or the other's mouth was immediately met with a sense of disgust, a transparent mask of disapproval: Oh, not *that* fucking story again? I've heard it ten fucking times. Get over it; it's *not that funny.*

We did this to one another often enough that we didn't want to be in the same room together anymore.

The division was severe, terminal. Our drive for mutual understanding drove us to hatred, alienation, as brothers.

Instead of transparency, we started keeping secrets.

There was a time when, if we needed comfort, reassurance, all we had to do was call each other, and we had a code: We would start out by saying, "OK, so check this out . . . " and then one or the other would tell his brother a story about what he'd done, what he'd tried to get away with, and how he was caught, and how he was now in trouble at work, or with school, or with someone in temporary authority, but it was nothing: I can get out of it, and it will blow over, but I just kind of need for you to tell me that everything is going to be all right, you know? I just kind of need to hear you say, "Aw, fuck those guys, man. You didn't do anything wrong; it will be fine." You know?

And so we would; we'd bolster one another's doubts, transgressions, and trespasses with reassurances, absolutions, or sympathetic confessions, because we had no one else, no system of trust based outside of one another's understanding of our animal compulsions, brought about by living with—and being raised by—Mingo, *pater noster.*

Dan understood me as thoroughly as I understood him, and now, when we found we knew each other thoroughly, we were disgusted with ourselves, and with the other. No more could we call one another and say, "OK, so check this out . . . "

It was done. We had broken all that had tethered us together, by wanting more of it. And so I moved out. And we didn't speak to one another for years. This is who Dan and I had been groomed to be, these two pillars of mutual disgust.

I tried to break out of it by moving as far away from Brownsville as I could; I had one clubbed foot in that life and the other in this one that I've tried to create in Seattle. But you can't run with two clubbed feet.

Dan is still my own personal hero, still my biggest brother. And for years, when we needed it we gave each other the biggest place of comfort I could ever think of: the absolution, the warmth of home, the understanding that whatever we did, the other person just understood, nodded his head.

That we became estranged after living together just makes sense now. It makes sense because we could always make sense of one another, but could not make sense of this conflict that was created within us by the twisted exaggeration of machismo that was my father's first principle. And it is also a copout. I feel that very likely we will never forgive each other, and that it was really our father's humiliation that divided us, the ghost of our Gramma's construction, this conflict and competition they evoked in us as brothers, how Dad sabotaged our personalities to make himself the best and biggest among his two brave sons, made himself the strongest and the weakest, so that we had to grow up and take care of him, and quickly, because he couldn't grow up or take care of us, let alone himself.

So now, even today, my older brother Dan remains my most immediate, my most beloved of human beings on this planet (with all the hellish opposites that this relationship can create). That we could no longer be around one another is the very reason I cannot forgive my father for what he did to us, how he underactualized us, how he prematurely sexualized in us this competition. And how in our eventuality, Dan and I are utter offenders to one another's good sense, disparate strangers on the street. How terribly sad. How terribly human. How pathetically biblical, and familial.

My brother Dan fell on the Dad-grenade, as the oldest boy. Took most of the blast, shielded me with his suffering, as the person closest to Dad besides Mom. How do you repay that?

In the end, I hope Dan knows how much I love him for that, love him still, and that he can still—even though we do not speak—hopefully carry that, in his heart; that however deep his resentment, misunderstanding, and hatred of me, how much his younger brother loves him, how I align him high among the brutal songs of trumpeting angels, the gilded testaments of broken saints, that Dan is still our family's hero. The caretaker of his and other people's families. That his song of sadness is still sung, and still remembered fondly.

And I have the hope that he will come to know that this debt, genetically imprinted, was deviously engineered so that it could never be paid back. That I could never even begin to reimburse him for what he suffered, except through witnessing and acknowledging it, as I have done here, and that—*that*—is what

I tried to tell you, Dan, though you swatted it away dismissively like it was nothing. That? That's nothing. Move in with me and Orlene. It will all be better. Come on in, move into that bedroom there, and have at the groceries. Just not the canned goods we keep under the bed, or my personal stash.

And then you later hated me for it, when I tried to explain, and kept failing at reimbursement, kept failing at being a man in your eyes because you kept me as your little brother, constantly in the debt of your good graces and goodwill, protected by your generosity, at the expense of your respect.

Please understand, Dan, that yours is a debt that could never be paid, by anyone.

EPILOGUE

On Dan's first day on the job at Queen Anne Healthcare, a nursing home here in Seattle, he meets Phil Franzo, who becomes one of his patients. Phil just happens to be suffering from a bowel obstruction the size of a baseball that day. This is Dan's first procedure at his new job.

The nurse's assistant is a wispy Filipino boychick who has already known Phil Franzo for a couple of years. "Now, Phil, this is Daniel. Daniel is going to help you, OK?"

"Mister," says Phil gruffly to Dan, lying on his back and holding his distended belly, "I'm full of shit, mister." He's a small man with black horn-rimmed glasses, vaguely Italian and diminutive, from the World War II era, with old man black hair peppered with gray. He's adorable, except for this belly swollen like he was an African child with parasites. "I'm full of shit," he repeats.

Dan has seen this before. It's a bowel obstruction, and it's a messy procedure.

Phil's stomach is distended and firm, like he's got a bowling ball growing in there. Dan removes his watch, straps on long gloves, and puts a bed pan along with a five-gallon bucket down by the bed, preps for what needs to happen. "Are you ready, Phil? This is going to hurt a little, but you'll be fine. Here I go."

The assistant raises Phil's legs, and Dan's gloved fingers enter Phil through the tradesman's entrance and grab hold of the hard, dried obstruction. Dan pulls it free, slowly, and then Phil's lower GI tract begins the process of emptying.

Not a pleasant thing, sure, but it helps Phil. He begins to feel relief, and the Manila boychick assistant says to Phil, "Now, Phil, you say thank you to Daniel; he just did a very nice thing for you. Say thank you, Phil."

Phil says, "Thanks, you prick."

Dan falls in love with Phil Franzo right there. He's Phil Franzo's primary nighttime caregiver, and they've both made a new best friend on Dan's first day of work.

After three years of not speaking to me, Dan and Orlene fly to Brownsville to visit family for the first time after nearly five years of living in Seattle and come back with the determination to move back to Texas, to pack it in and move back home.

But once back he breaks the freeze between us and calls me unexpectedly one afternoon and invites me to a large Sunday dinner at his favorite seafood restaurant, later that week. I agree to meet him. I've missed my bigger brother. He tells me to meet him at the nursing home, after he's off work at six o'clock, and I do.

I'm nervous as I make the drive to the nursing home, and in my eagerness to see him, I'm terribly early, but Dan is overjoyed to see me, hugs me forcefully when I see him, and his bulk and strength are very reassuring, as he envelopes me in his nurse's scrubs. He kisses me on the cheek, and I do the same, in return. I'm surprised at how much I missed him, how big the vacuum he left in my heart.

He brings me to the nurses' station and introduces me to his fellow nurses: his best friend Llambi, the Croatian kid who I'm surprised looks like he could be a surfer from Santa Cruz; and of course Alex, whom I knew from before; and then, one of his favorite patients, Helen Ellis. Helen Ellis is Dan's other favorite patient because of the stories she tells him, as a former model from the 1960s and an ex-junkie who once dated Jim Brown of the Cleveland Browns, possibly the toughest man who ever lived and played football. He used to beat the crap out of her, she tells Dan. He used to beat the crap out of anybody who pissed him off, especially women, she says. She doesn't seem conflicted about this, says it with a sort of antique awe, I notice.

Dan's not ready to leave yet, and he asks me to wheel Phil Franzo to his room while he does other nursing things, in preparation for his departure. Phil is in the lounge making a mess of his coffee and cold water, pouring coffee into the water, water back into the coffee, for no reason whatsoever.

"Phil! Philippo! This is my younger brother, June. He's going to take you to your room, OK? Say hello, Phil," says Dan to Phil, then runs off to finish his shift.

Phil says, "Hi, you prick."

I try not to laugh. I know all about Phil.

I wheel Phil to his room, get him next to his bed.

"Put me to bed, doll," he says.

"What did you say, Phil?" I ask, not sure I heard correctly.

"Put me to bed, doll."

"Phil, I'm not going to put you to bed. You can do it yourself."

"Bah, you're a prick, mister," says Phil, clearly disgusted, and starts to move from his chair to his bed.

A bit later, Dan and I are at the nurses' station saying goodbye to Llambi and Alex when Phil wheels himself by in super slow motion. Apparently, he didn't want to get into bed too badly and had shifted back to his wheelchair.

Phil rolls directly in front of the nurses' station and settles in next to a vegetative but still living Mary Ellen, aka Dances with

Whiskey, who is now eighty-seven years old, though, as Dan continues to tell her, she doesn't look a day over eighty.

"Fire this prick," Phil says to Dan and Llambi, pointing at me with his thumb.

We all burst out laughing.

"I want you to fire this prick," he repeats himself.

"Why do you want us to fire him?" asks Llambi, winking at me conspiratorially.

"Because he's a prick," Phil says.

I say, "Phil, your schtick's getting old."

He says, "Fuck you, you prick. You're fired."

❖

Dan wants me to move back to Texas with him in a year, he tells me.

Moaning over Alaskan king crab at a Magnolia restaurant, he tells me that it's done here; that he's felt it for a long time, for the both of us.

"Look, I'll never speak bad of this place. I love Seattle. But we're getting older, and you don't know how old you are until you see your parents again. Can't believe how old they got," he says while digging at the crab's interiors with a tiny, double-pronged fork. There's stringy meat all over our table. I have no argument. Things are coming down around my ears. My time is unstructured and I've been acting out like a borderline personality for months. But Dan doesn't know about that.

"Besides," he says, "I don't want to be here when Phil Franzo checks out. I love Philippo; I don't think I can handle him dying." Dan has served as a midwife to people's deaths in that nursing home on an almost weekly basis. He's like a death Sherpa now. He describes the process of death as similar to watching a ceiling fan wind itself down, as the body begins to shut down, until it just stops. To hear that he's grown this attached to one of his patients is considerable indeed. Franzo, a Brooklynite, had a stroke twenty years ago and has been at Queen Anne Health Care for eighteen years. He was slipping into more of a vegetative state until Dan and Llambi came along and engaged him in schtick, as boys.

"How's Phil doing?" I ask, wondering if there is something to his condition that I haven't been made aware of.

"Oh, Phil's doing great," says Dan, and then pauses. "I just don't want to see him go."

His face changes a bit, and he prepares to get into his Phil Franzo schtick mode: "You're a prick, Phil," Dan says in his regular voice.

"I was born that way, mister. You're a prick, too," Dan replies to himself in Phil's gravel pit voice, for my benefit.

"What's that make us, Phil?" says Dan as Dan.

"A pair of pricks," says Dan as Phil.

Then Dan imitates Llambi from across the nursing home, and yells out, "I'm a prick, too!" waving his hand.

"Triplets," says Dan as Phil.

Early on, when Dan was very new at this nursing home and he'd just met Phil, Phil would usually wheel himself into the smoking area and watch as people would come in and out of the nursing home at the three o'clock afternoon shift change.

There had been this twenty-five-year-old Somalian nursing assistant who'd moved to America with dreams of becoming an NBA basketball player. He would dress every day in an NBA outfit like he was going to play in a professional game, for the Lakers. Every day.

Phil would watch him walk in and out of work, and one day, Phil looked at him and said, as usual, "You're a prick, mister."

The Somalian kid took umbrage at this, his American fantasy so delicate and fragile. He got angry, yelled something in Africani at Phil, and actually punched Phil in the stomach, which was lying flabby and exposed because his robe was open while he smoked his cigarette. The punch left an imprint on Phil's stomach.

"Ouch, you prick," Phil yelled back.

Dan and Llambi saw this happen from across the hall and grabbed the Somali kid by the back of the neck and slammed him to the ground, unnecessarily putting their knees and weight on his neck until the cops showed up and sent the idiot back to whatever shithole Somalian village he was from, rescinding his work visa.

Phil watched as the cops showed up and the guys wrote up the abuse report, and then he remembered his manners, as he continued to smoke.

"Thanks, you pricks," he said, to Dan and Llambi.

"I can't watch him go," says Dan, in a moment of quiet, after we're done laughing.

"If you'd seen him when we got there . . . " he trails off, his eyes water and he swallows, hard.

This is significant. Dan has helped many patients that he loved to their end, helped their families endure the inevitable and painful reality of expiration, of death. Of dying. He's charted all this on his own, with just his own personal navigational tools, his own love for their humanity and dignity. They can't teach you that in nursing school.

But Phil Franzo, he is different. He has imprinted upon Dan as something other than a patient he has to Sherpa through that final door. Dan loves Phil, like family. For the first time in his professional career, Dan cannot watch one of his patients die. Maybe it's because Dan brought Phil back from the brink of a vegetative state, with the affection and the jokes exchanged between men, between them and Llambi and Alex.

Maybe all this happened because I was out of his life, and that gave Dan the freedom to love others in the same way he loved his little brother, and it made his life richer. Spread that affection around, in a way he couldn't before.

And so now, here is Phil, at this point, aware, knows he's making the boys laugh.

They brought him back to life. And now Dan couldn't watch him die.

⚜

Phil died in 2008. I had posted some variation of these stories on some sort of online blog at some point when I was wooing some girl who turned out to be a polyamorist. Long story. I got a message from Phil's grandson, out of the blue, who had been Googling his grandfather's name. The kid was twenty-two, from New York state, and uncomfortable writing. He had been online, trying to find out more about his grandfather, before he shipped out to Afghanistan. Phil had been in World War II, and the kid was trying to find the courage that his grandfather once had, to do his duty. We exchanged email for a month before the kid shipped out. I shared all this with Dan, forwarded him every email exchanged, mediated questions and answers between Phil's grandson and what was left of Dan's memories of Phil. The kid loved all the stories about his grandfather, thanked me effusively for taking the time to write them and post them. I had no idea they were still online.

Dan was noticeably saddened to be reminded of Phil. Llambi had kept him up-to-date, even though Dan had moved back to San Antonio, and had told him of Phil's passing. Phil had been cremated and his ashes spread into the Stillaguamish River, about an hour north of Seattle, his grandson had written. Dan did not know that part. The kid said he and his mother, Phil's estranged daughter, felt that Phil would have liked that, because he'd been locked indoors for the thirty years or so after his stroke. My stories of his grandfather made him laugh, he wrote me, and he said he'd print them out and carry them with him when he shipped out, he said.

I did that—helped close the circuit for Dan and Phil, though it broke my heart to watch him grieve Phil's passing.

And I broke Dan's, when I didn't move back to Texas.

CLOSEDOWN

Velva Jean got her divorce and moved out with Derek. She and Dad had been married for over twenty-five years, and it took a very long time for her to disentangle her furniture, her past, and make that move away from the house on Oklahoma Avenue.

She moved with Derek to an apartment across the street from our old high school, and she continued working at the JC Penney, then finally graduated from the University of Texas at Brownsville in 2004, with a degree in business administration. Derek had a very difficult time adjusting, started acting out in strange, weird ways. Eventually, he had to move in with Mare and Mark, in Corpus Christi, where he bloomed through high school, then imploded in college.

Mom never forgave herself for breaking up his home, and feels responsible for all of his weaknesses, his periods of self-harm, his struggle—like mine and Dan's struggle—with alcoholism and drugs. For us, it's our own fault, Mom felt. But Derek's, that was her doing. Neither Dan nor I buy into that: We also both feel responsible for Derek's faults as well, because we were not ideal models. I have a tendency now to collect little brothers, where once I was trying to collect fathers.

Mom eventually remarried and now lives in and works for the City of Houston with her husband Robert, from La Porte, who is a salsa music fanatic, plays the bongos. We could not have asked for anyone better to share in Velva Jean's life. He treats her very well, always pulls out her chair for her in restaurants. It makes my throat knot up, when I see him do that for her when I visit them. He never forgets, and Mom acknowledges it with terribly modest elegance, like it is the most natural thing in the world.

Dad actually quit drinking, has been sober now for fifteen or so years. After the divorce, he met up with and married his high school sweetheart, who also tried taming his savagery, but Dad is not to be tamed; he is to be understood, he feels. Maybe studied. He divorced her after a few years, moved in with a waitress and her daughter next, and when that didn't work out, he moved back in with his mother and was sleeping in the same bedroom he grew up in, at age sixty. We're all strangely protective of Dad now, look upon him like someone who deserves special care, someone who was wounded terribly as a child, someone who's been struggling tremendously with posttraumatic stress disorder his whole life, at the hands of his mother, whom he will not leave, and who we cannot blame.

Gramma is still alive, at the time of this writing, and quite tiny. You could never imagine the Gorgon of old, in that tiny frame. At Mamí's funeral in 2010, Gramma and Dad showed up unexpectedly, and Dad had secretly arranged for a mariachi band to play three of the most heartbreaking Spanish songs ever, and everyone—everyone—cried, Dan told me, and he had never been so proud of his old man. When Gramma arrived, she asked only for Dan, plucked her way through the crowd, pushing away well wishers, looking for her *Denny*. Dan had not seen Gramma in over twenty years, still regarded her as the Devil; but when this tiny, shriveled person came up to him and reminded him that she was, in fact, still his Gramma, Dan's heart broke open and he hugged her, in front of the whole family, and it was a moment I wish I could have seen, but I was in Seattle, on the ninth floor of Harborview, with my fiancée in a coma, and dealing with her New England family whom I could neither understand nor ultimately join.

I could not be there, for my mother's mother's funeral, and I have felt very terrible for that.

Dad even hugged Robert, my mother's husband, to everyone's astonishment, especially Robert's. When he told me about it later, I just laughed. "He's full of surprises, that Mingo," I said.

They're both very lonely, Dad and Gramma, because we all left, we all went forward into America, and it was as if they chose not to invite themselves along. So they've stayed there, on Oklahoma Avenue.

Gramma raises chickens. In the place where the pigsty once stood now stands a multilevel retirement coop, for her chickens. She does not eat them or sell them to be eaten, as she considers them her pets, gives them names and takes their eggs every morning. I like to think it's a sort of penance she's paying, for all the hogs she's killed, in that spot.

And for other things she's done.

My sisters have prospered in unimaginable ways. They all married very well, and each have lovely children, live all over the state of Texas. Both Syl and Mare are administrators or teachers in the school system there, which is quite stable, and Marge, as mentioned, became a research scientist, finished her PhD at Stony Brook in New York, then came back to Texas to raise her family, with Corwin. Mare was married to Mark, and they have a delightful daughter, Madison; Syl and Ruben have three daughters of their own. Let's see if I can get this straight, without calling my mother for help: There is . . . Danielle, Megan . . . and Olivia. That's right.

Derek had a bad go of it for a while, but he seems to be getting his life together now, I hear tell from Mom. He's not speaking to either Dan or me, or the rest of the family, really, and he depends on Mom more than anyone ever did, even more so than Dad. They're sort of caught in a mutual agreement to drown one another, and neither can let the other go.

The three of us boys can't be in the same room together, oddly. We've spent so much time apart, when we see each other these unconscious alignments tend to exclude one of the three, and it ends up in an argument. I was the odd man out for the three or so years Dan and I were not speaking, and Derek had moved in with Dan, after his accident in Austin, when Derek had fallen after a night of drinking and cracked open the back of his skull on the sidewalk.

That relationship turned into a simulacrum of the one Dan and I had in Seattle, except I was more clearly defined, didn't bow under the pressure of Dan's relentless conditions in the way Derek did, which bred a tremendous resentment on Derek's part, and so now, the only power Derek feels he has is to keep us out, all of us, at once.

Dan and Orlene are still in nursing, and Orlene has stuck with Dan through some very bad times, is very much a part of this family. While she has had every reason and opportunity to despise me, she does not, and that simply amazes me. I don't think I could be as forgiving as she has been.

Dan and I still go through periods where we cannot stand to speak to one another for years, but the love we have for one another is still there, always there. It just turns into sadness. From him, even though we don't speak, I know he still loves me. It will always be the way I feel about him: I might not be able to talk to him for a long time, but it doesn't mean I don't love him. Quite the opposite. It's simply that there is no one in the world that can drive me as absolutely bat-shit crazy as Dan can. No one who can make me so angry.

Family has a way of doing that.

And for helping each other: I spent twenty years trying to get away from them, trying to deny my connection to my family, and it was this last year when I fell apart completely, was utterly dysfunctional, that they all lined up and kept me alive through the worst event in my life, when my fiancée had a seizure while driving on December 4 and plummeted off the side of an overpass in Seattle.

But that is another book of its own.

ACKNOWLEDGMENTS

This book is the culmination of the support, abiding patience and dogged endurance of many, many people, especially my family: my older brother, Daniel Martinez, my younger brother, Derek A. Martinez, my sisters Mary (Mimi) Guess, Margie (Mimi) Moczygamba, and Sylvia de los Santos, my mother, Velva Jean Martinez, my father, Domingo C. Martinez, and especially my grandmother, *La Señora* Virginia Rubio. Partners and spouses are included in that, meaning Corwin Moczygamba, Mark Guess, Robert Swanagan, and Orlene Ezekiel. And whoever happens to be with Dad when this prints: you're special, too.

My friends who believed and encouraged me, and dealt with the prickly parts: Amy Niedrich, above all, then the McCartys, Andrew and Pam, of course, my dear friend Philippe Critot and the lovely Mrs. Critot (whom I've never met, but who yells at me when Philippe and I are talking on the phone). There's Kim McIver and her husband, John, who've been terribly encouraging since the late 1990s. And I owe a debt of gratitude for the following friendships: Camille Ball, Chris Arteaga, Eric Lawson, and Robb Garner.

Of course, there are the people who helped make this happen: Brianna Morgan, for helping with copy editing. Also, there's the best agent in the world, Alice Martell, who took me on as a completely unknown quantity: an author simply could not ask for a better champion, and my editors at Globe Pequot/Lyons Press, Lara Asher and Kristen Mellitt, and their keen sense of story and tenses. And I would not be writing this without the help of Jeffrey Gustavson, Odette Heidelman, Martin Rock, and Willard Cook at *Epiphany* Literary Magazine: thank you all, so, so very much for your vision and encouragement. Also, the staff at *This American Life* for bringing the Mimis to radio: Ira Glass, Robyn Seimyn, and Nancy Updike.

Finally, this book would not have been published if it weren't for Sarah J. Berry, who guided me through the darkest period of my life and brought me into the brightest. I can't imagine where I'd be if you hadn't been there, Sarah.

ABOUT THE AUTHOR

Domingo Martinez, 2012 National Book Award finalist, lives in Seattle, Washington. His work has appeared in Epiphany and he has contributed to *The New Republic*. He has read pieces from *The Boy Kings of Texas* on *This American Life* and an essay about being chosen as a 2012 National Book Award finalist on *All Things Considered*. An excerpt from *The Boy Kings of Texas* was nominated for a 2013 Pushcart Prize.